WOMEN'S V
FROM THE
SPANISH CIVIL WAR

Women's Voices from the Spanish Civil War

Edited by
JIM FYRTH
with
SALLY ALEXANDER

LAWRENCE & WISHART
LONDON

Lawrence and Wishart Limited
99a Wallis Road
London E8 2LH

First published 1991
This anthology © Jim Fyrth and Sally Alexander, 1991
Introduction © Sally Alexander, 1991
Foreword © Jim Fyrth, 1991
The Acknowledgements on pp. 348-50 constitute an extension
of this copyright page.

Photoset in North Wales by
Derek Doyle and Associates, Mold, Clwyd
Printed and bound in Great Britain by
Biddles Ltd., King's Lynn, Norfolk

Contents

Part 3: **With the Rearguard**

Part 4: **Supporting and Reporting**

Part 5: **The Other Side of the Lines**

Part 6: **A People in Retreat**

Part 7: **Afterwords**

Introduction

Sally Alexander

When I was a child in England in the 1940s and 50s my mother dreaded the coming of the third world war. Men were precious to my mother. She had grown up almost exclusively among women in the shadow of the first – the Great – war. 'We never saw a man,' she told us, 'no man ever came to our house.' She lived in the Berkshire countryside, the eldest of four children raised on a peacetime widow's pension and occasional charity – 'We idealised men because we didn't know any.' Her sisters and brother thought her fortunate because she was the only one who could remember her father, and the only one of his children he had known. My mother's father had survived the First World War only to die in military service in Africa in the 1920s before his wife, who had been a nurse before her marriage, could reach him to care for him. My mother's brother had been killed on the last day of the Second World War in Burma. Riding his motor-bike to welcome his commanding officer he was ambushed. So my mother wanted the third world war that she knew was coming – 'world wars come every twenty years' – to happen before my brother grew up. Korea and Suez were met with relief in my family because my brother was too young to go.

As far as I can remember this was my first understanding of war: that it was the time when men killed each other somewhere else, a time of telegrams and death when women were left to live in a world changed by men's absence or mutilation. Gradually I heard other stories: of crouching under the kitchen table with my mother and sister during an air-raid; of gas masks that were never used; of land girls, evacuees, women in uniform (but not fighting) and foreign lovers. My father's stories were quite different – he and his friends were the first out of Dunkirk; 'if you see the enemy, duck'; 'always be the first to surrender' – and they tempered (as I daresay they were intended to do) my childhood fears. If from my mother I learned about love and loss, then from my father the lessons were as negative if less tragic. He taught me about the disillusionment and impotence of the ordinary soldier, of the humour in self-deprecation (a powerful theme, reaching back through music-hall, of plebeian humour, reinforced in the 1940s, for instance, by the radio broadcasts of Al Read, some of the Ealing comedies in the late 1940s and early 1950s, and in the 1960s television show, *Dad's Army*), but also of the unexpected egalitarianism among men in wartime. It is a paradox that while each one of my generation has had her or his psyche marked by their parents' memories of war, and their senses blunted by the incessant stream of images of war, actual and fictional on television, few have had direct experience of war themselves. So I read these testimonies with the curiosity of ignorance. What was war like to live, and why did these women choose to go to Spain?

'...a deep hatred of fascism'

Loathing of fascism, dread of war and belief in democracy drove women to volunteer for Spain on the side of the Republican government, the Communist historian Margot Heinemann remembered fifty years later.[1] Fascism divided Europe, but anti-fascism was an international movement. 45,000 men from all over the world, 2,500 of them from Britain, joined the International Brigades. Like the men, the first women to go – from New Zealand, Austrialia, North America as well as Britain – were mostly Communists and socialists who had learned from the study of international politics in the previous ten or fifteen years the meaning of fascism.[2] For women fascism meant, continued Margot Heinemann, war, the abolition of civil liberties and the return of women to the status of second-class citizens and to child-bearing as their exclusive socially useful function.[3] Not every woman who went shared Margot Heinemann's retrospective circumspection. A passionate sense of injustice sent some. Patience Darnton, training to be a midwife in East London, 'realised at once – I don't know how I had the sense but I did – that this was "us" and "them" and this was a chance to do "them" down'. Lots of young women who had not fully thought through their political response to the civil war reached out to help the Spanish people because they were horrified by the spectacle of a military overthrow of a democratically elected government – the 'invasion' as the Republicans called it, and as Dorothy Parker reiterates here. Sheila Grant Duff, an English journalist working in Prague, received a telegram from the Paris editor of the *Chicago Daily News*, asking her to go to Spain,

> I had worked in Edgar's office in Paris and learned from him ... that the only decent aim for any footfree individual at that moment in history was the defeat of fascism.

The first British woman to enter the territory of the insurgents, her mission was dangerous, but exhilarating: to expose 'appalling slaughter' which succeeded Franco's entry of his troops into every Spanish town.

About half the nurses, secretaries and interpreters among whom Winifred Bates worked went for compassionate not political reasons: 'They were just nurses, courageous women, willing to work under the most dangerous conditions.' Others went 'only' for humanitarian reasons or to pursue their 'healing mission'. From these accounts it is clear, however, that once in Spain, political awareness was swiftly born. Even the Quakers – officially neutral – wrestled internally against restrictions on their public speech and actions. Ruth Cope, an American, wrote home, 'There is much we do not agree with and stay silent about.'

Pleading for medical supplies and food, she felt bitterly frustrated and shamed – as did so many British women – by her government's policy of non-intervention which, by facilitating Hitler's and Mussolini's aid for General Franco and the insurgents, paved the way for Munich.

With the exception of the few supporters of Franco (described by one defender of the 'patriots' as a 'shining light', a 'beacon') the dominant political impulse in support for Spain was anti-fascism, and fascism to democrat, humanitarian, socialist or Communist meant political dictatorship predicated on imperial aggression. Franco's rebellion – although widely anticipated in Spain after the February election of the Popular Front, fulfilled the worst fears of the anti-fascists, because it was illegal, brutal and lacked popular support. Since the 1920s anti-fascists had worked together in organisations like the League of Nations Union, the No More War Movement, the Women's International League for Peace and Freedom, the Peace Pledge Unions, the Women's Committee against War and Fascism and the Left Book Club. For each woman who went to Spain there were thousands of others who formed the Aid Spain Movement between 1936 and 1939.[4]

Nevertheless, Communists speak most insistently in this as in most English-language history and memoir because their initiatives led the huge popular movement in support of Spain. Communists believed that the struggle against fascism was the class-struggle writ large, and fascism the inevitable if – hopefully – final phase of capitalism. In accordance with the strategy of the united or popular front, their analysis was muted and aid for Spain was articulated in terms of democracy versus fascism, a formulation persuasive to generations who could remember the First World War, were alarmed by the prospect of a second but still idealistic enough to imagine in 1936 or 1937 that it could be stopped.[5] For if, as Ellen Wilkinson argued to the largely unsympathetic House of Commons in 1938, the civil war in Spain was the 'point of truth' for Spanish people, then many in Britain felt that struggle to be their own. 'Our fate as a people is being decided today,' wrote Ralph Bates, novelist and Communist (his collection of short stories on Spain, published before the outbreak of civil war in 1936, marked the beginning of the identification of Spain with 'contempt for luxury and death' and the 'instinct to revolt' which seized the imagination of so many intellectuals among all classes in the 1930s), Storm Jameson, novelist and anti-fascist remembered in her *Autobiography*).[6] And in 1986 Winifred Bates, teacher, writer and wife to Ralph, reiterated: 'If we could have stopped Hitler from taking Spain, we could have stopped him spreading his evil over the rest of Europe and Britain.'[7]

Civil War in Spain

While there is no question of the political and moral prescience of those anti-fascists who led the support for Spain in Britain during the 1930s, their courage should not blind us to the realisation that from the perspective of an Andalusian agricultrual labourer, Asturian miner or industrial worker from Barcelona or Bilbao, the divisions of the civil war were more complicated than the opposition of fascist and anti-fascist. When the Popular Front won 4.7 million votes in February 1936, 4 million voters opposed them. Revolutionaries of both sides – Falangists in opposition, and Communists, left-Socialists and Anarchists in the Popular Front – declared that this was merely the first step towards social revolution. The fascist Falangist party founded in the early 1930s, had formed links then with monarchists and Catholic Carlists as well as with more traditional forces of reaction, the church, landed gentry and army. In their wish for social revolution, the elimination of large landed estates, the nationalisation of the banks and democratic control of factories, the Falangists sometimes had more in common with Communists, Anarchists and Syndicalists than with the élitist monarchists and right-wing Catholics. On the other hand, religious faith could motivate sections of the peasantry, haunted by the spectre of church-burnings, anti-clericalism and the destruction of private property to support the nationalists; or fear of the populism or brutality of Franco's 'Crusade' might persuade sections of the professional or business classes in the towns to support the Popular Front. The populations of the large industrial cities were the most ardent defenders of the Republic, although the brave if tragic defence of towns and villages by the untrained Republican militias, who were gunned down as they fled unarmed and without cover, are testimony to the depth of Republican feeling elsewhere. Political divisions within one family evoke the confusion and tragedy of civil war for the Spanish people.

Ronald Fraser spoke to Juan Narcía the son of a mining engineer in Asturias, sympathetic to the nationalists until he was twelve years old when he saw the corpses of three of their victims brought down to his village in garbage carts.

> When they killed some of them – people who had fled, who were living in the mountains as guerrillas to a certain extent – they celebrated their success with a sort of fiesta, with plenty of food and drink.[8]

Of his four older brothers, the eldest, Jose, was a doctor of liberal beliefs who voted left republican; Francisco, a lawyer and clerk of the town-hall was an 'extreme conservative'; Timoteo a dentist, was a member of the Communist Party; Leopoldo, the fourth, a member of the Falange. Before the war 'we all got on as brothers,' Juan told Fraser, but as his mother was an ardent Catholic and only his father 'a moderate man' there were 'violent political discussions'. When war broke out the brothers joined their respective organisations. Timoteo was executed by the nationalists in Algeciras where he had 'attempted to organise resistance to the military uprising'. When Juan's father heard the news, 'From that time until his own death seven years later, he never raised his head again. He was completely over-whelmed with grief ...' Both during and after the war there was a silence among the brothers about Timoteo's execution: 'No one wanted to talk about it. After the war it was a question of keeping alive; there was considerable fear.'

Women's Work in Wartime
The women writing here do not explore the depths of contradiction and change in Republican Spain, nor do they explore their own motives or selves. This is wartime writing, immediate and often urgent in description. Nurses, administrators, relief workers, teachers of literacy were each inspired by the strength of the Spanish people's resistance to Franco, their determination to eliminate illiteracy and to create a democratic culture, but they were saddened too by the suffering they saw. Letters home cajole or plead for funds and supplies – 'it's no consolation to me to know,' begged Madge Addy, a Manchester nurse in Uclés, that aid has been sent to Barcelona, 'we

have a hospital of 800 wounded *here* ... so please get them to concentrate on us.'

All describe the surface of events. Blood spattering walls and floor, staining clothing, bodies and pavements red, clogging nails. We hear the unnatural silence before the wounded arrive and feel the exhaustion of the nurse who throws a dead body off her bed before she collapses in sleep. There is much horror: packets of chocolate dropped by Mussolini's fascist planes are picked up by hungry children whose hands are then blown off by the hidden explosives. The nationalists commandeer an ambulance which whirls wildly round machine-gunning civilians at random. Retreating ranks of refugees are bombed by Hitler's Luftwaffe. These non-combattants too experienced battle-fatigue and shell-shock. The symptoms were loss of memory, uncontrollable shaking, indifference to death. Some letters home read as though writing were itself necessary to expel unthinkable experience. Sometimes there is only the comfort of geography of atmosphere: 'Walking down twisted cobbled streets with only a narrow strip of star-pricked heaven above us, lighted only by the glow of two cigarettes,' wrote Florence Conard, 'tired as I was, the stillness of that Spanish town crept into me and rested there.' But there is love too – for the soldiers wounded and dying some of whom were scarcely more than boys, for lovers and husbands briefly and sometimes unexpectedly encountered, and for children, friends and family left at home.

The men's war was very different from the women's. John Richardson, an eighteen year-old volunteer from Luton, described in a letter the last attack in the battle of the Ebro:

At dawn we went over the top and the world went mad. Machine-guns sent a hail of bullets at us. Snipers shot at us, shells and trench mortars burst all round. But we reached cover at the bottom of the valley where we lay all day unable to move because of snipers. The heat of the sun became unbearable. The ground scorched and our clothes stuck to our backs. We had no water and my mouth and throat were swollen and hard with thirst.

At 10 p.m. we got the order to attack. We reached the very summit without a mishap. A little while later came the signal for real business. We rose with a yell and rushed forward throwing hand-grenades as we ran. But the machine-guns rained death on us, red-hot lead. Hand-grenades burst all round. Time and time again we attacked only to be driven back. The fortifications were too strong. Solid concrete pill-boxes lined the hill-top and we were only flesh and blood.[9]

The most dramatic accounts in this anthology come from the women who nursed that 'flesh and blood'. 'Bodies torn and limbs smashed' were repaired often with blunt instruments, anaesthetics given by unskilled helpers, injections and bandages applied with shaking hands in hospitals swiftly set up in olive fields, caves, or under a bridge or in a tunnel as the Republicans retreated and the bombers pursued even the wounded. Twenty-four- or forty-hour shifts were followed by tea and cigarettes, as food was scarce and often had to be shared with starving refugees and soldiers. Any likely sturdy person could be hauled into an operating theatre to stroke a man's forehead, to hold an instrument or limb as he underwent an operation. These desperate, tragic times were not without their moments of black comedy. What to do with the limbs hastily amputated, flung on the floor, chucked out of windows, dumped in moats of castles where they blocked the sewage and fed the rats, was a macabre preoccupation.

Not everyone who had volunteered for Spain had been allowed to go. The women writing here represented many others left behind. And those who did go had to be content with conventional women's work mostly, because war confirms the sexual division of labour. Some had wanted to fight. Valentine Ackland, poet, Communist and hitherto campaigner for peace, wrote immediately news of the insurgents' rebellion reached Britain to offer her services. She had a scheme for fifty women like herself, with their own cars, who could spearhead medical as well as military aid.[10] Kay Ekervall, writer and secretary, recalls how she (and her boyfriend) longed to volunteer but were turned down, in spite of training to use a machine-gun until her shoulders were sore.[11] Felicia Browne, artist and Communist, trained in machine-gunning, went to the front and was shot dead. And stories were told, behind the frontlines of battle, of women brave and eager enough to take pot-luck with the militias.

Women in Spain

In the first months of civil war women had been recruited into the Popular Front militias, ill-equipped and untrained as they were. Women defended their cities and villages by hand, alongside men and children. They built barricades, poured boiling oil on the insurgents and in less pressing moments did as their government directed them to do, and delivered food to their husbands at the front instead of in the fields.

The visible and symbolic presence of women on the Republican side was vital, even after they had been prohibited from fighting. Dolores Ibarruri – Pasionaria – was only the most well-known of women leaders in the Popular Front (admired by British women, as they make clear below, because she was beautiful, of the people, self-educated, principled – *and* a mother.) The position of women in Spain was a flashpoint of political conflict. Catholic and conservative opponents of the Republic linked women's emancipation to the destruction of the family, private property and the anti-Christ, while how far women's emancipation should go was as much a bone of contention among Anarchists, Socialists and Communists then as now.

Spanish women won the right to vote in 1931. In 1934 the Republican government passed Spain's first divorce law. Young women celebrated their new-found freedoms by wearing trousers and make-up, seeking training and work alongside men, and addressing men as comrades and friends as their women leaders did. But some women wanted the changes to go deeper into the structure of relations and feeling between women and men who formed the Republic and were disappointed to find their explorations checked or suppressed. Pilar Vilvancos tells Ronald Fraser about her village in Aragon where the men would permit no women on the village committee, and where her cousin was vilified for living 'like an animal' because he lived with a woman out of wedlock. None of this deterred Pilar from falling in love with a Major, a Republican hero, 25 years her senior, and defying family and friends to live with him:

> I liberated, emancipated myself. We slept together, we became the couple we were to remain all our lives, for we never married. I believe that people respect each other more without marriage. Not being married is a freedom – not a freedom to do as one pleases but the freedom to be oneself in a human relationship.[12]

Feminism, Pacifism and Anti-fascism

In Britain Spain was never a feminist issue, but a democratic and humanitarian one. In these respects the Aid Spain movement drew a lot of support from both women's organisations and individual feminists. Selina Cooper, for instance, Lancashire radical suffragist, aged 72 in 1936, argued with Sylvia Pankhurst and others that fascism meant 'back to the kitchen sink for women'. After a visit to Nazi Germany in 1935 Selina discovered that fascism also meant living in constant fear without the protection of civil liberties. Women must oppose fascist brutality she wrote in her report, because they are the 'creators of life and it is their business to preserve it.' She lost no opportunity after her return, to speak to meetings of women and socialists about what she had seen and learned in Germany in spite of the lack of enthusiasm from her Labour Party for what they regarded as a dangerously pro-Communist analysis.[13]

In the predominantly feminist pacifist movement anti-fascism drove a wedge between those who recognised that fascism could only be reversed by force, or at least the threat of force, and those who believed that no regime, however vile, ever warranted deliberate killing. Storm Jameson's *Autobiography* traces the agony of a liberal socialist driven inexorably to the realisation, mostly by the angry frustration and curt mockery of more knowing European friends, that fascism was not going to respond to pacifism, or goodwill, anymore than it respected national frontiers. Vera Brittain, on the other hand, whose *Testament of Youth* had shaped so many people's understanding of what war meant to women, never abandoned her pacifism solemnly vowed in a hospital in France in 1916. 'War,' she argued, in line with her mentor the Revd Dick Shepard, 'however "righteous" its alleged cause, was contrary to the will of God and spiritual welfare of man.'[14]

It is doubtful whether this conflict of opinion, echoing that between socialists and feminists before the First World War, and causing estrangement among women of different nationalities in the international women's movement for peace in the 1930s, will ever be resolved. But women's experience in Spain reminds us why women are unlikely to glorify the results of war. The stern reality of watching so many die (it was often a surprise, how long it took a strong young man or child to die), or starve (the descriptions of refugees wild with hunger are among the most horrible), or people faced with impossible choices (one woman preferred to kill her child, she said, than be separated from her husband) and the gradual defeat of Republican hopes meant that the war these women describe is closer to emotional suffering than the heroism of armed combat we are more familiar with from men's memoirs and reminds us why women are so often drawn into humanitarian and pacifist movements.[15]

The recovery of women's memories of their work in Spain is part of a movement gathering momentum throughout Europe in the past ten or fifteen years, to rediscover the conditions of fascism and movements opposed to it through the release of popular memory. Children whose parents lived and worked under fascist regimes in Italy and Germany, Austria and in Vichy France have probed painfully the sluggish memories of collaboration, acquiescence, silence in fascist nations, through film, television fiction and history writing. The will to forget has been understandably powerful, but the anger of later generations, their determination to know what happened in Europe during their parents' lives has been tenacious too. Women's participation in anti-fascist movements has been largely suppressed too. Every voice in this book has something to tell us of the struggle

Introduction

between fascism and its enemies and it would be wise to listen to them all if the tragic outcome of the 1930s is not to be repeated. For the conditions which gave rise to fascism – political and economic inequalities, militarism, unemployment, racial prejudice – still have deep roots in western democracies in the 1990s.

Notes

1. Margot Heinemann, 'Remembering 1936', *Women's Review*, October 1986.
2. Bill Alexander, *British Volunteers for Liberty*, London 1983, ch.2; Hywel Francis, *Miners Against Fascism, Wales and the Spanish Civil War*, London 1984, ch. 2; Jim Fyrth, *The Signal Was Spain, the Aid Spain Movement in Britain*, London 1986, Parts 1 and 2; Joe Jacobs, *Out of the Ghetto*, London 1979, ch. 10.
3. Claudia Koonz, *Mothers in the Fatherland, Women, the Family and Nazi Politics*, London 1988; Luisa Passerini, *Fascism in Popular Memory, The Cultural Experience of the Turin Working Class*, Cambridge 1987.
4. For a brief account of the anti-war movement in Britain in the 1930s, see Noreen Branson and Margot Heinemann, *Britain in the 1930s*, London 1971, ch. 19. On women's involvement see C. Bussy and M. Tims, *Pioneers for Peace*, London 1965; Sybil Oldfield, *Spinsters of this Parish, The Life and Times of E.M. Mayor and Mary Sheepshanks*, London 1984, ch. 13; Vera Brittain, *Testament of Experience*, (1957) London 1979, passim. For personal views of socialism and fascism see Harold Laski and John Strachey in *Why I Believe*, London 1940. Jim Fyrth, op.cit., argues that the Aid Spain movement awakened understanding of fascism and appeasement and brought politics to the level of actions at which anyone could take part (p 309).
5. Communists argued for a 'People's Front' of all anti-fascists from conservatives to left Socialists. The Labour Party in Britain would not co-operate with Communists (nor with Liberals). They had not forgotten the 'class against class' phase of the Communist International which had designated them 'social fascists' until the International's volte face in 1935. For a socialist of the Independent Labour Party's outline of popular front politics see Fenner Brockway, *Workers' Front*, London 1938. For a left-Labour view see G.D.H. Cole, *The People's Front*, Gollancz, London 1937. See also Jim Fyrth (ed.), *Britain, Fascism and the Popular Front*, London 1985.
6. Autobiography of Storm Jameson, *Journey From the North*, (1969) London 1984, p. 316.
7. Winifred Sandford, 'Caring Through Cruel Times', *Women's Review*, April 1987.
8. Ronald Fraser, *Blood of Spain, The Experience of the Civil War, 1936-1939*, Harmondsworth 1981, pp.431-3.
9. Alexander, op.cit., p. 208.
10. Wendy Mulford, *This Narrow Place, Sylvia Townsend Warner and Valentine Ackland, Life, Letters and Politics, 1930-1951*, London 1988, p.88.
11. Kay Ekervall, Telling Myself, *Women's Review*, May 1987.
12. Fraser, op.cit., p.289.
13. Jill Liddington, *The Life and Times of a Respectable Rebel, Selina Cooper, 1864-1946*, London 1984, ch. 22.
14. Jameson, *Autobiography*, op.cit, Part 2; Brittain, *Testament of Experience*, op.cit., and *Testament of a Generation, The Journalism of Vera Brittain and Winifred Holtby*, ed. Paul Berry and Alan Bishop, London 1985, p.228.
15. I am thinking in particular of George Orwell, *Homage to Catalonia*, John Summerfield, *Volunteer in Spain*, London 1936, James Pettifer (ed.), *Cockburn in Spain*, London 1986, some of which read, to me, like Boy's Own adventures. For the latest study of women's support for fascism, Claudia Koonz, op.cit, is a brilliant if sobering re-appraisal.

Foreword

Jim Fyrth

Sunday 23 August 1936: a group of young people is standing outside Victoria Station in London, surrounded by a large crowd which has come to see them off. Ten thousand, marching from Hyde Park, parade past them, some pressing flowers into their hands. Mayors and mayoresses from six London boroughs, and representatives from the London County Council, the Trades Union Congress and the Labour Party are there with good wishes to this first medical unit from any country to go to the aid of the Spanish Republic.

Gaumont British News records the event for cinemas across the country. The voice of the commentator says, 'The brave adventure of these ambulance men has started, and we too wish them the best of luck.' But seven of the 'ambulance men' are women, and they are to meet up with another, a doctor, on the journey. From the very first those creating the images and forming the public consciousness of the war are putting women into the background.

The Spanish war was part of my generation's experience. The meetings, collections for medical aid, showings of the film *Defence of Madrid*, the departure of a friend to join the International Brigades and his return with a length of his intestine missing, the last great rally when, on the night that Barcelona fell to Franco, thousands poured out of the old Queen's Hall in London and marched to Downing Street chanting 'We demand arms for Spain' – these things helped to mould my political consciousness. Yet it was only very much later, when I was writing the history of the Aid Spain movement in Britain and the medical units which it sent (*The Signal Was Spain*), that I realised the importance and courage of the women who went to Spain, and the extent to which the great campaign to aid and support the Republic was a women's movement. Of course at the time I knew of Isabel Brown, the charismatic working-class Communist who could charm money out of an audience, even their bus fares home, and the Duchess of Atholl, the high Tory mistress of Blair Castle who organised help for the Basque child refugees, foodships during the terrible winter of 1938 and even a children's knitting club to make blankets for refugees. But the main images and memories of the conflict were masculine. It was, after all, war.

Then, when I interviewed people who had served in the hospitals, and dug through the International Brigade, Quaker and other records, the women began to emerge, and their letters, diaries and memoirs to accumulate. It became clear that they must be returned to their rightful place in history. Hence this book.

When I have spoken of the project, people have asked rather doubtfully, 'Were there many women?' How many is many in such a case? We know the names, or have reliable records, of some 170 women from Britain, the USA and the other English-speaking countries who served in the medical or relief services. There were others, who make a shadowy appearance in diaries, letters or people's memories. Unfortunately the records of some of the committees which sent them cannot be found.[1] There were also Felicia Browne, who was killed fighting in the Republican militia, and Marion Merriman who was a full member of the American Abraham Lincoln Battalion. And we know of more than thirty women who went as journalists, delegates or broadcasters.

Is a minimum of two hundred people 'many'? Certainly no other conflict in which their own countries were not directly involved has ever drawn so many women to give so much.

Our women come from English-speaking nations. We have not included the French – probably the largest contingent – nor the Czechs, Scandinavians, Poles, Dutch, Belgians, Latin Americans or others, or the refugees from fascist countries. That would be another major work; while a collection which reflected all the facets of the lives of the Spanish women themselves would be something else again.

We have made one exception. Aurora Edenhoffer (Fernández at the time) was a young Spanish woman who served with the British and American nurses from the early days of the war until the fall of Catalonia, when she crossed into France with them, and spent the Second World War in England. Her memoir is unique, and we have included extracts.

There were outstanding women of whom we could find no personal records; Dr Audrey Russell, who helped to evacuate the Basque children to England in the spring of the 1937 and worked in Spain with refugees for most of the war, and afterwards in France; Angela Guest served the Spanish Medical Aid Committee at the front, and looked after the Medical Aid villa at Valencia (back in England she was one of those arrested for throwing red ink – symbolising the blood of Spain – on the Prime Minister's doorstep); the Welsh nurse Margaret Powell who was decorated by the Republican government for her services; Ada Hodson, the matron of a Johannesburg hospital who had been decorated in the first world war and who was loved and respected by all who knew her in Spain. There are many others whom we wish were included.

How did the women get to Spain? When Franco led the army revolt in July 1936 there was a quick response in democratic countries. One people after another had fallen under fascist and right-wing dictatorships; now the Spanish people were standing up and fighting back. The effect was immediate. The Spanish Medical Aid Committee (SMAC) in London was formed within two weeks of the attempted coup. Three weeks later it had raised the money and recruited the staff to send a small hospital unit to Grañen on the Aragon front. With it went five doctors or medical students. One was a woman, Ruth Prothero, who had come to Britain from Germany as a refugee in 1934. There were four nurses and three women who went as secretaries, translators and administrators; two of them – Margot Miller and Aileen Palmer – were Australian.

Throughout the war the SMAC sent supplies, equipment and personnel to Spain. Early in 1938 it reported that it had sent 44 nurses, as well as a woman radiologist and a woman physiotherapist. Some two hundred local Medical Aid Committees throughout Britain drummed up support. Most of its nurses served in the International Brigade hospitals. Seven, originally at Grañen, worked with a Catalan surgeon (one of them married him), others went to hospitals set up by the SMAC at Uclés and Huete in Central Spain. Those with the Brigades ranked as private soldiers and were paid ten pesetas a day. Otherwise they were unpaid. (American nurses ranked as officers and were paid more.)

Two other British medical groups went out in 1936. The Independent Labour Party sent an ambulance and supplies to the left-wing POUM in Barcelona, but there were no nurses. In September the Scottish Ambulance Unit left Glasgow for Madrid. There were no nurses, but the group was led by Fernanda Jacobsen, secretary to Sir Daniel Stevenson, the industrialist who was the prime mover of the unit.

In February 1937 Sir George Young, a former diplomat and Labour parliamentary candidate, formed the London University Ambulance Unit which, with the help of British and American Quakers, ran the 'Southern Hospitals' in Murcia and Almería. The unit and hospitals recruited some twenty nurses from Britain, Elizabeth Burchill from Australia, Dorothy Morris from New Zealand and one Irish nurse.

Meanwhile American, Australian and New Zealand nurses were arriving in Spain. The Australian Spanish Relief Committee was formed on 26 August 1936, three days after the first British Medical Unit had left for Spain. It recruited four nurses, who reached Spain in December, all of whom are represented in this book.

In December the New Zealand Spanish Medical Aid Committee recruited three nurses, two of whom are represented here.

December also saw the American Medical Bureau to Aid Spanish Democracy recruiting its first Hospital Unit, which arrived in Spain, led by Dr Edward Barsky, in January 1937. Of the eighteen in the group eleven were women. Altogether the AMB sent 117 men and women. There were also those who made their own way to Spain. These included Señora Urquidi, the Australian wife of the Mexican *chargé d'affaires*, who organised hospitals and ambulances, and Celia Seborer (Greenspan) one of the Americans in this collection, who worked with the Spanish blood transfusion service.

Most of the relief workers were sent by the British and American Quakers, but some went for Save the Children or the National Joint Committee for Spanish Relief (NJC). The British Quaker Spain Committee, an offshoot of the Friends' Service Council, was formed on 3 September 1936, and its first relief workers were setting up canteens for refugees in Barcelona by Christmas. The first American Quakers began work in Spain in May 1937.

The Non-Intervention Agreement, which forbad war materials to be sent to Spain, did not apply to medical supplies and food, although when ships carrying these were bombed or torpedoed the British, French and American governments would not protect their own flags. In January 1937 the British government banned its citizens from volunteering to fight on 'either side', and volunteers had to cross the Pyrenees by night. But this did not apply to medical or relief personnel.

The 'Non-Intervention' policy was adopted by the French and British governments, largely under pressure from Britain, a month after the conflict started. To isolate the war, arms were not to be sent to 'either side'; the legitimately elected government was banned from buying arms equally with the military mutineers. Germany, Italy and the Soviet Union joined in the agreement, but the Soviet Union withdrew in October when it was clear that Germany and Italy were sending arms and men to Franco. 'Non-Intervention' starved the Republican government of arms, while Hitler and Mussolini were able to supply Franco virtually unhindered. The policy was a major reason for the defeat of the Republic.

Many of the women and men who went to Spain felt that they were helping to uphold the honour of their country, tarnished by 'non-intervention' or worse – support for Franco in high places. But they achieved more than that. Besides helping to save lives and relieve suffering, the nurses took part in medical advances which have saved countless lives in peace and war. Among these was the storage of blood for transfusion, one of the great medical advances made in Spain; also new techniques in surgery which helped to conquer the demon of gas-gangrene, one of the greatest killers in war, and the beginnings of mobile front-line hospitals (as featured in the TV programme *MASH*), which ensure that the wounded are operated on as soon as possible.

The personal cost was often high. Ruth Ormesby, a Catholic nurse with Spanish Medical Aid, died trying to escape from a fire in the SMAC flat in Barcelona. Some of the nurses were wounded. Few escaped illness – typhoid, breakdown, malnutrition. A number of the Americans faced witch-hunting in the McCarthy years; they had, after all, been 'prematurely anti-fascist'.[2] (Many came from Jewish homes, so this was hardly surprising.)

Nurses and others working in danger and discomfort sometimes looked rather contemptuously at those journalists and delegates who came, were fêted, saw and went away. Yet their contribution too was vital. It was they who spoke in parliament and at meetings, reported to the aid committees and caught the eye of the world's press. They were the link between those at the war and those at home who were forming committees, collecting food, giving money, caring for refugee children and putting pressure on governments.

How authentic is the picture which these extracts paint of the Spanish war? Letters home were censored. Sometimes they were written as propaganda to conjure up supplies from supporters, although there is no reason to think that those who wrote them did not believe what they wrote. Memories select what they recall, and colour it with later opinions. Individual extracts may give a slanted view, but we have not excluded any for this reason. Martha Gellhorn warned me against Lillian Hellman: 'That woman', she said, 'wrapped the Spanish Civil War round herself like a Dior creation'. We hesitated, but decided that no one should be excluded because of self-aggrandisement – or any other failing.

Yet whatever the limitations of individual extracts, taken as a whole they give a tremendous feeling of what it was like to be engaged on the Republican side, and a view of the war which it would be difficult to find anywhere else.

Some aspects of the war experience are unavoidably under-represented. The tragic disputes between Anarchists, Socialists, Communists, liberals and other groups were disillusioning to the Anarchists Jane Patrick and Ethel MacDonald, and to the Australian Mary Low, who was with the POUM. Those who were working in hospitals and relief centres were more on the margins of the political in-fighting.

At a more personal level, few contributions give any impression of relationships between men and women in the medical services, though these young men and women, thrown closely together in heightened circumstances of death and danger, lived no differently from what others might do today. A number of nurses married International Brigaders, doctors or others whom they met in Spain. Sometimes a few words hide heart-break, as when the Australian nurse, Una Wilson, writes, 'I have let my surgeon go back to the front without me. We have worked together right through the war. I let him go back to that.' Or joy, as when Madge Addy writes, 'Wilhelm Holet was waiting at the dockside ...' And there were brief encounters, happy or unfortunate. Nor was sexual harassment unknown, and Marion Merriman records the trauma of rape. The SMAC in London was constantly worried that 'goings-on' might detract from its appeal, and the police Special Branch in Britain was ready to pick up any scandal going.

The picture from Franco's territory is sketchy. He had relatively few supporters in Britain, and they tended to be older, richer and in higher places, so less likely to volunteer.[3] The two groups which might have been expected to send volunteers did not do so. Mosley's British Union of Fascists boasted that it had not sent a penny or a person to Franco,[4] though from Ireland General O'Duffy took a contingent of 'Blueshirts'. From the large Catholic community in Britain, only Gabriel Herbert went with Franco's medical services, and she went to liaise between British supporters and the services in Spain.

Franco was not willing to accept foreign volunteers in the medical or relief services, apart from the Germans and Italians who went with their own armed forces. Gabriel Herbert suggested that this was to prevent the confusion of many tongues, but the Republican experience belies this. No British Quakers were accepted in Nationalist territory. Six American Quaker men did go, but their role was confined to handing over relief supplies to the Auxilio Social, the Nationalist relief organisation.

Here then are the voices of some of the women who played a part in the Spanish war, to remind us if we have forgotten, or to tell us if we never knew, what moved and inspired, and what was the experience of, some of the best spirits of their generation.

Many people have provided us with material for this book. Besides those whom we thank in the 'Acknowledgements' (below) we thank those who have helped us to trace writing by the women who were in Spain.

In Britain: Bill Alexander (International Brigade Association), Michael Alpert, Tony Atienza (IB Archivist), Audrey Canning (Scottish Gallacher Memorial Library), Max Egelnick (Marx Memorial Library), Josef Keith, Sylvia Carlyle and Edward Milligan (Library of the Religious Society of Friends), Tim Heald and Wendy Mulford.

In the USA: Victor Berch (Special Collections Library, Brandeis University), Robert G. Colodney, Bernard R. Crystal (Butler Library, Columbia University), Walter J. Lear (Institute of Social Medicine, History Center), Rosalita J. Leonard and James R. Lynch (Bretheren History Library and Archives), Ray Marantz, Richar Ogar (Bancroft Library, University of California), Elizabeth Shenton (Schlesinger Library, Radcliffe College), Sam Sills (Abraham Lincoln Film Project), Mildred Rackley Simon, Abe Smorodin, Ben Iceland and Irving Weissman (Veterans of the Abraham Lincoln Brigade), Jack Sutters (American Friends Service Committee Archivist) Quentin D. Young (Health and Medicine Research Group) and Francesca Patai.

In Australia: Amirah Inglis and Judith Keene (to both of whom a special 'thank-you') and Michael Saclier (Archives of Business and Labour, Australian National Library).

In New Zealand: Ann Cherrington (*New Zealand Nursing Journal*), George Jackson and Yvonne Shadbolt.

And any others whom we may have unintentionally left out.

Notes

1. 56 British women and one South African are named as serving for Spanish Medical Aid Committee, (International Brigade Archives, Marx Memorial Library, London). There were four Australian women and three New Zealanders in IB hospitals. Records of the Abraham Lincoln Brigade show that the American Medical Bureau to Aid Spanish Democracy sent 61 women. British Quakers had 26 women in Spain at different times. There were at least two Canadians, one a nurse, one a journalist. US Quakers had six. (Records of Friends' Spain Committee, Friends' Library, London and American Friends' Service Council archives, Philadelphia.) Various sources indicate that Sir George Young's Southern Hospitals had, in addition to American Quakers, seventeen British, one Australian, one New Zealand, one American and one Irish woman working at different times. We also know of five women with the NJC and Save the Children. This makes a total of some 170 women. Unfortunately the records of the SMAC, Sir George Young's unit and the NJC have not been found. A considerable number of women also went to Spain as journalists, observers and delegates.
2. Many volunteers from Eastern Europe suffered persecution, anti-semitic prejudice, and in some cases death, during the Stalin era.
3. A Gallup poll in Britain in March 1938 showed 57 per cent pro-Republic, 7 per cent as pro-Franco and 19 per cent as undecided. A repeat in January 1939 showed 72 per cent for

the Republic, 9 per cent for Franco and a steady 19 per cent as undecided. Support for Franco was greater among older and higher-income groups.

4. *Blackshirt*, 16 January 1937. Lack of Roman Catholic involvement, information from Terence Sheehy, former editor of the *Catholic Herald*, via Douglas Hyde.

Note on the Text

Many of the writings in this book are taken from longer works – diaries, letters and memoirs. It has rarely been possible for us to include pieces in their entirety. Editors' cuts are indicated by […]. Where writers used dots as a literary device these have been left unbracketed. Editorial additions and translations are also square-bracketed. In a few cases extracts have been taken from more than one text by the same writer; these are indicated by three asterisks across the page. There are also a few cases of minor editing where an interview was in question-and-answer form and we have written it up to run on continuously, or where the person interviewed repeated herself unnecessarily.

Every choice of extract, each cut or editorial alteration involves a value judgement, and some readers may disapprove of our judgements. Where this is so we can only refer them to the originals which are given in the Acknowledgements. For our part we have taken every care to avoid distorting the sense, viewpoint or intention of the writer, or the balance of the original. No writer has been omitted because of her viewpoint.

Some of the writers in this anthology refer to the 'Moors' and condemn the use of black troops by Franco, or the use of Islamic troops in what purported to be a Christian crusade. This refers to Franco's use of North African mercenaries, part of the Spanish Army of Africa, and reflects a degree of racism, even among left-wing and other progressive people, which would be unacceptable today. It also reflects the particular circumstances in which Spain was created through the expulsion of the Islamic rulers and peoples of Spain between the eleventh and fifteenth centuries. This *Reconquista* so dominated Spanish national consciousness that Franco's use of 'Moorish' troops deeply offended the Republic and its supporters.

Chronology

1931
13 April   Spanish monarchy falls: Republic declared.

1934
9-10 October   Franco puts down Asturian miners' rising.

1935
August   Comintern adopts Popular Front policy.
14 November   Conservatives win British General Election.

1936
16 February   Popular Front wins Spanish General Election.
3 May   Popular Front wins French General Election.
18 July   Army revolt against Spanish government.
27 July   National Council of Labour launches Spanish Workers' Fund.
1 August   Spanish Medical Aid Committee formed in London.
23 August   First British medical unit leaves for Spain.
26 August   Australian Spanish Relief Committee formed.
3 September   Quaker Spain Committee set up in London.
4 September   Irún falls: northern Spain cut off from France.
9 September   Non-Intervention Committee meets in London.
17 September   Scottish Ambulance Unit leaves Glasgow.
12 October   Formation of International Brigades.
22 October   First British ambulance to Franco.
December   American Medical Bureau to Aid Spanish Democracy formed.
Australian nurses arrive in Spain.
New Zealand Spanish Medical Aid Committee formed.
25 December   First Quaker canteen opened in Barcelona.

1937

January	British medical group links up with International Brigades.
	First American Hospital Unit arrives in Spain.
February	Sir George Young's ambulance unit formed.
Feb-April	Hospitals and feeding centres set up in southern Spain.
6 February	Battle of Jarama begins.
8 February	Fall of Málaga.
26 April	Guernica bombed.
May	Second American medical group arrives in Spain.
4 May	Anarchist and POUM uprising in Barcelona.
18 May	Negrín replaces Caballero as Spanish Prime Minister.
23 May	Basque children land at Southampton.
28 May	Republican La Granja offensive begins.
May	First American Quakers arrive in Spain.
19 June	Fall of Bilbao.
6 July	Republican Brunete offensive begins.
July	First Quaker supported children's colonies.
24 August	Republican Quinto/Belchite offensive begins.
21 October	All northern Spain in Nationalist hands.
15 December	Republican Teruel offensive begins.

1938

9 March	Major Nationalist offensive in Aragon.
15 April	Nationalists cut Republic in two.
1 June	First International Commission relief reaches Spain.
25 July	Republican offensive across River Ebro.
21-23 September	International Brigades withdrawn.
29 September	Munich agreement.
29 October	Farewell parade of International Brigades.

1939

26 January	Fall of Barcelona.
25 March	Surrender of Madrid: defeat of Republic.
April-June	Last British and American medical and relief personnel leave Spain.
June	Refugee ship *Sinaia* sails for Mexico.
3 September	Outbreak of Second World War.

Books for Background

Paul Preston: *The Spanish Civil War 1936-39*, London 1986 (readable and reliable).

Hugh Thomas: *The Spanish Civil War*, Harmondsworth 1968 (standard text; not reliable on medical and relief services).

Jim Fyrth: *The Signal Was Spain; The Aid Spain Movement in Britain, 1936-39*; London 1986 (for medical and relief services and aid movements). There is as yet no history of the American medical aid.

Amirah Inglis: *Australians in the Spanish Civil War*, Sydney 1987.

Judith Keene; *The Last Mile to Huesca; An Australian Nurse in Spain*, Sydney 1988 (the diary of Agnes Hodgson).

Bill Alexander, *British Volunteers for Liberty Spain, 1936-39*, London 1982 (history of the British International Brigaders).

A.H. Landis: *The Abraham Lincoln Brigade*, New York 1957.

There are many memoirs by individuals. Two by women are:

Marion Merriman and Warren Lerude, *American Commander in Spain*, Reno 1986.

Lini de Vries, *Up From the Cellar*, Minneapolis 1979.

Others are referred to in sources at the end of the book.

Two anthologies of Spanish War writing are:

Valentine Cunningham (ed.): *Spanish Civil War Verse*, Harmondsworth 1980.

Valentine Cunningham (ed.): *Spanish Front; Writers on the Civil War*, Oxford 1986.

(Women are under-represented in both these. We have avoided duplicating pieces which appeared in them, even when it meant sacrificing the best available.)

An anthology of Scottish memoirs is *Voices from the Spanish Civil War*, (ed.Ian MacDougall), Edinburgh 1986.

Glossary of Initials

Spanish Political Parties and Trade Unions:

CNT: Confederación Nacional de Trabajo; anarcho-syndicalist trade union grouping.
FAI: Federación Anarquista Ibérica; Anarchist Federation.
POUM: Partido Obrero de Unificación Marxista; far-left socialist party.
PSUC: Partido Socialista Unificado de Cataluña; effectively the Catalan Communist Party.
UGT: Unión General de Trabajadores; Socialist trade union grouping.

Aid Organisations:

AFSC: American Friends' Service Committee.
ASRC: Australian Spanish Relief Committee.
AMB: American Medical Bureau to Aid Spanish Democracy.
FSC: Friends' Service Council (Religious Society of Quakers) (Britain)
NACASD: North American Committee to Aid Spanish Democracy.
NJC: National Joint Committee for Spanish Relief (British 'umbrella' aid organisation).
SMAC: Spanish Medical Aid Committee (Britain: same initials for New Zealand).

Others:

AIA: Artists' International Association.
IBA: International Brigade Association (Britain).
TUC: Trades Union Congress (Britain).
VALB: Veterans of the Abraham Lincoln Brigade (USA).

Gijón
Bilbao
Santander
Hendaye
Perpignan
Portbou
Burgos
R. EBRO
Huesca
Grañen
Zaragoza
Belchite
Barcelona
Segovia
R. JARAMA
Brunete
MADRID
Teruel
Toledo
Uclés
Benicasim
R. TAQUS
Valencia
Albacete
Alicante
Córdoba
Murcia
Sevilla
Málaga
Almería
Gibraltar

SPAIN

100 km.

Part I

FROM GAMES TO WAR

In the Beginning …

Aileen Palmer

Aileen Palmer, *Secretary of the Victoria Writers' League (Australia), was in Spain with her parents in July 1936, typing and translating for the* Olimpíada Popular, *the anti-fascist games planned to counter the Berlin Olympics. After the army revolt the Palmers were evacuated in a British destroyer. Aileen then joined the first British medical unit for Spain as secretary and interpreter. In May 1938 she returned exhausted to London. In August 1939 she reported on the Spanish refugee camps in southern France.*

In the beginning was Barcelona … before the war burst, when the furtive rich sat in the shady cafés, looking out. Then I was also a tourist, an outsider, sitting in cafés, and watching the river that never stopped flowing and passed me by: the Ramblas, whirling thoroughfare grown from an ancient river, like all the sunken roads that wind from the Catalan hills to the sea …

Then the storm. First it was just a cloud that thickened on the far horizon of Madrid. Monday: 'Calvo Sotelo is dead,' Frieda announced, as she joined the usual group at the fonda in the early afternoon.

'Viva,' the student said. 'There's a fascist out of the way.' Frieda turned on him.

'No, you fool, don't you see what this means? It's what the fascists have been driving for all along. Their whole policy of provocation has been directed to this end. Now they have a slogan, a rallying-cry: "The Reds have killed Sotelo." '[1]

The days passed, heavy with foreboding. Arthur used to spend long vigils on the streets after midnight, with groups of workers waiting for arms to be handed out if the fascists should rise. Every day, travelling in by train to Barcelona, you saw reinforcements of Civil Guards pouring into the city: for which side?

Then the sultry Saturday afternoon: July 17th; and, in the evening a visit to Radio Barcelona, where Hermann was to speak about the *Olimpíada Popular* – the People's Olympiad to be held in Barcelona, as a protest against the holding of the official Olympic games that year in Berlin, that was then the centre of Nazism and racial prejudice.

At the radio station government communiqués were pouring in – reports of fighting here, fighting there – an impassioned crescendo of voices. What was going on then was all very obscure to me, trying to pick up the thread in my hazy Spanish.

It hadn't happened in Barcelona yet: would it happen now? Others were more on the alert than I was, but even so when it happened it caught them unawares.

I had been asleep for some hours in Hermann's flat when two of his friends burst in. They had been out on the street all night.

'It's begun. They're fighting in the city now. We've seen the first dead'

Their voices were subdued, they were somehow overcome, as if it was all something different from the possible military revolt they had envisaged and discussed beforehand.

The soldiers had come down in the early hours of the morning, marching down one of the main boulevards, and taking possession of the strategic buildings by entering with a shout of 'Viva la Republica!'

No one realised they were enemies at first, and no one resisted. But when the situation was grasped, the government of Catalunya passed out what arms it had to the workers who lined the streets, and, even without arms, the workers rose, tore up paving-stones, built barricades and fought …

Below us in the city the guns boomed out, but by afternoon Barcelona's fate was decided. We were as happy as if the fate of all Spain had been decided that day. Fighting continued elsewhere, but it was remote, unreal.

In the afternoon we walked down into the city as far as the Plaza de la Universidad. People were strolling about the streets as though it were just any Sunday afternoon – sitting in cafés exchanging the latest news, or just ordinary gossip.

And then a lorryload of Civil Guards would pass, and the people would greet them with the clenched fist salute, cheers and applause – the Civil Guard. They were good fighters, and in Catalunya the old traditionalists with the shiny Napoleon hats had remained loyal to the elected government.

By Monday the fighting was over in Barcelona, except for occasional burst of sniping in the tortuous streets back off the Ramblas. But Barcelona was a changed city.

The city that had roared with traffic all night long was wrapped in stillness by early evening. If you walked in the streets after darkness fell, you were liable to be warned to separate and return home:

'The fascists have got hold of a Red Cross wagon, and they're driving it round the streets, machine-gunning the crowds.'

It was the newly formed Citizen Guard, men in ordinary working-clothes with old-fashioned rifles, who patrolled the streets, maintaining order in the town.

But with daylight the voice of the city burst forth again in greater volume than ever before. There was a continuous circulation of traffic on the Ramblas: commandeered cars and lorries, roughly daubed with the letters that stood for the parties and trade unions who had banded together in the defence of the city – CNT, PSUC, Estat Catala, POUM – armed guards sprawled along the running-boards, or seated on the bonnets – horns tooting continuously the one-two-three signal of the CNT, radios pouring over the streets their floods of oratory ('La Republica ... la Republica ...'), and the songs that had become the continuous refrain of those days, 'Himno de Riego' and 'Els Segadors' ...

A Real War

Winifred Bates

Winifred Bates *taught in East London in the 1920s. From
1931 she and her novelist husband, Ralph, lived off and on in the
Pyrenees. In July 1936 Winifred began working as a journalist
for the United Socialist Party of Catalonia, and from July 1937
was a personnel officer for British, Commonwealth and American
nurses. In late 1938 and 1939 she toured Britain and the USA
raising funds for food and refugees. Later she worked in China as
a translator. Back in England she became a leading teacher of
Esperanto.*

One day when I went down to the village I was told that something
had happened in Spain; the villagers thought it might be a
general strike. Two days later they told me that it was a military
rebellion, that the soldiers had marched out of their barracks early on
the Sunday morning and attempted to take the civic buildings and
telephone exchanges. According to the radio news they had been
stopped. 'It's all right,' said the villagers in their friendly way, 'the
government's got it well in hand. The soldiers are still holding out in
Seville and Zaragoza, but the government is in control almost
everywhere and the navy and air forces are with the government. The
trouble can't last long.' I wanted to go to a town on the main road to
buy more food than could be obtained in the village, and asked, as
usual, for the use of the hotel car. I was told that I could not have it as
no vehicles were running; the government had controlled gasoline
from the first day,

I returned to my home in the hills to think it over, and decided that
this was something more than some local labour unrest. […]

We went to Barcelona, the local county council courteously
supplying the car in which we travelled. What I saw on that journey
fully bore out what the villagers had told me. The government had it
well in hand. The town councils had placed men on traffic control
along the highway, men whose duty it was to stop cars and examine
papers, and luggage if they so wished. There was no chance of a thief
taking advantage of the situation by robbing a church or a rich house and

getting away to France with the loot.

I took a room at a hotel opposite the Francia Station. I looked up my friends and heard their accounts of 18 July. One morning, sitting outside the hotel over my coffee, I read in the newspaper that thousands of Italians had landed on the southern shores of Spain. I looked at the other tables. 'Italians!' exclaimed a man indignantly, 'Then we are being invaded! It's not a civil war; it will be a hard and real war.'

'And it'll last two years,' remarked the man next to me. […]

I went to the anti-fascist women's committee and found out about the work they were doing, training girls in factories, looking after refugees from the war zones, arranging classes in reading and writing for illiterate women, getting out a bright little woman's paper fortnightly. When English or American visitors arrived in the city I usually spent a while with them. If they wanted to visit the new schools, hospitals or clinics I sometimes went with them and a woman from the anti-fascist committee as interpreter. I had the honour of dining with the delegation of English clergy who visited Spain.

Then I was asked to broadcast my comments in English over the government station. I did this more and more often, till I was doing it every night.

Mediterranean

Muriel Rukeyser

Muriel Rukeyser, *the American writer, was in Barcelona for the anti-fascist Olímpiada Popular. She was evacuated with the American, Hungarian and Belgian teams, in a small boat. Some team members volunteered for the Republican militia.*

I

At the end of July, exile. We watched the gangplank go
cutting the boat away, indicating: sea.
Barcelona, the sun, the fire-bright harbor, war.
Five days.
       Here at the rail, foreign and refugee,
we saw the city, remembered that zero of attack,
alarm in the groves, snares through the olive hills,
rebel defeat: leaders, two regiments,
broadcasts of victory, tango, surrender.
The truckride to the city, barricades,
bricks pried at corners, rifle-shot in street,
car-burning, bombs, blank warnings, fists up, guns
busy sniping, the town halls, towers of smoke.
And order making, committees taking charge, foreigners
commanded out by boat.

I saw the city, sunwhite flew on glass,
trucewhite from window, the personal fighting found
eyes on the dock, sunset-lit faces of singers,
eyes, goodbye into exile. Saw where Columbus rides
black-pillared: discovery, turn back, explore
a new found Spain, coast-province, city-harbor.
Saw our parades ended, the last marchers on board
listed by nation.

I saw first of the faces going home into war
the brave man Otto Boch, the German exile, knowing
he quieted tourists during machinegun battle,

he kept his life straight as a single issue –
left at that dock we left, his gazing Breughel face,
square forehead and eyes, strong square breast fading,
the narrow runner's hips diminishing dark.
I see this man, dock, war, a latent image.

The boat *Ciudad de Ibiza*, built for 200,
loaded with 500, manned by loyal sailors,
chartered by Belgians when consulates were helpless,
through a garden of gunboats, margin of the port,
entered: Mediterranean.

II

Frontier of Europe, the tideless sea, a field of power
touching desirable coasts, rocking in time conquests,
fertile, the moving water maintains its boundaries
layer on layer, Troy – seven civilized worlds:
Egypt, Greece, Rome, jewel Jerusalem,
giant feudal Spain, giant England, this last war.

The boat pulled into evening, underglaze blue
flared instant fire, blackened towards Africa.
Over the city alternate lights occurred;
                              and pale
in the pale sky emerging stars.
No city now, a besieged line of lights
masking the darkness where the country lay.
But we knew guns
bright through mimosa
singe of powder
and reconnoitering plane
flying anonymous
scanning the Pyrenees
black now above the Catalonian Sea.

Boat of escape, dark on the water, hastening, safe,
holding non-combatants, the athlete, the child,
the printer, the boy from Antwerp, the black boxer,
lawyer and communist.
                              The Games had not been held.
    A week of Games, theatre and festival;
    world anti-fascist week. Pistol starts race.
    Machine-gun marks the war. Answered unarmed,
    charged the Embarcadero, met those guns.

And charging through the province, joined that army.
Boys from the hills, the unmatched guns,
the clumsy armored cars.
Drilled in the bullring. Radio cries:
To Saragossa! And this boat.

Escape, dark on the water, an overloaded ship.
Crowded the deck. Spoke little. Down to dinner.
Quiet on the sea: no guns.
The printer said, In Paris there is time,
but where's its place now; where is poetry?

    This is the sea of war; the first frontier
    blank on the maps, blank sea; Minoan boats
    maybe achieved this shore;
    mountains whose slope divides
    one race, old insurrections, Narbo, now
    moves at the colored beach
    destroyer wardog. 'Do not burn the church,
    compañeros, it is beautiful. Besides,
    it brings tourists.' They smashed only the image
    madness and persecution.
    Exterminating wish; they forced the door,
    lifted the rifle, broke the garden window,
    removed only the drawings: cross and wrath.
    Whenever we think of these, the poem is,
    that week, the beginning, exile
    remembered in continual poetry.

Voyage and exile, a midnight cold return,
dark to our left mountains begin the sky.
There, pointed the Belgian, I heard a pulse of war,
sharp guns while I ate grapes in the Pyrenees.
Alone, walking to Spain, the five o'clock of war.
In those cliffs run the sashed and sandalled men,
capture the car, arrest the priest, kill the captain,
fight our war.
The poem is the fact, memory fails
under the seething lifts and will not pass.

Here is home-country, who fights our war.
Street-meeting speaker to us:
                '... came for Games,
    you stay for victory; foreign? your job is:
    go tell your countries what you saw in Spain.'
The dark unguarded army left all night.

Muriel Rukeyser

M. de Paîche said, 'We can learn from Spain.'
The face on the dock that turned to find the war.

III

Seething and falling black, a sea of stars,
Black marked with virile silver. Peace all night,

over that land, planes
death-lists a frantic bandage
the rubber tires burning monuments
sandbag, overturned wagon, barricade
girl's hand with gun food failing, water failing
the epidemic threat
the date in a diary a blank page opposite
no entry –
however, met
the visible enemy heroes: madness, infatuation
the cache in the crypt, the breadline shelled,
the yachtclub arsenal, the foreign cheque.
History racing from an assumed name, peace,
a time used to perfect weapons.

If we had not seen fighting,
if we had not looked there
        the plane flew low
        the plaster ripped by shots
        the peasant's house
if we had stayed in our world
between the table and the desk
between the town and the suburb
slowly disintegration
male and female.
If we had lived in our city
sixty years might not prove
        the power this week
        the overthrown past
        tourist and refugee
Emeric in the bow speaking his life
and the night on this ship
the night over Spain
quick recognition
male and female.

[...]

This Earthquake!

Felicia Browne

***Felicia Browne**, artist and sculptor, was the first Briton to be killed fighting for the Spanish Republic. In 1934 she won a prize for her design of a Trades Union Congress medal commemorating the centenary of the Tolpuddle Martyrs. She travelled widely, working as a kitchen hand, and was an active member of the Artists' International Association and of the Communist Party. In July 1936 she went to Spain. With the army revolt she joined the Republican militia. While trying to blow up a rebel munition train her party was outnumbered. Felicia stopped to help a wounded man but both were riddled with machine-gun bullets. An appreciation published by the Artists' International Association is reproduced below.*

The newspapers can be relied upon to make capital out of the fact that she was a woman, and she was the last person to wish to lay any undue stress upon the significance of this fact. But it has significance. She had it in her to represent the very best type of the new woman, but the kind of upbringing to which she was automatically subjected and and the forces with which she had to compete in a society where commercial values are pre-eminent, seriously and unnecessarily delayed her in harmonising all the remarkable powers within her.

She had most of the best human characteristics, but she conceived her own variety more as a source of opposition than of enjoyment. She was without guile, duplicity or vanity; painfully truthful and honest, immensely kind and generous, completely humane, loving any aspect of livingness, and as capable of enormous humour as she was deeply serious. She was gifted at every craft that she tried, a witty letter-writer, an amusing cartoonist, a vital and interesting companion, and socially much too gracious to belong credibly to the twentieth century. She was enormously well read, with a literary visual capacity which would have made her an excellent illustrator, particularly of Dante and Kafka, by whose strange and elaborate cosmogonies she became fascinated in the last year. She loved and appreciated good music and poetry, and whenever she got it, good food and drink – though materially she was remarkably careless and hopelessly generous. [...]

But if her fighting was the expression of her deeply conscientious but less happy side, at least she had intellectual faith in the future. And she found happiness at the end, as far as one can judge from her letters, in a real sense of comradeship with her fellow militiamen. Intellectually she was quite clear about what was necessary for the next few years of her life. In a letter to a friend written just before she went to Spain she said, 'You say I am escaping and evading things by not painting or making sculpture. If there is no painting or sculpture to be made, I cannot make it. I can only make out of what is valid and urgent to me. If painting or sculpture were more valid or urgent to me than the earthquake which is happening in the revolution, or if these two were reconciled so that the demands of the one didn't conflict (in time, even, or concentration) with the demands of the other, I should paint or make sculpture.'

Notes

1. José Calvo Sotelo, leading monarchist and Minister of Finance under Primo de Rivera dictatorship (1922-29); allied with Gil Robles, leader of CEDA, alliance of right-wing parties, also of pro-clerical *Acción Popular*. On 13 July 1936 Sotelo was shot dead by a Captain of the Civil Guard, while in custody, in revenge for the murder of Lieutenant Castillo, a socialist member of the Republican Assault Guard. The Francoists used Sotelo's death as a proof of the breakdown of law and order, thus justifying their rebellion.

Part 2

WHERE THE WOUNDED WERE

The First Medical Unit

Thora Silverthorne

Thora Silverthorne *came from a Welsh mining family. She trained as a nurse at the Radcliffe Infirmary in Oxford, where she joined the student Communist Party. Later, at the Hammersmith Hospital, she recruited nurses to a trade union. In August 1936 she joined the first British medical unit for Spain. She married Kenneth Sinclair-Loutit, the unit's administrator. Back home she started the first trade union that was solely for nurses.*

There were six nurses – we were done up in little round nurses hats, blue macintoshes, black shoes and stockings – absolutely as nurses were in those days. [...] The men wore uniforms; khaki uniforms for some reason. [...] We had gathered at the old Trade Union Club, which was at the end of New Oxford Street. I don't know how we were taken to Victoria Station, but then there was a great demonstration, a walk-past of people with banners wishing us a good journey to Spain. We all stood outside Victoria Station, in Buckingham Palace Road; we stood in a row and they gave us flowers. It was a very lovely occasion. That was an indication of the support that there was at that time. Then we got on our train and went to Paris; and we all got to know each other – because we didn't know each other; we were a motley crowd. We stayed in Paris for about a week. We went to a magnificent demonstration in the Buffalo Stadium. They had terrific crowds, and they were giving us a terrific reception, shouting. It was a wonderful evening, a terrific send-off. [...]

[In Spain] We went off to Grañen in lorries; very dusty roads. We had lots of sweeties; we'd taken toffees and licquorice all-sorts, and I had masses of them in a case. Now and again people would give us great big green water-melons – lovely; and we'd cut them up: it was hot and dusty, and we were very glad of them. The moment we got off the lorry and (were) giving the little kids sweeties — they'd come round us like flies.

The house we chose, or we were given [in Grañen], was the doctor's house, because it was the biggest building. It was empty. There was nothing, only dirt and filth and rats and a stinking courtyard.

Everything was absolutely stinking. We were a sort of pioneer unit. For the first week or so we scrubbed and cleaned. The great thing was we were all young and enthusiastic people, and we cleaned the place up. We set up an operating theatre, which was my little province, because I'd done a lot of theatre work, and a couple of dark little wards. But English nurses are marvellous at carrying English hospital traditions into other places. [...]

We were up against things which young people had never seen, and yet we coped. I had two very good friends who died on the table. One was just alive, and I went back to the ward with him, staying with him and holding his hand and talking to someone who was unconscious; talking and crying because he had died. That would break me now. I could not stand it any more.

Hospital Ingles,
Grañen (Huesca),
Aragon,
Via Barcelona, Spain.

25 November 1936

Dearest All,
We are very busy – the attack on Huesca has actually begun – and will be for some time I'm afraid. [...] We've been working hard for the last few days and doing very good work. We've been doing major operations and working 14 hour days.

A nurse is just going back to England and taking this with her to post in London so it will get through in a few days. [...]There's very little to write about. We live a very enclosed life; our wireless has been taken away: (censorship of news!). Papers from England don't come frequently and we are altogether cut off.

The news re Germany's and Italy's support for Franco, Russia's decisive move, are all very frightening. We are heading undoubtedly for world war. I hope I get home first! [...] I must fly – Mollie is going – it's 3.30 a.m.

All my love,
Thora.

Seccion Sanitaire
14th Brigade International,
Spain.

9 March 1937

Dearest All,

[...] Did you know that Comrade Ball of Reading (son of the chemist Dad was friendly with) was killed on this front.[1] He'd behaved very well: the commandant praised him highly. Said he was due for promotion for his splendid behaviour. Please give my very sincere sympathy to Comrade Ball's father; tell him his son died with many other fine fellows but not in vain. The English comrades did much towards keeping our front: they set a splendid example and greatly raised the morale of the other battalions.

We have become accustomed to air raids although they still worry me a great deal: I dread them. The planes were over last night, dropped bombs but did no damage. Considering the number of raids suprisingly little damage is done. The swine deliberately attempt to bomb hospitals – it's inhuman. The other day, an English nurse who works in a village some distance from here came along to stay the night with us for a change.[2] She was very shocked. She'd had a nasty experience the day before. She was sitting talking to a comrade when a bomb was dropped quite near them. She was thrown off her chair and her companion was killed. Then she saw a bunch of kiddies killed by another bomb. Its really awful but I can assure you its absolutely true – the nurse told me all about it. Poor dear, she was badly shaken up.

This war is just bloody but if possible has made me even more violently anti-fascist. Their methods, even for war, are horrible. I can imagine by this time Shon is almost on the point of coming out. Please don't let him: I just couldn't stand the strain of knowing he was in danger too ... God, I'd love to see you and talk to you. I miss you more and more. Do try to write more frequently. I don't know when I'll get home[...]

We are in quite comfortable quarters and our food is reasonably good.

Sometimes we have to work 20 hours and then slacken down. None of us mind, our morale is very high. [...] I hope you are not worried about me, please don't. [...] I'm starved for news of you every one. Please tell me all the little bits about Bet and Muffy and the rest.

All my love and thoughts.

Red Front,
Tho.

Bread and Chick Peas

Aileen Palmer

407, Muntaner,
Barcelona.

8 December 1936

Dear Family:
At last I am down on Barcelona leave after over three months up at the hospital, and it's beginning to come back to me that there was a world before Grañen. [...]

Our hospital is not on a very dangerous front – as you probably know, the Aragon front has changed less than any since the beginning of the war. So far, however, there has been no move towards sending us to Madrid, though our administrator offered that we should go if desired, as we are the best hospital close to the front line, have established a certain reputation in the sector, and are the first good station to which cases requiring urgent operation can be brought. Our work is, of course, very spasmodic – for instance, two nights running, after days of idleness occupied, rather fruitlessly, with our own internal affairs, you have cases requiring laporotomies – operations on the guts – brought in after midnight, and the chief surgeon, theatre nurse, anaesthetist (who is also the administrator) and maybe one or two others such as myself who hang around to make tea and help clear up working till well after three or four. Then another day when no wounded arrive, and people quarrel for lack of occupation, and because they dislike the shape of each other's ears.

You don't realise how the place has got you down till you get away to a place like Barcelona. I go round the streets in a daze, feeling like a prisoner emerging to blink at the light. Barcelona all looks very clean and newly painted – not hectic, as before we left, or dully resigned, as when we were here before, but just steady winter sunshine and bright colours. Taxis are back on the streets – neat, efficient-looking, black and red ones, run by the CNT – and the driver scrupulously insists that you wait for the ha'penny change when you pay your fare. I've seen Barcelona with at least four different faces now, and I can't get used to the last one. [...]

Servicios Sanitarios 35-E,
Plaza de Altozano
Albacete,
Spain

3 April 1938[3]

Dear Family:
Writing this is an ambulance in a magnificent garden, not in the house
of an absent marquis, but of a Catalan poet. In this case there was no
confiscation as the *dueño* [owner] was apparently a sympathiser of the
popular front and resides still in Barcelona. When we arrived
yesterday we found a *mayordomo* [butler] and an *ama de casa*
[housekeeper] guarding a lofty mansion, fountain playing in the
square in front, frogs croaking and goldfish in the ponds. Hard to
believe, looking from the terrace at the top of this winding stair over
acres of blossoming orchards, that not far off there is a war, and
bombs hurling destruction.

...The house presents a quaint picture a little later, reminiscent of
scenes early in the war. It is somewhat the atmosphere of a ship or a
smart hotel, you almost expect to see people moving about sipping
cocktails. Stretcher-bearers and first-aid men are playing billiards,
others are looking at magazines in the library, tired doctors, nurses
and stretcher-bearers have fallen asleep on the plush lounges that are
still protected by spotless linen coverings. But instead of cocktails
people are having their supper of bread and *garbanzos* [chick-peas].

...So far this letter probably sounds rather frivolous. You have read
of fascist advances on the Aragon front and you know that I must have
been taking part in a retreat. But this all just goes to show that we are
not in any state of panic or abject depression. The situation is certainly
grave. All along the roads we have seen the pitiful pilgrimages –
peasants driven from their homes by the annihilating bombs,
uprooted Spaniards trecking eastward to the coast with their flocks
and herds if they have any, and with their ramshackle mule-drawn
carts piled up with mattresses, bits of furniture, bits of food,
sometimes taking their hens and chickens which are all they have,
sometimes people who have nothing at all to eat, women carrying
children and making the long trek on foot, not knowing where they
will get anything to eat but placing their faith in the relief
organisations till they get to some more tranquil town where they have
a relation or someone and they will be able to find a corner to settle
down. They are mostly people who have never moved from the

villages where they were born and have grown up, and have suddenly seen the whole world they knew turned into a heap of dust and crumbling shards ... It is a long painful journey for all of them, I have seen people on the road yesterday, the names on their little donkey-carts showing that they came from villages taken a fortnight ago by the fascists. All these people, though, are moderately cheerful, and determined to save all they can from the wreck, above all to save themselves from coming under fascist domination. [...]

It was just about this time last year that I managed to send back a message to you from Madrid – just about my birthday. I have done richly in birthday presents this year and am very grateful to you all.

My love to all of you,

Aileen.

I Shall Never Forget

Annie Murray

Annie Murray came from a family of Aberdeenshire farmers. She trained at the Royal Infirmary Edinburgh, and was one of six nurses with the second British contingent. They joined the hospital at Grañen. Annie was one of the last British nurses to leave Spain in February 1939. During the Second World War she was in charge of an air-raid station in East London, and later became matron of a children's nursery in Stepney.

During the first attack I was on night duty, and because of this, the war made a deep impression on my mind; for sick people are usually more ill at night, and our senses being more acute at night to the gruesomeness and the awful suffering of the men, especially those with abdominal wounds and haemorrhage, for which one can do so little, became burnt on my mind. In those days many of the soldiers were under twenty years of age, and I shall never forget those young men with their bodies torn and their limbs smashed.

But, in addition to caring for the men from the battlefield, there was the civilian population of the neighbouring villages to care for. When the fascists bombed the little towns in the hills, the people came running to us over the rough ground, over stones and rocks till by the time they reached us their feet were torn and bleeding. Often they carried each other. Once a blind woman of eighty years came stumbling in; she was so patient and she never complained. A bomb had dropped on her cottage whilst she was in the fields. When someone began to sympathise, she said, 'Well, I've lost my house, but there's many a woman who has lost her children. As long as there is fascism we shall have this.' The nurses used to take turns, a day each, to wash and bandage the feet and take care of this fugitive civilian population

Once we had fascist prisoners. There was a boy of sixteen who was a lieutenant, who greatly feared the nurses. He was surprised at the attention he received. When they were picked up they were starving, and two of them died from their starved condition, which prevented their wounds from healing. They were pleased with any food we gave them. The two who could get about had permission to walk in the court yard, but they did not believe they had understood aright and at first refused to go out. The older ones had made up their minds that they would not speak to us at all, but they gradually broke down under our treatment. Most of them volunteered for service in the Republican Army when they were better. The Moors were fighting against the Spaniards on that front. One was brought in by our ambulance; he had been left out five days by the fascists with a terrible leg wound of which, in spite of all our care, he died. He had German money on him, out-of-date German marks of no value, with which the fascists had paid him for giving his life in the cause. One night a German, who had been left behind in fascists' territory, crawled across to us with a dreadful leg wound. After an amputation he recovered. We nursed all who came to us.

During the Ebro offensive we had a hospital train in a tunnel near the fighting area and where the number of wounded was very high.[4] I had the anxious experience of having my brother Tom, a commissar in a machine-gun company of the British Battalion of the International Brigade, and my brother George who had been wounded and recovered on another front. George was number two company's intelligence officer. It could be understood that when stretchers were brought in I would rush to see if either of my brothers was on one of them. Fortunately this never was the case. Early in the war my brother George had been wounded at the battle of Jarama by a bullet that went straight through his chest, missing his lungs by quarter of an inch, which kept him at death's door for several months. On the road to recovery he spent part of his convalescence in my hospital and it was of course a special satisfaction that I had the opportunity of helping to restore his usual vitality. Thereafter he went back to the front. […]

Whilst leaving Barcelona (during the final retreat) we had the horrible experience of witnessing little children whose hands had been blown off while picking up from the streets packets marked 'chocolate' in Italian, which were in fact anti-personnel bombs dropped from Italian fascist planes. If there was any experience of the war in Spain needed for any reinforcement of our anti-fascist hatred this was it.

A Woman's Work in Wartime

Winifred Bates

In July 1937 I got in touch with the committee in England that was sending medical supplies and personnel to work in the hospitals. I agreed to write news for them, to visit the hospitals and find out what the personnel needed in their work, deliver supplies to them and take photographs.

Then began for me a time of hard work, intense living and an education in the wonders of the human mind and behaviour. The personnel of the British Medical Unit was scattered about Spain from Murcia to Aragon. My first problem was transport. [...] Many a time I waited on the Madrid road and begged a ride. Once I made the mistake of thinking that telegraph wire would make a good seat. I sat at the back of the truck and every time it went over a bump I went up in the air and came down hard on my coil of wire. For days afterwards I could not sit down in comfort. Another time I put up an umbrella to keep off the driving rain; that was the last of the umbrella. On these journeys I used to carry a blue flannel dressing gown which I wrapped round my shoulders and head in the manner of a shawl, until the happy day when I bought a real sheepskin jacket with the wool inside. It probably looked just as funny but I kept warm. I reached the Teruel Front in January by ambulance, truck and car.[5] The roads were so deep in snow that at one hill we had to get out and, roping the ambulance, six of us let it down the hill while the driver tried to guide it straight.

Another of my problems was where to sleep. I could write a volume on beds I have known. I have tried those wobbly hospital beds, which made you feel as though you were in a hammock, and went down under you if someone tripped against the leg. I have slept on springs without mattresses, and mattresses without springs. I have slept in all my clothes and my camp eiderdown *and* shivered all night. I have slept in every kind of hotel bed, clean and dirty. I have slept in luxurious beds in houses from which people had run away before the war began; I have slept on kitchen benches and I have slept in the car.

Whenever possible the girls at the hospitals made me comfortable, sharing their beds and rooms with me. One night at the Teruel Front I arrived very late and was taken to the top floor of a large building. There were about 150 men in beds placed close together. In one corner were four double iron beds walled off by large pink and white counterpanes. In these slept the eight Spanish nurses. They were undressing when I arrived. One of them went and made me a cup of coffee; another found two pieces of dry bread and a seven pound tin with a tiny scraping of jam in the bottom. They gave me a knife, and the coffee in a condensed milk tin, which had had the rim filed off; then they sat on their beds and said, 'Eat your supper,' and they talked and laughed. If some one giggled too loudly as girls will, one of them would say, 'Hush, my companions, discipline; remember the sick men.' They made a bed for me in the pharmacy, which was just a large cupboard. It was like sleeping in a chemist's shop with all the stoppers left off the bottles. There was no window so I left the door open. And they had actually found me some sheets. Outside in the mud and slush and snow the army ... their brothers and fathers ... was holding up the enemy. [...]

It soon became clear to me that life for the nurses would be easier if they had someone to do liaison work and be in charge of them. So I suggested to the committee that I should do this. I became their 'Responsable': 'someone responsible for', but I would rather translate it 'friend'. This proved to be the most interesting work I did in the war. [...]

The girls who went to work in Spain as nurses, secretaries and interpreters were drawn from different parts of Britain and different kinds of families. About half of them when they came out were quite unaware of the historical importance of the war and its international complications. They were just nurses, courageous women, willing to work under the most dangerous conditions. The other half knew what it was about, had read a good deal on it, and were not surprised when they were called upon to nurse Moorish and Italian prisoners as well as Republican Spaniards.

I grew to know and respect some forty of these compatriots of mine; and I knew some of the American girls well too. It was my job to listen to them, to talk to them, to comfort and advise them. I shared little intimacies with them; I knew about their love affairs, past and present. They told me how the war was affecting them. I listened to their minds beating out the problems that knowledge brings. I suffered with them and laughed with them. [...]

Then I had to listen to tirades that they let forth about each other. So-and-so doesn't work hard enough or is a selfish pig and Miss ABC thinks of herself first, second and last. Equally violent were the speeches of praise about each other. I know at least ten nurses who, according to their colleagues, are 'the very best nurses that ever went to Spain'. They had an amazing respect for each other's courage and professional ability, and they did not forget to say so … to me. I would let all these high-powered speeches go on and on, knowing that it was good for them to talk themselves out. That was what I was for, a kind of soft buffer against which they could fling their war-ragged nerves and be soothed. […]

They were amusing too and we learnt to laugh at each other's idiosyncracies. There were girls who never seemed to be able to keep enough clothes hanging together to look clean and tidy and there were others who always looked spick and span under all conditions. There were girls who would break ice on the water to wash in and girls who preferred not to wash for weeks unless forcibly encouraged by their friends. There was a girl who never learnt any Spanish and persisted in giving orders, rebuking stretcher-bearers, coaxing cooks and flirting with soldiers in her own native tongue. 'And I told him not to do it that way …' she would say, and to the day she left she never seemed to realise that she had not made herself clear. There was one who worked in a dilapidated old monastery building. One of her patients was a man who was paralysed. At night the rats got into his bed and ate his feet and she would put her hand in his bed and pull them out. Yet that same woman when working at the front made a fuss because there were no toilets. […]

A nurse was dressing one morning and had got as far as her slip; as she was reaching for her uniform the roof of the house fell in on her. She was buried in the debris and her head was badly cut. A doctor and half the hospital staff rushed to rescue her. As she was dug out she said quite seriously, 'Oh, doctor, I'm so sorry I'm not dressed.' And she made the men search in the ruins for some clothes, while the blood streamed down her face.

Then there were the girls with frustrated sex emotions who told me the most lurid tales about the other girls. 'No, I didn't like it there; SUCH women, you've no ideAH. There was ONE girl who NEver slept in the nurses' quarters. DISgraceful. After all, one must think of the dignity of English womanhood.' I listened patiently. If she felt like that she had better say so. She was intensely sincere, and her professional work on the wards was excellent. By careful probing I found out whom she was talking about; she was not anxious to tell me.

I had to spoil the story by explaining that the woman concerned was married to an orderly at the hospital and sinfully 'crept out every night' to sleep with her husband. Most of these high faluting tales that I heard were not told in a spirit of gossip or spite, but as a kind of outlet for girls who really needed a chance to let off their feelings. [...]

There were girls from every political party. I did not ask them what they were directly they arrived, but it came out after a while. I wanted them to acquire that same spirit of unity amongst political parties that the Spaniards were achieving. [...] Whatever party they came from they were a credit to it.

I also came into contact with girls of varying religions. There were two Roman Catholics, devoted to their duty. One of them was not very strong and had to go to England for a rest. Twice she came back. She always wore a silver cross and carried her prayer book; these were the days of religious tolerance in Spain. Said the Spanish girl who worked beside her, 'If I'm not a Catholic, there's no reason why you shouldn't be.' The other girl died there and took her place beside many others of her persuasion who believed it worth while to risk all for Spain.[6] There was a Scottish Presbyterian who told me that the rich people in her church ought to be made to buy food for the children. 'Jesus taught us that we should feed the poor and the hungry,' she said, 'and look at these poor little mites.' Her religion was perhaps a little severe, but it brought tears to my eyes when she told me that she had written to her church and asked the pastor and congregation to help feed the hungry children. [...]

When the famous Ebro offensive of 1938 began I went up to that front. I found our people working in a large cave in the side of a mountain. It was not far from the river and only the worst cases were brought in there. Men died as I stood beside them. It was summer time and they had been in long training before they crossed the Ebro. Their bodies were brown and beautiful. We would bend over to take their last whispers and the message was always the same: 'We are doing well. Tell them to fight on ... till the final victory.'

It is so hard to make a man, and so easy to blast him into death. I shall never forget the Ebro. If one went for a walk away from the cave there was the smell of death. [...]

These are but a few of the incidents that left me changed and scarred. 'A woman's work in war time.' It was leading me along bitter paths.

Last of all it led me to the concentration camps in the south of France, where my friends had fled after being driven out of Spain. There I saw the people I had lived amongst for years, all kinds of people; teachers, doctors, lawyers, nurses, dressmakers, shop assistants, street car drivers, hotel keepers, waiters, musicians and artists, journalists, carpenters, mothers with tiny babies, thousands of little children, priests and farmers and soldiers, all waiting in unspeakable misery, waiting to see what the civilised world was going to do about them. [...]

We with passports other than Spanish, Czechoslovakian, Austrian, German or Italian were free to go home. But we all agreed, we women who had found work in wartime, that we should never be free again until we had found a way of stopping war. The war taught us that there will be no freedom for the individual until his neighbour is safe. It taught us that the root of all war is greed. When we got over our dislike of each other's creeds and opinions we found that our ideals were similar. [...] We left our war work hoping and believing in a not too distant future when decent minded men and women will get together and demand that this monster Greed will be struck out of our social institutions by peaceful legislation. [...] Had you seen little children machine gunned from the sky by aeroplanes paid for by the monster Greed, you would not hesitate a minute.

Them and Us

Patience Darton

Patience Darton *became a nurse because it was so difficult for a woman to become a doctor. Horrified by the poverty she saw during her training, and by the unequal treatment given to paying and non-paying patients, she volunteered for Spain. Afterwards she was asked by the London County Council to instruct all its nurses in war nursing. She married an International Brigader.*

I realised at once – I don't know how I had the sense, but I did – that this was 'Us' and 'Them', and this was a chance to do 'Them' down. If I got there I could do something. In England I couldn't do much as a nurse. [...]

The hospital was very fond of me. They wanted me to stay on the staff. It was a very strong Anglo-Catholic hospital – very nice, marvellous treatment; very nice people, but they thought this was an emotional extravagance for me to go.

My mother was absolutely terrified. She thought that I'd be raped and not found. My father I'm afraid I didn't consider very much. But he didn't like the idea. I mean, he didn't come into it, poor man. I finished my training, I got my midwifery, and I came up (to London). I thought I'd go to the *Daily Herald*, 'That's a Labour paper, they'll know how to get me to Spain'. So I went to the *Daily Herald* and they couldn't think what to do with me. They were very interested. They gathered round, the journalists and editors, and said, 'Try the *News Chronicle*.' So they put me in a taxi to the *News Chronicle*. I hadn't been in a taxi before, and this was very nice. The *News Chronicle* was running a collection for the medical services in Spain, and they knew the address of Spanish Medical Aid. They sent me round there, and there was George Jeger, who took me on straight away.[7] He didn't check up at all. I went back home and told my mother, without asking. She swallowed hard, and tried to think that 'This is the pioneering spirit of the family.' I wouldn't want my son or daughter to go either. I would have felt the same. It's different when you're a mother. [...]

I landed in Barcelona in bright sun. It was February in England, very soppy and snowy, and there it was bright sun, and oranges and tangerines in the trees, and lovely flowers and soldiers standing guard at the airport, very slack, very sloppy ... A little soldier was so pleased to see me coming to help that he picked the flowers and gave them to me. I sent a postcard back to Mother saying, 'All is well, they give me flowers.' [...]

In the end, after a lot of toing and froing, they thought they'd better send me to the little hospital we had up in Aragon. Now Aragon in those days was in the part where there were separate armies belonging to the different parties, and I was in the Carlos Marx Division, a Catalan division. We had the POUM on our left flank and the anarchists on our right. And the anarchists didn't like us doing anything. In fact they were very rude about us. We used to bathe in the river, not near the village, but up and away. They didn't like us because we wore bathing dresses, and anarchists were very very old fashioned about women in those days. In fact they didn't think women should learn to read and write, and they didn't like women in bathing dresses, so they stopped us. They said it frightened the mules! I shall never forget it. The POUM on our left hand had a group with Orwell, but I didn't know who he was.[8] He used to come over on Sundays to see the local English talent, with two of our other English chaps. I didn't know who they were, but I was interested. [...]

The Ebro was where we attacked again; a really big formal attack, not just a holding thing; us doing the attacking. We were right up on the side of the Ebro, in a cave on the south side of the river. The fighting had crossed the Ebro so we didn't get the people back until it was dark, because the bombing and the shelling were so extreme, that you couldn't get them back until it was dark. Then they all streamed in, terribly bad, much worse than we usually had – ever so much worse. The cave was very uncomfortable; it was very dark, very low and all uneven. The metal beds were all higgledy-piggledy over the floor and you could barely see – we hadn't got lights. We had lights for the theatre, run off of one of our ambulances, but we hadn't got lights in the cave, and we had to do our work by little tiny oil lamps, cans – ordinary tin cans – with a wick in them with oil. It isn't much light; a miserable little fickle light, and you couldn't see across the cave, and you kept banging yourself on those iron beds that were all higgledy-piggledy. [...]

In the middle of the night – when it had been going on for three nights – somebody had come in and was sitting talking to an officer who was very lightly wounded. He was sitting and talking and laughing loudly and smoking with this chap who had come in from outside, and I couldn't stand this. I went over and said, 'Look this is no way to be talking and laughing in these circumstances.' In the road outside were all the people going up, the kids going up, the last call-up, fifteen-year-olds had been called up, singing in the road, going up to cross the Ebro – terrified of what they were going to come back like. I heard these kids singing to keep their morale up in the road outside in the dark. And I said, 'How can you do that? Can't you hear what's going on round you? Can't you hear those children singing? How can you be laughing and talking?'

The chap said, 'I'll tell you. Sit down and have a cigarette.' So I sat down and had a cigarette – rolled a cigarette – and he told me that he was the local mayor.

There hadn't been a path to the village. It was just a little lost place. They'd heard there was going to be an election, but it hadn't stirred them, because always before the owner of the village, the owner's agent, had voted for them; so many souls, so many votes. Then, afterwards, they'd heard something about the next village. They were measuring up the land. So they went over to see what was happening. The land was going to be divided up. So they came back and measured up their own land, because the owners had fled quite quickly after the beginning of the war. He was elected the mayor. So he'd learned to read and write and he'd organised this village. Then he had a letter for the mayor which said he was to go up to Barcelona. He went in a car for the first time, a car with leather seats, and he went to Barcelona. There was a big meeting for all the local people, and they were told there was going to be a secret advance. They were to be ready to take refugees coming the other way. They were to pass them through and get them out of the way, to see they were safe. They would have food ready for the army, and he said, 'That's what I've brought, here's your food.' He'd brought a lot of fruit up from his village, and he said, 'That's why we've got to fight; that's why I'm here and that's why I'm laughing.'

The Best Part of My Life

Joan Purser

Joan Purser was from a farming family in Worcestershire, where she rode with the Croom Hunt. She qualified as a nurse at University College Hospital, London. She volunteered for Spain and was flown to Albacete, headquarters of the International Brigades in December 1938, where she met the other British medicals with the XIVth (French-speaking) Brigade. Joan married an International Brigadier whom she had met in Spain.

A lbacete was a seething mass of people who had come from all over the world, and who were being sorted out in a big barracks. We were briefed and threatened and generally initiated into the International Brigades. You were in the army and if you didn't behave yourself you would be shot. We were given a pep-talk by a Frenchman who was dying of TB, but really sincere and honest. [...]

At Grañen we were by a river.[9] There had been a great outcry because there was a VD hospital in the village. The Spanish *chicas* [young women] who had done the washing in the river had gone on strike, and said they wouldn't wash things from the VD hospital. They were frightened, and we had no sheets at all. There were these piles and piles of dirty sheets ... Aurora,[10] who was a wonderful person, asked what we should do? We decided the only thing we could do was to set an example and start to wash the sheets ourselves. We got into this river – I still have rheumatism from the icy cold water. We weren't skilled enough to lie on the banks like the Spanish women, so we went on a rock and started rubbing these sheets on a rock; and all these girls stood there. They were laughing at us because we were so inept. But one by one they joined in and got the sheets washed. [...]

At Teruel we had a hospital in what had been a factory and a warehouse for making material of some kind. The cold was appalling, and half way up the mountain towards Teruel the engine of our ambulance seized up. We just ran out of water. We could hear water down under the snow somewhere, down the side of the hill. We had an American driver. We got a primus stove out and a bucket, and we started melting the snow. Well, you can't get that much water melting snow; and the driver got angry, and picked up this bucket and pitched it down the ravine. We'd lost what little water we'd got, but eventually managed to get the thing going – at least he did, and we went on towards Teruel. [...]

When the place was evacuated there was one man – an Austrian doctor who was supposed to have a leg amputated. I thought he would die on the journey he was so ill. We got him down in the cellar and kept him there for a couple of days. Then he went off in an ambulance. I was walking along the beach in Benicasim,[11] as we were going through, and suddenly this young man came up on crutches and put his arm round me. He'd still got his leg on, and it was the most satisfactory thing that ever happened to me. [...]

Towards the end I had just had enough. I came back on September 9th 1938 and went down with typhoid fever two days later. People were dying of typhoid fever back in Spain, but I was lucky to be back in England and nursed in my own hospital. I was there for three months and was very lucky to survive because we were all suffering to some extent from malnutrition.

Spain was the best part of my life. I had no personal possessions, none of this clobber.

Enfermera

Aurora Fernández

Aurora Fernández *was a student in Madrid when the war started. She volunteered for nursing and served alongside British and American nurses until the end of the war. She escaped into France and came as a refugee to Britain, where she lived and worked during the Second World War. She married Joe Edenhoffer, the Czech driver for General Walter (Swierczewski) commander of the XIVth (International) Brigade.*

It was a lovely sunny afternoon in Spring 1937 when a huge lorry covered by canvas stopped at Fernández de la Hoz in Madrid, where my friend Gloria and myself were living. When we heard the claxon we came down. The driver climbed from his seat and greeted us with the usual '*Salud, camaradas*'. He was tall and had a small beard. Later I learned he was Scotch. Another two men, tall and smiling, were waiting in the lorry. One of them was Dr L[en] Crome.[12] We headed for El Goloso. 'Have you got your things with you?' asked the doctor in broken Spanish. Yes, we had taken some things for an absence of a month. In Gloria's case it was going to be a month. In my case I came back to Madrid after 42 years.

We were in the Medical Service of the 14th Brigade. [...] In El Goloso, very near the Madrid Guadarrama Mountains, we stopped at the hospital. There was an enormous amount of people but no patients. They all seemed very busy carrying things, parcels, sanitary equipment. Dr Crome said a few words in English to a very nice woman who turned out to be a French nurse and she took Gloria and me to a room full of parcels and wooden cases and two beds and said in Spanish, 'Here, sleep.' We thanked her, left our things and looked round to see if we could help. We joined people putting things in lorries; it was my first experience of preparing the front line hospital for the next offensive of the Republican troops in La Granja.[13]

After a few days we were told by the head nurse, a Spaniard, that we should go with some lorries and ambulances (all from England or France, very nice and modern) to the Sierra, there in the Club Alpino a hospital was being organised and we should get to know it. Gloria said she would like to stay as she was expecting a visitor [her fiancé] from Madrid. I went without her. The Club Alpino was fitted very nicely, portable beds, on them new sheets and blankets. We started making them and getting everything ready ... A nurse was sitting preparing swabs for the steriliser. She turned her head and said one word: 'Nurse'. It was not the usual '*Enfermera*', but the real English word 'Nurse', and I felt all hot and colour mounting to my face. 'She thinks I'm a real nurse, perhaps the white apron and the head-dress makes her think so,' and, unable to say a word, not even in Spanish, I came near her. 'You are shy, SHY, don't you understand? But you speak English, come on.' And to make me at home gave me a chair, put a piece of cotton wool in my hands and began, 'Look, in England we make swabs like this ...' Little by little I lost a bit of my shyness, she was very nice, about forty with light hair and lovely blue eyes. I never got to know her name. [...]

After the offensive in La Granja ended we were divided into two groups, I was 'put' in one of them going the long way to the Aragon front. [...] Our group included two negro Spanish girls who used to live in the Club Alpino and were evacuated and joined the Sanitary Service and made the long and difficult trip to Aragon. [...]

We were all so tired by the slow travelling and the occasional food; drivers were exhausted after those horrible dusty roads or terrible hairpin bends in the mountains; we did not wash or undress, and after a week that seemed a month we arrived at Puebla de Hijar where the real front line hospital was to be installed.[14] [...]

On the way to Aragon I met many English nurses. Two of them were specially near to me. As an example of courage, deep knowledge and professional touch, besides her cheerfulness (so necessary in our lifestyle), I recall Joan Purser. She was a wonderful theatre nurse and doctors valued her very much, including the Spanish ones. The other one I met on my way to Aragon was Ada Hodson, much older. She really 'mothered' me with a patience and dedication that was really moving. She was, unlike the other nurses who picked up a lot of Spanish very soon, unable to express herself in this language. She felt it a great handicap, although it was marvellous how she knew what was wrong with a patient, what he needed, better than me who could speak to them. [...] Ada and I became inseparable, always together. She was very brave. Once we had a hospital in tents and while seeing to a patient a fascist plane flew over and machine-gunned the tents. Ada was wounded in the right arm, but she carried on working for a week until she got infection and a high fever and collapsed. She was taken to England and recovered and came back. While she was in England she had an inheritance and bought a complete 'autochir' [a kind of mobile operating unit], and brought it back to Spain in the last months of the war. She was not in any political party. She happened to be in London on a holiday from South Africa where she was a Matron in a hospital in Johannesburg, and packed her bag and came to Spain. [...]

I never met anyone so dedicated to help the suffering. I still remember many of her pieces of advice: When you feel very tired, when you feel 'the worst' ... 'keep smiling!' 'Never leave a boy to die alone. Go there and hold his hand and talk to him.' 'Those wounded who shout, *"Enfermera, curandera ven aquí."* ' ["Nurse, healer come here."] They are ALIVE, go and watch those who are keeping quiet, they might be bleeding.' 'Keep always a clean apron for the visiting time to look clean and nice and never argue with the doctor in front of the patients!', and so on, and so on. [...]

English nurses such as Patience Darton, Ada Hodson and others from the USA and Canada, taught us how to prepare trollies or trays for the doctor's visit or to know the instruments for operations, or how to prepare the bandages. I must stress the non-obtrusive way in which this was done in order not to hurt anybody's feelings. They did not say, 'I'm going to tell you how to do this ...' but rather, 'Come, *let us* get this ready.' [...]

We were always short of someone to give injections so they taught us very patiently how to do it. I was astonished at myself when I gave the first intravenous to a patient telling him in the calmed voice I have heard from English nurses, 'Don't move, it'll soon be over.' Or if a calcium injection was administered, 'You'll feel hot, don't worry, it'll pass.' It might sound silly nowadays but in 1937 it did not.

Another important activity between 'offensives' was of a political character. We had a young Commissar who organised a Party group in the hospital. He convinced me I should join and I joined and went to meetings. [...] The Commissar did not inspire me at first with a lot of trust after my experience in Madrid, but on one occasion when we had lots of wounded and we needed blood, he offered himself. The doctor said he looked very tired and perhaps it was not wise, but he insisted and gave his blood for a young soldier who eventually lived to be evacuated. That impressed me very much. He did it as if nothing happened. It is true that we all gave blood in direct blood transfusions, nurses, even doctors, and stretcher-bearers, but ... a Commissar!! [...]

One autumn day, bright and sunny, our team of doctors and nurses arrived at the 'pueblo' of Grañen. [...] In Grañen I felt more confident of myself. I did not tremble so much for fear of doing the wrong thing. Ada was by my side and we understood each other very well.

She used to tell me not to be so terrified of the rats which came to the end of the barrack where we slept on the floor, separated from the 'ward' by a sheet hung from the ceiling using bandages instead of strings ... Ada used to chase the rats with our torch and sometimes we used to take our mattresses and sleep in the open outside the barracks. [...]

In Grañen we did not have wounded but a typhoid epidemic. [...] A group of young Spanish doctors joined us. They had just joined the army in war duty. One of them came to do the usual visit in the morning and Ada informed him (I translated) that they were typhoid patients. He looked at every one carefully and then he said: 'Two enemas every day.' I saw surprise in Ada's eyes but she answered with the usual, 'Yes sir.' Then she sent me on a long errand. I protested, 'But the enemas.' 'I'll manage.' When I came back the 'job' had been done. Well, following day, doctor said the same: 'Two enemas daily,' and Ada sent me on a longer errand. I was a little 'offended' that she should not 'trust' me with such a menial job so I hurried and came back before she thought I would and I found to my great surprise she was 'doing' as if she would give the enemas but only pretending. She saw me and smiled and said, 'Look, dear, I've been nursing typhoid patients for years. That doctor may be clever but enemas for them would be their death.' Thank goodness that doctor was only a week with us. In any case we had to get ready to move on to what was going to be the battle of Teruel. [...]

After much travelling and many hairpin bends and the snowbound roads sometimes blocked for days our lorries and trucks got to a small mountain village. Trembling with cold we turned an old water mill into our hospital. The Teruel attack had begun. I must say we did not have any news of any sort in those days. No papers, no radio. We guessed how the battle was going by the number of wounded and when they stopped coming we knew that we had either retreated or the front had calmed down. The hospital functioned very well in the mill ... But we had a great torture: lice. It is true lice had bothered us in the summer and autumn, but now the chance of having a wash was very small due to the cold weather so we scratched and scratched day and night. Sometimes it was impossible to sleep and I had the idea to pinch a little ether for anaesthetics and pour a little on so the lice slept and also myself. I think it was an English nurse called Lillian Urmston, who was very efficient and good, and told me not to do that, 'Everyone is smoking here and you could go up in flames.' [...]

Lice also tortured the wounded. I remember getting ready a soldier for operation. He had an open fracture and I proceeded to cut his trousers and underpants (he had two pairs of underpants), for I knew already I must not move his leg, and I remember his sad eyes and him telling me, '*Enfermera*, don't cut my underpants I shall never be able to get another pair so warm and it is cold in the b...... trenches.' [...]

I think one of the hospitals where we worked in greatest harmony was the one installed in a huge natural cave near the Catalan village of Bisbal de Falset. [...] Spanish soldiers in that cave with hardly any light used to shout, calling out to us. They were in a hospital for the first time in their lives. Some never saw a hospital before. [...] So those wounded soldiers called '*Curandera!*' – 'Healer', for they were used to the women in the village who 'knew' about curative plants and secret healing methods. Ada was by then very tired and besides other nurses looked much older, so the soldiers who had noticed how wonderfully she 'healed' their wounds and with such love and care tended them began to call her '*Abuelita*'. ... One afternoon while we were having our cup of tea Ada said with a very happy voice, 'The wounded like me even if I don't know how to speak Spanish. They call me "Florita".' We all kept silent but a stretcher-bearer who knew a little English began to laugh. 'They call you "*Abuelita*", which in English is "Granny".' Ada, pale, almost crying got up and as she was, with her white dress and apron, with her sandals, got out of the cave and left by the path into the bright Spanish sun. 'I am going to England,' she muttered.

We were all very quiet for a while and then Joan got up and followed the path where Ada had disappeared. After many hours, it was already evening, Ada and Joan came back. Ada came to me and said, 'You see, I am not going to England because my boys need me, even if they do call me "Granny", well it is like as if they were part of my family, don't you think?' I hugged her, crying my eyes out! Dear Ada! [...]

The Ebro battle was like a breath of fresh air to a dying man. I did not realise it then, but I remember English nurses talking and suddenly stopping when I came among them. My ears caught the words, 'and this is the end or very near.' Apparently they did not want to frighten us young Spaniards.

English Penny
Penelope Phelps

Penny Phelps came from a London working-class family. She went to Spain early in 1937 and was the only English nurse serving with the XVth (English-speaking) Brigade during the Battle of Jarama. She was sent as Medical Officer to the Garibaldi (Italian) Brigade during a typhoid epidemic. After contracting typhoid herself she returned to England and spoke at Medical Aid meetings. Back in Spain with the XVth Brigade she served at the Battle of Brunete, where six of her medical friends were killed by a shell. She was sent home to recover from the shock. Returning to Spain she served with a Spanish unit during the retreat of spring 1938, and was severely wounded. During the 1939-45 war she worked with physically handicapped children and in industrial personnel.

I went to Spain in January 1937 under the auspices of the Spanish Medical Aid Committee accompanied by two other nurses. I was interviewed at Albacete and told I would be joining the International Brigades. My destination, however, was kept secret from me since I was, by then, under military discipline. As the guns were rumbling all the time my first night was rather disturbed.

The next day we were on the move taking mobile theatre equipment with us and getting it ready inside a school. Casualties began to roll in and our work went on until the early hours of the morning.

The wounded arrived in ambulances, on open lorries or any other available transport. They must have had a very hard time because the roads in this region are rough and it is mountainous. We were quite near the front.

I slept until 9 a.m. and then we had to begin operating until 6 o'clock the next morning. I kept thinking we had just about finished, but more and more casualties arrived and the small hospital became overcrowded. Many of the wounded were left out in the yard from lack of space inside the school building, which must have been extremely stressful because it was very cold and there was often snow on the ground.

The fighting went on continuously day and night and when the electric lights failed we had to resort to torches. There was no heating except from a small gasoline stove and sometimes it was so cold you would be glad to be in the operating theatre full of people.

Sometimes I was so tired I felt I could not go on; then one would have a Spanish cigarette and some black coffee and begin again.

When one went out for fresh air there was a tendency to stumble over bodies, some dead and others wounded, the latter crying out for '*agua*' [water].

At our next location in Chinchón near the Jarama river we attended to some of the wounded from the English Battalion. They were grateful to hear an English woman's voice.

The conditions here were difficult, with shortage of essential materials and medicaments. Our instruments were becoming blunt. We did not have enough anaesthetics and had to give local ones for operations which required ether or chloriform, a most unpleasant experience for the patients.

While stationed at Tarancón an incident occurred which I must tell you about. On the Madrid-Valencia road was a petrol station where lorries refuelled. Taking a breather during a lull when casualties were not arriving I sauntered along the road; the guard by the petrol station signalled to me, and as he could speak a little English I chatted with him. I then went and sat down at a little coffee shop and watched children playing and thought how beautiful they were with their dark eyes.

Suddenly, without warning, there was a huge explosion. My hands automatically went up to my ears and my chair went from beneath me. Bombs had fallen and I dashed across the road, through a bloody mess of mules and fallen masonry, to get to the children.

By this time the petrol station was a sheet of flames. It was my first experience of picking up an injured child and I shall never forget it. As the child regained consciousness and struggled in my arms, I had to hold it tight which was difficult because one leg was hanging on by a sinew. I hurried along to the hospital and the child was operated on.

In the middle of the operation one of the doctors came in with another child. However, its burns were so severe that all we could do was to give it morphine so that it should not wake up in agony.

I have become used to picking up children who may be injured but I shall never forget that first horrendous experience.

While at Chinchón I had to go up to Madrid in order to replenish our dwindling stock of medical supplies, and I took some patients in the ambulance who were being transferred.

Just as we were crossing the Arganda Bridge Franco's fascists began machine gunning us (though we were clearly marked with the Red Cross).[16]

We escaped by going at a terrific speed round hairpin bends; I shall never be frightened by road-hogging again! The dispatch rider in front of us was killed and we had to leave him, as stopping to pick him up would have been suicide. We got through all right in the end.

At times we were short of food such as milk and eggs, the little butter we received was rancid; but we ate it to make the dry bread go down. These are just part of my experiences. It is difficult for you to realise what is going on out there. War is a great atrocity. The responsibility lies with those who started this war

But 'Spain is red,' a friend said to me. 'Yes,' I replied, 'It is red with blood. Blood is splashed over the streets and the gutters run with it. For weeks my finger-nails were stained by the blood, and my arms were spattered up to the elbows with it.'

While the people of England are arranging festivities for the Coronation they should spare more thoughts for Spain! I do not know what our government is doing, they do not appear to want the Spanish people to win. We must endeavour, therefore, to help to improve the awful conditions that exist out there.

El Escorial

Portia Holman

__Portia Holman__ was from New South Wales, where her father was Labour Prime Minister. She read economics at Cambridge and was studying medicine in London in 1936. She visited Grañen for the SMAC in December 1936, and returned to Spain during the summer vacation of 1937. She later became Senior Psychiatrist at the Elizabeth Garrett Hospital in London, with a special interest in children.

We went to the Escorial, very near Madrid, which again was a very beautiful place, but where the patients had arrived almost before the hospital.[17] I remember being impressed by the way we packed up all we had for the hospital, the beds, tables, drugs, the instruments, in the morning, drove a hundred miles and got them all ready and were working by evening.

This was a place where the casualties came in very fast. Either they were badly injured or they were suffering a great deal from exposure. Although it was early summer, in the mountains it was very cold, and I remember having a ward full of patients with pneumonia. They were very ill, and in those days pneumonia was regarded as a fatal disease. One thing that arrived from England was a large tea-chest full of something called Prontosil. I'd heard of Prontosil. It was one of the first chemo-therapeutic drugs. But there were absolutely no instructions. However, since most of my patients were going to die anyway, I thought there was no harm in trying the Prontosil on them. I supposed you gave it like you give most medicines, three times a day. So that's what we did. Well it was most effective, and the majority of the patients recovered. And my friend Molly Murphy, who was a senior nurse, and I spent most of our time filling hot-water bottles and cleaning lavatories while the patients improved,

At that time there was a schism between the Communists and the apolitical, or the moderate left, if you like, members of the team who did not wish to associate ourselves with members of the International Brigade; that was Richard Rees, Julian Bell, John Cornford, and Molly and I and the Boulting brothers,[18] and one or two others whose names

I no longer remember, were a little minority who were rather disliked by the majority who were very definitely Communist or pro-Russian. This led to internal problems which made us all very, very sad as we had come to help the Spanish people. But anyway we all did what we could according to our convictions.

Rain

Rosaleen Smythe

Rosaleen Smythe, from Leicester, went to Barcelona to work at the SMAC centre. Early in 1937 she joined the British medical personnel in the 35th Division, performing secretarial work in hospitals. Her brother Jim also served in Spain with medical aid.

It has been raining for days and days. This prevents attacks. The river is rising hourly; it has reached the door of the hospital, which is only a wooden hut. Operating room and triage are divided from the wards by sheets. My office is in triage.[19]

We had orders to pack up and move off, but the floods have prevented the lorries from coming up. For two and a half weeks we have been in a state of package. We have scarcely any food and what there is is bad. We each keep a bit of quite mouldy bread under the pillow to nibble at night. Oh for something to put on it. We are allowed a small piece of cheese and a small piece of sausage. There is tense excitement when trading sausage for cheese begins. We have to go half a mile to the kitchen for food in the mud and the dark. As we are expecting to move we have discharged the civil personnel. I have been doing the kitchen work with the two American nurses, Esther [Silverstein] and Irene [Goldin]. We also serve in the dining-room. There is very little wood round here. We can hear the guns all day. We have half a tank of drinking water left. The lorries have not yet got through the mud.

The wards are filling with influenza cases. The other hospital has been bombed and we have orders to turn ours into an infirmary. Dr Saxton has to chlorinate the water every morning. There is absolutely no sanitation of any kind.

The cases are increasing. We have no clean water, no fires, no heating, no lavatories.

The village has been bombed, the hospital, garage, and one or two houses. We had fourteen patients in the hospitals. One of them died. A cavalry man had to have his leg amputated. They have been bringing his horse to the door of the ward to see him. We had one pregnant woman hit in the leg. We took in patients from the infirmary and the day after it was evacuated it was bombed to pieces.

Existence is a misery. Rain is coming in. Rats run across the floor. Our rations are tinned meat, chick peas and five almonds each. We are afraid to undress night or day because of the bombing.

We have no milk, eggs or potatoes for the typhoid patients (yet owing to good nursing only 8 per cent died). I cannot say enough about the splendid way Ada Hodson, Patience Darnton and Lillian Urmston are working. How Ada makes us laugh when she tries to drink the peculiar liquid which is neither tea, coffee nor cocoa, but a mixture of all. Lillian's morale is never destroyed; I admire her. We gave Millicent a special case to look after. Andy is a jewel. He has organised the stretcher-bearers and sees to the sanitation, the little there is. By now Dr Saxton has started a canteen in which we sell mouldy bread and jam, cognac and Malaga wine.[20] In the evenings, by the light of a few candles we put on a gramophone. The records we have are Beethoven's Fifth Symphony, one movement of Schubert's Unfinished and one Haydn. We play them over and over again to the drip, drip of the incessant rain. We put on extra pullovers to go to bed in, we have given our blankets to the patients.

A bitter cold wind and a frost has set in. Those poor chicas [young women] have to clean the few bed-pans in the icy river water.

Today the lorries tried to get down; we could have cried when they returned empty. Yet everyone is being very brave. The nurses are splendid. The bombing has begun again ...

True Comradeship

Phyllis Hibbert

Phyllis Hibbert *joined the British medical unit during the Battle of Jarama, early in 1937. She served until the summer of 1938 when she returned home to care for her invalid mother.*

It was not until I served with the British Medical Unit in Spain that I learned the true meaning of the word comradeship.

For the last few months I was with a mobile unit on the Aragon and Teruel Front, and we were never more than four kilometres from the front lines. We were bombed and machine-gunned from the air; we were continually being forced to retreat with the Republican troops and to set up our hospital in any building available.[21] We had no means of heating in the bitter cold of the winter, we had to deal with as many as 200 cases a night, and we sometimes worked in the most appalling conditions, for forty hours at a stretch.

And yet during all those terrible months I never heard a word of complaint, never encountered anything but willingness to help on the part of the staff of all European nationalities, who were sometimes reduced to communicating with each other by means of rough sketches and diagrams.

Most of us had left well-paid jobs to come out and serve the cause of humanitarianism. I say humanitarianism because 60 per cent of the nursing staff had no definite political views, but were merely democrats with a desire to succour the suffering.

And there was not one of us who had ever, in the course of years of nursing experience, come across such a relationship of deep human sympathy as existed between the medical staff in our unit and the wounded, on whichever side they had been fighting, whether they were Moors, or Spaniards, French or Italians.

* * *

We have set up hospital in an old convent in a front-line village where a siren blows when the war planes are coming. I am busy in triage when I hear the warning and presently the drone of engines is very clear. I go on working, giving injections and bandaging wounds, struggling to remain cool but I cannot keep my hands from trembling. A false calm covers my terror when the sound above becomes suddenly louder, and I know instantly that the bombers have swooped to make sure of their target, that the next moment will bring death and destruction. Perhaps the first one will fall right here and save us the anxiety of waiting. Perhaps it will just miss us. It is a gamble. Suddenly I hear a whine which becomes a shrill whistle and then – crash, crash – ear-splitting explosions. The walls shake and plaster rains down on us. I run to the wall and press my rigid body close. I feel three times my own size. I suddenly remember the helpless wounded on the stretchers in the middle of the room; I rush to them. I grab one end of a stretcher and shout to the doctor to take the other and we move them one by one close to the thickest wall. We cover their faces with blankets as a protection against flying glass. Then I stand shaking against the wall. Oh, will it never stop? One explosion, drowning the sound of others, tells us that one dropped very near; a lightning flash illuminates the room. I feel a terrific rush of air which knocks me over. … Now I feel calm … For five minutes we wait hardly daring to breathe; then it is all over. Half an hour later the sirens blow all clear. The relief is overwhelming. Everyone talks in loud, excited voices. The work of rescuing has already begun, digging and tearing at the ruined houses for those tragic ones who were too late. They carry out a two-year old baby … quite dead, a young girl in hysterics, two lifeless old women, all from the same house.

Small Beer

Nan Green

Nan Green worked for Spanish Aid in London while her husband George was serving in Spain. In July 1937 Wogan Philipps, who had returned wounded from ambulance driving, offered to send her children to A.S. Neill's school, Summerhill, if she would go as a medical administrator. She served until late in 1938. At the Ebro crossing she was secretary to Leonard Crome, chief Medical Officer of the 4th Army. George was killed on the last day on which British Brigaders were engaged. In 1939 Nan went with a ship-load of Spanish refugees to Mexico. She worked in China in the 1950s. On return to England she became Secretary of the International Brigade Association, which she represented at trials of Franco's prisoners.

I found myself at Huete, in what was called 'the English Hospital'.[22] To my profound astonishment, I found George there.

Now George had left for Spain with the firm intention of joining the International Brigade as soon as he had delivered his lorry, and I had only a vague idea that he was still in the medical service. [...]

A little while before my arrival he had burned the skin of one arm by getting under his ambulance to examine a choked feed of petrol on a mountain road, and freezing petrol had run down his arm, taking off an area of skin. He had been sent to Huete for treatment and was almost recovered. Meanwhile he was appointed Political Commissar of the hospital.

It was pure chance and good fortune that brought us together now. I had not had the ridiculous idea that I was going to Spain 'to join my husband' and though I had a deep-down hope that we would meet I had no expectation of this incredible bonus. It was sheer unadulterated joy.

George was a good Commissar. [...] Part of his job was to promote the welfare of patients and staff, and on this day he had arranged a concert for such patients as could walk or be carried to the large 'recreation hall' – formerly, perhaps, a chapel in what had been a monastery. He had bought himself a 'cello; a Bavarian lad with an injured leg played the violin (by ear); the village plumber was an excellent guitarist though equally illiterate musically, and a Catalan patient, also with a leg injury, played the *bandurrión* (a sort of mandolin). George taught them tunes, and they already had quite a credible repetoire. A departing patient had left behind an accordion. Early in the afternoon George showed me this, and said I should play it with his orchestra that evening. 'But I can't play the accordion!' I protested. 'You will by tonight,' he replied firmly. The keyboard side was of course easy since I had piano lessons as a child. I learned a dozen or so chords during the afternoon and dutifully took my place in the orchestra that evening (it must have sounded dreadful).

Next day I was introduced to my job: Assistant Secretary. The chief Administrator was British, as were the surgeon in charge, theatre sisters, ward sisters (who included three New Zealand nurses) and one or two ambulance drivers. Somewhat to my disillusionment, I found that there were wheels within political wheels, colouring the relations and actions of this group of people. The anti-Communism of the Conservatives and the Labour leadership had its reflection here, and I came to suspect (though never to prove) that the Foreign Office had its finger in this and other pies.

Nevertheless, tremendously devoted work was done and the Spanish people (patients, mostly peasants, staff and the villagers of Huete) were a glorious example and lesson to all.

The training of village girls as nurses and wardmaids was speeded by their eagerness to learn and their devotion to the work, far out-running the expectations of our nurses. Like Cromwell's men, they knew what they were fighting for, and loved what they knew. I have never forgotten an old grandmother to whose cave-house (half of Huete's houses consisted of caves hollowed out of the hillside in the village) I went, trying to recruit women for the hospital laundry and linen room. Her daughter, for whom I was searching, was out and she was surrounded by several grandchildren, one or two of whom were of school age. On the whitewashed wall of the cave were stuck some children's drawings done in coloured crayons. 'Look', she said pointing proudly to them. 'Before the Republic there wasn't a pencil in this village, and now all the children go to school. Yes, my daughter will come and help! Those wounded men are fighting so that our children can learn.'

This is a chronicle of small beer. I can only tell what I saw and experienced. [...]

A fiesta was planned, I think it was to commemorate the October Revolution, in which the hospital invited the entire village to participate. In preparation for this, a bar was set up in what had been the crypt of the monastery and was now the garage for ambulances. To make an inspection pit, some flagstones had been removed, uncovering some human bones. An American artist, one of our patients, devised a banner to hang at the back of the bar, depicting caricatures of Franco, Hitler and Mussolini and, to point the lesson, had hung some of the bones beneath the banner. The point was raised, might this not antagonise the villagers, to whose ancestors maybe the bones belonged? In the aftermath of my personal repudiation of the Christian religion, I was vehemently in favour of leaving the bones there. 'I don't like finding myself on the opposite side to my wife,' said George, and proceeded to remind us of the meaning of the Popular Front. The bones were taken down and re-interred, and I swallowed my lesson without too much difficulty. [...]

In December, George at last attained his desire and was discharged to go to the front and join the British Battalion. At almost the same time, I was appointed Administrator of a hospital for convalescents at Valdeganga,[23] which had in the past been a hydropathic hotel, being located by some hot springs of chemically-impregnated water which emerged from under the ground nearly boiling. It had been a health resort for rich people; there were marble bathtubs with silver-plated taps in the shape of swans heads.

My job at Valdeganga was not an easy one. The accounts and records were in a state of confusion. The hospital was paid so much per head of patients – consequently if the number of patients fell we got less money per month to remain solvent, and to remain solvent we had sometimes to lay off staff, mainly girls from the nearby village which was an anarchist stronghold. Angry deputations on behalf of the temporarily unemployed followed. Rightly or wrongly we suspected Huete, which was supposed to send us its convalescents, of hanging on to them unnecessarily for the sake of *its* solvency. [...] The village girls, mostly wardmaids and kitchen hands, slept together in two dormitories and as it was winter, and a mountainous situation (snow fell that Christmas, very unusually) they often shared beds for warmth; scabies broke out among them. It became necessary to decontaminate them, their clothing and their bedclothes simultaneously. The majority of the girls possessed only one pair of corsets, which they refused to give up. The Austrian Medical Officer bullied them; I was for persuasion; Frank Ayers, the Political Commissar, explained and explained and explained, and we eventually won the battle.

I am sorry to say that the Medical Officer [MO] had become a drug addict, and was appropriating the hospital's supply of morphia; to obtain more, he had to have my signature for a requisition. When I began to suspect him, he invented an unknown addict among the patients and protested that 'These people were so cunning that it was impossible to trace them.' He also made passes at me, not I am sure for my beaux yeux but to neutralise my hostility.

I believe that due to the altitude we were all infected with a touch of the 'mountain sickness' and lived in a permanent state of mild excitement. The physiotherapist (an excellent one), a refugee from Austria who had done all her training in England and had joined the Communist Party there, possessed a teutonic political rigidity and started a whispering vendetta against Frank the Commissar because he flatly refused to remove some anarchist literature from the patients' library. This was at the height of the Soviet-inspired hatred of 'Trotskyism', which spilled over into the Communist movement everywhere and made heresy-hunting a righteous crusade for many members.

Wise old Frank Ayers [...] ignored the vendetta. The Medical Officer now did something which turned us into open emnity. Frank was summoned to make a short visit to England, to report to the Spanish Medical Aid Committee on the needs of the hospital service. He had been keeping a little book of memoranda on the behaviour and characters of the medical personnel with whom he had been in contact. He considered whether to leave this with me to keep in my office safe, but decided it would be asking too much to expect me not to read it. I don't know whether I would have done so or not, but at all events it would have been a great temptation. Consequently he gave it to Anita with whom he had started to fall in love. His confidential reports would be safe with her, since she didn't know a word of English. Anita was the assistant housekeeper at the hospital, a former film star whose personal beauty was matched by her nature, and who had volunteered for the medical service from the outbreak of war. She was assistant to an elderly, sly and sycophantic woman called Felisa who wanted to stand well with the Medical Officer and, to curry favour with him, reported that Anita had a book hidden under her mattress. Frank had only been gone a few days when the wretched man reported her to the civil police, as a spy, who had stolen Frank's book to give to the enemy. Police came in the middle of the night and whisked her away to prison in the town of Cuenca, some miles away.

I charged off to Cuenca next morning and after several tortuous days of interviews, depositions, counter-depositions, enquiries and table-thumpings, succeeded in obtaining her release, returning in triumph with her to the hospital, from which she was promptly fired by the MO and went to Valencia, her home town. He now turned on me, first inventing an accusation of embezzlement against me on the flimsy ground that I did the book-keeping in an account book which had, when I first took it over, nothing in it except a figure, on the first line of the first page, of 1,000 pesetas. As this meant nothing, I had simply turned the page and started my accounts on the second page, ignoring the first. He called a meeting of staff and patients and, having filched, or caused to be filched, the account book from my office, began a heavy diatribe against me. 'What has happened to the thousand pesetas?' He failed to make the accusation stick – it was too silly, but mud had been slung and sides were taken. The atmosphere deteriorated. Eventually he drove me to the medical HQ in Albacete where he made God knows what allegations about me to the authorities (some of which followed me round to my later jobs though I did not know it until much later). Unable or unwilling to verify these charges, the authority (I don't remember who) interviewed me with the pretext that for a Medical officer and his administrator to be at loggerheads was bad for the hospital, and I was therefore ordered to resign. [...]

Frank had returned from England to wind up the English section of the hospital at Uclés.[24][...] He took me and Anita with him. We found: a line of concrete pipes leading down the hill from the hospital (an ex-monastery, far larger than the one at Huete) to what was intended to be a new septic tank; money had been sent from England to complete the job but some of it had been temporarily 'diverted' to pay the hospital staff. A dry moat round the whole building, into which they had been throwing soiled dressings, and bits of amputated limbs, was now the home of a large rat colony; there was an empty ward with a notice over the door to say it was to be the Leah Manning Ward, and a general state of hostility towards us. There was no job for me. Anita took charge of the barely furnished little house which had been given over for a British nurses' home. I undertook, to the best of my ability, while I waited for the official call which Frank had demanded from Barcelona for me, to raise the morale of those poor British girls who had been thrown into this shambles: one of my daily jobs was to delouse them when they came off the wards. They were not permitted to go on night duty. I remember one of them weeping – she had a patient who was paraplegic, and one night a rat got into his bed and gnawed his leg which of course had no sensation in it. She had procured four big tins, filled them with disinfectant and set the legs of the bed in them. The night nurses had removed the tins because they 'looked untidy'. I also manufactured a shower bath out of a biscuit tin (into which holes were punctured) which was set on a wall in the corner of the garden; standing on a chair I used to pour jugs of water while the girls washed themselves below. [...]

Soon the official call came for me to go north. How to get there? The road was cut. The Spanish authorities refused, quite rightly, to give me any sort of safe-conduct papers. I can't remember how, but Frank managed to arrange for me to travel to Marseilles on a British battleship, (the *Sussex*) as ostensible escort to one of the English nurses who was being invalided home. The excruciating gallantry with which the officers of the *Sussex* provided for our comfort (starting with cups of tea in delicate china and thin white bread and butter with raspberry jam for our first meal on board, not to mention the stationing of a seaman outside our cabin, ready to escort us up the companionway to the deck, carrying anything such as a book we might have in our hands) made the three-day voyage dream-like in contrast to the rough, sparse rations and conditions we had been used to. Three times we were asked: 'Has anyone shown you where the BATHROOM is?' At Marseilles I saw Penny [Phelps] on to her train, purchased a long list of medical supplies with which I had been charged by Frank, and went to the British Consul for a permit to return to Spain. He severely accused me of 'using the British Navy as a taxi-service to get about the Mediterranean', which was of course precisely what I had done. However, after some persuasion he gave me the required document. I flew back to Barcelona; it was the first time in my life that I had ever been on an aeroplane.

There was a job ready and waiting for me. I was to go to the front, as secretary to the Chief Medical Officer of the 35th Division.

The Monastery at Uclés

Louise Jones

Louise Jones *was one of the first nurses at the large Medical Aid hospital at Uclés. After her return to England she, with four other nurses, tried to deliver a letter to Mrs Chamberlain, wife of the British Prime Minister, urging her to use her influence with Signora Mussolini to end the bombing of Barcelona.*

I have been working in Spain for six months, but not until I came to the new hospital did I realise the Spaniards' need for help.

It is a very large building, and at the moment it is very cold. There is no heating, and there is no attempt made to heat the place because there is no money. Patients, of whom there are 800, cannot be washed, there are no bowls, no soap, no towels, some of the patients have not been washed for weeks.

There are no clean sheets; the dirty sheets cannot be washed because we have no soap. To add to our difficulties it is winter and no means exist for drying washing. The patients lie in bed naked for they have no pyjamas. It can be readily understood that in such circumstances even with the best will in the world it is impossible to prevent the beds from becoming verminous and the discomfort of the patients is acute. In face of it all their courage, patience and cheerfulness is marvellous.

The food is very poor, we are all rationed. Kathleen Hobbs and I share a room in the nurses' quarter, but the building is an ancient one and we wage a constant warfare against the rats. We feed with the Spanish nurses. They themselves cannot eat the food, so you can imagine what we feel like. We have a small loaf of bread to last us 24 hours, and black coffee in the morning with very little sugar. But the *chicas* [young women] are very keen and anxious to learn all we can tell them. They are having medical lectures and can already name every bone in the body, and every spare moment I am pressed into giving them lessons in dressings, fomentations, bandaging etc. The idea of the London Committee to use the new hospital as a training school for Spanish nurses was excellent. We are trying to fix a room as a classroom, but would like some simple books to put into the hands of our Spanish colleagues.

At the moment Kathleen Hobbs and I each have a ward with 104 patients in it. To help us are three *practicantes* [medical orderlies], four Spanish nurses and four *chicas*.[25] Our crying need is for more English nurses, and from a nursing point of view it is absolutely necessary to have at once supplies of sheets, towels, material for making pillow cases, pyjamas and sleeping clothes. Basins to wash the patients and urinals etc, are urgently needed.

We *do* most urgently need support for all these things from England.

Short of Everything
Madge Addy

Madge Addy, *a nursing sister from Manchester, was senior British nurse at the Uclés hospital. The North Manchester Spanish Medical Aid Committee raised large sums to buy equipment for the hospital. In the last months Madge was the only British person left at Uclés, and she was the last British nurse to leave Spain. She crossed the country in great hardship and danger and was allowed to leave Spain only after pressure on the British Foreign Office secured her a visa.*

Hospital
31 August 1938

Dear Nat,[26]
I am back at last and oh! what a wonderful welcome I have had. From the director downwards everyone has been to see me, and thank me for the work I have done for them in England. [...]
Oh I nearly signed on the Stanleigh they were so wonderfully good to us. I am loaded with presents from them, lovely things and we were two days in Valencia and all got to know each other very well indeed. I had kept to my cabin and the bridge for the voyage and the Captain came and ate with me, he's an absolute darling and I'm afraid he has fallen good and hard. I thought it would be better to keep out of the way and not let them feel the restraint of a woman being about. The Captain was terribly anxious once we got in the three mile limit, but we got in without a raid. Wilhelm Holet was waiting on the dockside with a car. [...] *Wilhelm (Holet)* gave a party in his lovely apartment and I was the hostess. Oh Boy! what a party there were eight men and one other lady and we broke up at 4 a.m. We left the next day Sunday for here at 2 p.m. The whole crew were there to see us off. Apart from personal presents, I think they gave me half the ship's stores. [...]
    We are short of Drs and *practicantes* etc because every male who was fit and could possibly be spared has been sent to the front. All the dear little boys out of the office are gone, most of the *practicantes*

[medical orderlies]. I know you will do your best but do be sure to put on your parcels for *Nurse Addy's Hospital*. I know it sounds rather selfish because things are needed everywhere, but I work here, and I see the suffering and want here, and it is no consolation to me to know it has been sent to Barcelona because they also are needing it. *After all we have a hospital of 800 wounded here, a Manchester Ward, and a Manchester nurse, so please get them to concentrate on us.*

I was very grieved indeed to find everyone so much thinner than when I left. The Drs and nurses look thin and pale, and food is terribly scarce, and the administrator tells me that things will be worse and the food situation more acute when the winter comes. So he has asked me to ask London if they can send a regular supply of tinned milk out for the wounded as they cannot obtain it here. [...] Really Nat, I have been writing until 2 a.m. in the morning, goung round the dispensary getting a list, the theatres and stores and I have never had one minute in my off-duty since I got back. [...]

With antifascist greetings,
Yours in the fight,
Madge.

c/o Alameda 15 iii,
Valencia
Spain
7 October 1938

Dear Nat,
[...]I have said good-bye to the 'Manchester Ward' as a permanent member of its staff, and tho' I am going on each day to do No 18's dressing, and will always help Porta whenever he wants me, I felt very sorry. I have been happy there but we are the proud possessors of a small medical electricity and ultra-violet ray dept, and the director has asked me if I will take charge of the dept as they have no one else, and combine it with the X-Ray theatre ... This is a splendid step forward, and many a man will regain the use of limbs, which before through lack of many things have just gone useless. [...]

I have written to my husband to ask if he will divorce me. [...] I am going to marry Mr Holet. I am very much attached to him, and although he holds a very important position here, he is unaffected and simple in his tastes, and is liked by everyone. [...] In the meantime Spain and the hospital come first. I have pledged myself to both for a year, then I am hoping to be able to turn my thoughts seriously to some kind of happy future. Write soon, my love to you all,

Yours in the fight,
Madge.

Same Address
Spain
17 October 1938

Dear Nat,

[…] I am working very hard at the moment and come home dog tired every night. I go on the 'Manchester Ward' prompt at 9 am and do the temps and pulses (there are 33 of them) then the dressings and then toddle off to the 'Fiero Therapia' where I have now got thirty patients for massage. Porta has lent me the sanatario orderly of the ward to help me and he does most of the vapour massages. We work on until about 1.45 pm and then I come up to the house to eat. Back at 4pm to the 'Manchester Ward' where I again take all the temps and pulses, give the injections, subcutaneous, intravenous and intramuscular, odd jobs like passing catheters, flatus tubes etc, and that brings 8 pm when I am only too glad to come to the house.

What is making us so busy on the M[anches]ter Ward is that we have got some typhoids. We had five, one died, it worries me terribly that they are with the other men, but we have nowhere else for them. I have got them all a piece of mosquito netting for their faces, but they are delirious more or less and keep throwing it off, and oh! if you could only see the flies. Their mouths are black with flies and I am constantly urging the nurses to keep cleaning out their mouths, flitting[27] the ward every time I go on duty but still the flies swarm. […]

To make matters still more cheerful we haven't had any cigs for weeks.[…] Really it is hard to keep cheerful without a smoke, and we have neither milk or sugar, we have plenty of tea but it is pretty ghastly without sugar or milk. […] It seems that when you get here you are forgotten. Letters are coming very slowly.

My love to you all, forgive this long grumble.

Yours in the fight,
Madge.

17 January 1939

Dear Nat,

[...] Oh how I wish you could know some of these doctors. They work on and on with little or no material and very seldom grumble or complain at the lack of it. It really makes my heart ache, when perhaps we are discussing the war, and they say, 'Yes! but the fascists have got much more material than we have.' How ashamed I feel when I think that England and France if they cared to, could give them such assistance. I mean officially of course. I am not criticising the help that comes from the workers, I mean official action! I cannot of course discuss the war, but there is a word in Spanish, it is *triste* which adequately describes the people now. All Spain is '*triste*', and I feel the state this country has been reduced to is an everlasting disgrace to all nations who call themselves civilised, and I feel sure you agree. Really when I think of all the misery in China, Spain and Czechoslovakia, refugees from Germany and Italy, I wonder how much longer people are going to stand for it. [...]

Talking about paper, the committee sent out a gross of Izal toilet rolls, but they cannot be used for the purpose they were intended for. The director said to me, 'Madge, we were very glad indeed for the paper'. I said, 'What paper?' and he said, 'Well it was really toilet paper, but we are using it in the office, come and see.' And at every desk, by each typewriter is a roll of Izal toilet paper, and the clerks are typing away on it! That will give you some idea of the shortage of everything. [...]

Yours in the fight,
Madge.

Learning to Walk Again

Lilian Kenton

Lilian Kenton came as a refugee from Austria to England where she trained as a masseuse. In 1937 she and her English husband, Lou, volunteered with the SMAC, and were sent to the convalescent home at Valdeganga in Central Spain. There Lilian worked very successfully as a masseuse and physiotherapist.

My work begins when the surgeon and nurses have nearly finished. When the actual wounds are healed I have to see that the limbs function well again. The patients and I have built a gymnasium. We made as much as we could ourselves to save buying. We took parts of an old clock, an old bedstead and an old car to make the apparatus. We fixed up rings with weights on them for arm and shoulder exercises. We found wood and made wands and a weight-lifting bar and constructed a neat stand on which to keep this apparatus. One of the patients upholstered the massage table and we have a sunny massage room of which we are proud. There are various types of wounded cases that come under my care. There are ordinary flesh wounds with scars that must be eased by massage and heat treatment, stiffened joints which have been in plaster and cases of paralysis resulting from head wounds. I had a patient with a head wound who had completely lost the use of his arm. I told him to give me the Popular Front salute. This was something he wanted to do; and in a short time he was moving his arm. When he could lift it just a little I teased him and said that he was still showing fascist tendencies, that he must try to close his fingers. After massage and exercise and good fun, I saw the happy day when he was completely cured; he went back to the Madrid front. I have to think of all sorts of jolly ways of making the men use their limbs even if it hurts them. Men who limp must be taught that limping will not cure them. I tell men with injured fingers to go and help the girls peel the potatoes and they do. In such ways we have the complete co-operation of the staff of Spanish women who work the hospital. There is a story that I tell men with amputated limbs, a true story that makes them laugh and gives them courage. There was a man shot through the leg in two places and he could not walk. When he was taken to hospital it was found that he had been shot through an articicial limb. He had managed so well with it that he joined the army and had gone to the front and nobody knew anything about it till he got hit.

Across the Ebro

Lillian Urmston

__Lillian Urmston__ was from Stalybridge where her father was a steel worker. Lillian went to Spain because she saw that a war was coming and wanted to gain war-nursing experience. In the Second World War she served with the RAMC, was evacuated with the British forces from Dunkirk, served on troopships and in the Western Desert, Eritrea, Sicily and Italy.

We moved forward to just a few kilometres from the river Ebro. We took a huge cave – our first bomb-proof hospital, and installed 120 beds. [...] For a few days the wounded poured in. Ambulances were continually arriving, day and night. Then rumours began to circulate that hundreds of wounded were lying on the other side of the river, and could not be brought across. The fascist aviators were bombing the pontoon bridges all day long, and all night long our fortification battalions were repairing them. Also, almost all the territory which we had taken was within range of the fascist artillery. We were all sick with horror at the thought of this unnecessary suffering, and begged our chiefs to send us across the river ...

The following morning, at 1 a.m., the Spanish Medical Director told me to pack equipment and be ready in 20 minutes to move *across* the river. I hurriedly issued orders, and in a very short time we were ready. I was to go, along with Dr Jolly,[28] the Spanish doctors and *sanitarios* [medical auxiliaries], and set up as large a hospital as possible. [...]

Just as dawn was breaking, we were crossing the newly-repaired pontoon bridges. We had just reached the other side, and our ambulances were toiling along the hastily prepared road, when we heard the familiar cry of '*Aviación!*' Ambulances were pulled up at the side of the road, under the shelter of the cliffs – and we lay in ditches, tense with expectation and apprehension. But it was only our usual early morning caller, the observation plane. We continued our journey for exactly 25 minutes, and then twelve huge bombers came into sight. We all pulled into an olive grove, just off the road, and hastily camouflaged our ambulances and autochir. Then, a brief whistle – no movement – and we all lay down under trees and bushes. The planes bombed all along the river banks, and roads and crossroads. Our anti-aircraft guns were going magnificently, and managed to bring down one bomber.

Suddenly came the familiar rat-tat-tat of machine guns – they were strafing the helpless people who happened to be anywhere in view. At last came a number, six I think, of our pursuit planes, and engaged in a glorious dog fight. It is a most stimulating sight, this, to see our small planes tackling these gigantic bombers. After an hour of this the bombers soared higher, and disappeared. We were all relieved. And weren't we hungry! Rations of bully beef and bread were issued, then we again moved off. At 2 p.m. we reached Santa Magdalena, a huge white hermitage set high on the hills. Rather a landmark – but the only available habitation. We cheerfully acted as charwomen, then quickly set up a hospital. We were again interrupted by a heavy bombardment – luckily the bombs did not fall too near. By 11 p.m. our hospital was complete, and a steady stream of ambulances started to arrive. We only received the more severely wounded cases and our beds were quickly filled. Work was carried on four days and nights with but slight respite, but conditions were satisfactory. All day long we had the enemy planes overhead. Bridge and roads were bombed daily, and many ambulances were smashed and rendered unfit for use. Work continued but under greater difficulties. Food and medical supplies could not be regularly brought across the river – so belts were tightened and brains racked to provide a solution to the problem of medical supplies. Many and varied were the ideas produced. One day about 9 a.m. we were again 'disturbed' by the whistle of shells overhead – the fascists had concentrated on us their heavy guns. [...] After three days of intermittent shelling, the powers that be ordered *evacuation*. Quickly all wounded were sent to a safer hospital, and at 2 a.m. we commenced another journey, determined to find a safer hospital. For 10 kilometres we drove without lights, owing to the road being under artillery fire; many pairs of eager eyes scanned the landscape, watching out for the occasional flash of enemy guns. A tunnel had been discovered at Flix, a one-time beautiful tunnel on the edge of the river. The whole was now a mass of ruins. Again, as another dawn was breaking, we came to our new tunnel hospital. [...] An accumulation of many years' soot and grime enveloped the walls and roof. We stumbled along in the dark, continually falling over railway lines. Everyone was cold, tired and hungry – but the hospital had to be prepared. [...] We all worked furiously, digging, scraping and scrubbing, and soon we had ready another hospital complete with

65 beds. But oh! wouldn't a coat of whitewash work wonders in our hospital? No time for rest – a furtive dab with a powder puff, a meal of bread and black coffee, and again all ready for work. Wounded were already being brought in, so we must carry on. We had no satisfactory lighting system – one lamp for three operating tables, and a few candles in the huge ward. After two days, candles and oil were finished. We used to do injections and all other work by the light of matches. Many and varied were the comments passed by the wounded and many and varied the attempts made to cheer up the atmosphere of the place. [...] By degrees many minor luxuries were installed in our tunnel although bombings were frequent! Occasionally a bomb fell directly above us and then we were all enveloped in soot. Rather bad luck if one had just shampooed one's hair in the river Ebro!

The Cave by the River

Leah Manning

Leah Manning *had been president of the National Union of Teachers since 1929. She was Labour MP for Islington East between 1929 and 1931 and for Epping from 1945 to 1950. Sh₍ was Honorary Secretary of the Spanish Medical Aid Committee. In the spring of 1937 Leah helped to arrange the evacuation of Basque children to Britain and in the summer of 1938 visited Spain to report on the hospitals where British personnel were working.*

I suppose that in all the history of modern warfare there has neve been such a hospital. It is the safest place in Spain, beautifully wire for electric lights and with every kind of modern equipment. Th: hospital is evacuated twice a day. It is tragic to add that a larg proportion of the evacuations are by death, because only the grave: cases are brought here from the front, and the only ones who remai for longer than the first day or two are abdominals and seriou amputations. [...]

Patience Darton and Ada Hodson were working there when w arrived. Patience was just coming on duty for the night and, as w went into the cave, the stretcher bearers brought in an Englis comrade from the British Battalion who was gravely wounded in th abdomen. He had had his spleen removed and Reggie [Saxton], ha given him a blood transfusion. As I stood by he opened his eyes an spoke my name. I recognised him as a comrade whom I had met at by-election in South Wales, a miner from Tonypandy named Harr Dobson. Dr Jolly told me that it was not possible that he could live, i fact they thought only a few hours, so I determined to stay by hir until the end. Actually, it was fifteen hours before he passed away bt I did not leave him during that time and he seemed very happy t have me there. Reggie gave him another blood transfusion and as h was group three, of which they had none in hospital, Winifred's bloo was used. Patience Darton gave him two salines and two adrenaline during the night and we did everything possible for him, but withot avail. This was one patient, but Patience, with two *sanitarios* [medic auxiliaries], was on for twelve hours, every case extremely grave and every case needing amost equal attention. It was a fantastic night, as I sat by this dying comrade, passing along the high winding road on the side opposite from the cave, hundreds of *camions* [trucks] passed by with singing reserves and loads of material and ammunition on their way to the Ebro, whilst winding down to the path to the glen at the bottom, came the ambulances with dead, dying and wounded men. [...] It is a night which I think I shall never forget. Rosita[29] and Winifred slept in the open with Nurse Hodson and the next morning, after saying goodbye to the various *equipes* who were looking forward to crossing the river and saving the comrades from the long, long wait on the opposite banks of the Ebro made necessary by the terrific aviation which destroys bridges and boats and the opening of sluices in Alto Aragon, which sweeps them away, we set out on our journey to the Evacuation Train. [...]

From the Ends of the Earth

May MacFarlane

May MacFarlane's *mother and aunt were both radically-minded Australian women. In 1934-35, after doing Christian Mission work, she went to the Lidcombe State Hospital where she was shocked by the condition of the patients, many of whom were destitute men, victims of the depression. There she met Mary Lowson and Una Wilson. When a nursing unit for Spain was proposed the three of them volunteered. She now campaigns for pensioners' rights, and was one of the 'Red Matildas' in a recent documentary film.*

The first time the bombs were dropping around the place dust and plaster came down with the vibration, and I was just totting up whether I'd cover the wound up or not. I said, 'Well, I can't cover everything up, I can't cover anything else.' And the surgeons went on as if they hadn't heard the bombing. So I thought, 'That solves my problem.' They just went on as if they hadn't heard it. That was the first time we heard bombing, but when we had two operations on the go, you see, we just carried on as if they didn't exist. And one time, I think they were working on town power then, and during raids they cut off their town power, we tried to get our generator going, and it wouldn't go. My surgeon was already starting to close the abdominal cavity, so I used a cigarette lighter to give him light for his job. But the other surgeon was still groping for holes in the intestines, so Una had the torch for him. When I put out the cigarette lighter I burned my fingers. [...]

The fascists were trying to capture the Madrid-Valencia highway again, and we'd set up a hospital on the outskirts of Colmenar.[30] On the 11th of February [1937] the onslaught started, and wounded were brought into the hospital. A lot were dead when they were brought in, and they were parked in the corner of the yard until there were about six dead. Then a little old man with a donkey cart would cart dead up to the cemetery and deposit them in trenches they had up there; and we had hundreds. In the first few weeks I estimated there were about 300 died at the hospital. In the early days there were wounded in the foyers outside the theatre, sitting up the stairs; the wards were full and most of the yards at the front were full of wounded on stretchers waiting to be cared for. There were wounded everywhere, and the first few days we did nothing but the most urgent ones ... usually bullet holes in the belly, which means sometimes the gut was torn to ribbons. The place was a mess, wounded everywhere. One man that was put on the table, his foot was practically severed. I had to hang on to the boot and the foot while the surgeon snipped the little bit of skin that was left, and it gives you a nasty feeling when all the weight suddenly falls on you. The French cook that we had there would occasionally bring in a plate of sandwiches and a jug of coffee, and we went on working as far as possible with instruments in one hand and a sandwich in the other to tide us over. But Una and I, after the surgeons had finished work, we always had a lot of cleaning up to do. We were very much overloaded, because we had hours of work to do after the surgery had stopped. This happened over and over again, these long hours. I suppose the first two weeks we might manage two or three hours sleep in twenty-four hours.

Later Una and I decided to have a tiny little ante-room alongside the theatre where we had two beds there. If you put a third bed there there wouldn't be any floor space left. The first time we went to use these beds there was a dead man in each bed. She got someone to remove the dead men. The mattress was all bloody, so she turned it over, but the blood had run through. It was a ghastly business, but you just retreated to the theatre where you could do something for people, seeing all these wounded around. [...]

The Spanish people got no medical attention unless they could pay for it, and peasants couldn't pay for it. So they went without medical care for the most part. It was a shocking state of affairs. We had a ward for women and children, and had a clinic almost every day – well, when possible – for the civilian population to come up and see medicos, at no cost of course, but we did what we could for those in need. And I remember one old granny had an ovarian cist, and we operated on her, and when we removed it it filled the wash basin.

There had been some typhoid on the front, and we undertook to inject the whole civilian population. The local authorities in the village organised the people. We went down to their council chamber in a team, with dozens and dozens of needles, and this anti-typhoid vaccine. We went through the whole village.

At the hospital and in the trenches and everywhere the illiterate people, our domestic staff in the hospital, were taught to read and write. There were always enough Internationals (with knowledge) at their finger tips, and they always taught others to read and write. When possible there were always schools on hygiene, on nursing, on languages, on political subjects, to explain the reasons for war. There was always that kind of co-operation in the People's Army.

S.2 Albacete
27 December 1937

Dear Mum,
I have just received your air-mail letter dated Dec. 4th and as usual I feel ashamed that I keep you waiting so long for news.

No, *our* Colmenar was not bombed – it was Colmenar Viago – there are many towns in Spain with the same name. For instance, I know of 3 or 4 Villanuevas. Yes, many small villages were bombed early this month, but they were not 'front line' villages or places where we had soldiers or anything else of military importance. In Tarancón the fascists after bombing the town, swooped down and machine-gunned the streets. Many women and children were killed. Just the usual fascist tactics of destruction to terrorize the civil population. [...]

Bombs never worry me – I shall have to be very unlucky to get hit, but I quite understand how anxious you feel when you don't know what is happening,

The only anxious time I had was on the Brunete front where the fascists bombed and machined the road from the front almost continuously from planes. Dr Langer and some of my other friends had to visit the front every day. The ambulance drivers had a very gruelling time. [...]

I live in hopes of getting your parcel of cake and pudding etc. If you posted it on the 4th it was not likely to arrived here before the first week in January. I will be 29 next month, I shall write to Valencia and make enquiries about it.

I am now working in a clinic with a Canadian doctor.

The weather now is quite cold – fog occasionally, very often frost and the thin ice lasts all day. We had a fall of snow last week, it is the only time I have seen it and everybody laughed at my excitement.

I had an air mail letter from Mary Lowson while she was in Melbourne. Her tour seems to be going on alright. Hope she brings back plenty of food – right now I would like some Aussie plum jam, the sort I used to turn up my nose at, when I was a kid – I have not had butter for 7 or 8 months now, the only drink of natural milk was some scalded goats milk at Villa-marrique last August. […]

I would love some 'Rex' Camp Pie right now – but since I can't have it I shall go to bed – it is 12.

My love to all

(sgd) Maisie Mac.

I Could Never Smile Again

Una Wilson

Una Wilson *was from New Zealand. In 1930 she moved to Sydney, Australia, where she worked as a theatre sister in the Lidcombe State Hospital. She was profoundly disturbed by her Spanish experience, and by the political hatreds and suspicions encountered there.*

Muntaner, 407,
Barcelona
14 July 1937

Dear Phil,[31]
[...] My diary speaks the cold truth, and I think it is better for you to get it that way ... what's the use of hiding the dreadful experiences we have, you must take the good with the bad; and now for the extracts:

23 February: We had some frightful cases today, just the remains of once healthy men. My God! how brave they are. Every day we are bombed but I am too tired to care what happens. I am in charge of the theatre and sometimes there are as many as ten doctors in it. It is too much really. They are very good to us, of course, and are everlastingly telling me what an excellent theatre Sister I am, etc. They are dears, really, but I am too tired for compliments. Our two chiefs, Doctors L. and D.[32] are very worried about the amount of work we have, but it seems impossible to get another sister who knows the theatre. Thank God I've got Mac. [May MacFarlane.]

25 February: Never in my life have I felt so utterly tired, miserable and unhappy. I would be grateful to be caught by one of the machineguns which play about in the air. We seem to wade about in a river of blood without a break. Everyone about me receives mail, and still none for me. I have given up hope of letters.

27 February: I have just had three whole hours sleep, but when I wakened I could not speak, my voice had gone completely. I looked in my little mirror and was shocked. My face is ashen and wrinkled. Hell! I'm ugly.

29 February: Today two men came in whom I knew. The boy, ————, whom I had met at ————, a small town near the front. A tall, handsome lad of about 21 years, the kind a mother would be proud of. One of his legs was blown right off, and the other so injured that Dr D. had to remove it. I usually manage to hide my feelings completely where my work is concerned, but on this occasion I could have wept for hours. We gave him a transfusion, of course, and did all we could to save him, but when I called up to the ward a minute ago to see how he was, he was already dead and taken away. Died of shock. Dr D. did a wonderful operation, too. Then, later this afternoon, another Englishman I knew, a 'Commandant', a tall, fine-looking man of about 35, called to me across the theatre (I was attending another table) and I recognised him immediately. What a change. The last time I saw him he strode up to me with a smile, a happy healthy man, and this afternoon he lay there stripped of his clothes, ready for operation, covered with mud, his face lined with suffering, a huge wound in his side with his intestines falling from it. He died under the anaesthetic … and so it goes on, day after day, this awful slaughter. We heal their wounds and back they go to the front to be shot to bits. Isn't it fearful? How I hate war, hate it like hell. I feel tonight that I could never smile again. […]

8 April: I'm off duty. Have lost my memory. At least I cannot remember clearly what happens from day to day and everything is very tangled. Great is the concern now. I notice that Dr L. and Dr D. are very upset about me. I am being taken swimming, riding, walking and God knows what. A tennis court has sprung up and also a ping-pong set. When I was asked one day the things I would most like, these were what I mentioned, in fun, of course. Everyone puts themselves out to amuse me and this evening Dr D. came home leading a new brown pony for me. He said, 'Una, is there anything else you want to make you happy?' I certainly am rather ill. My hands shake like a leaf and I cannot sit still for more than two or three minutes. If anyone talks to me too much I feel like killing them …

Something terrible happened to me this morning. You see, for weeks now our huge courtyard, every corridor and every bed in the place has been filled with dead and dying. The ambulances have to unload right outside the gates for they cannot get in for bodies. I rush out of the theatre from the dispensary to get something, and I must step over bodies all the way; some dead, some dying, all with horrible wounds awaiting attention, my heart breaks for I know that lots of them must die before we can attend them. The groaning keeps up day and night. While we work we hear it and forget that we haven't slept ourselves for days and nights. My last sleep was on the 24th, at about 10 p.m., for about four hours. Mac had had a sleep so she relieved me for a while. I went to our room about 9 a.m. but found that two wounded occupied our beds. In Mac's was a very young boy with a waxen-like face from loss of blood. He had a severe head injury, in fact his brains were oozing out on the pillow and under the bed was a huge pool of blood. In my bed was a dead man. I turned back the bedclothes and found he had been shot through the stomach. My bed was filled with blood. I had him removed, turned my mattress over and flopped onto it. Shortly afterwards I was awakened by bombs dropping. I looked across at the boy in Mac's bed. He was dead. My whole body ached so much from sheer fatigue I just went to sleep again. In about ten minutes, however, was asked to hop up, that they wanted my bed for a patient. I jumped up and ran to the theatre, where I found Dr D. (with whom I have worked since coming to Spain) I said to him: 'D., I simply must sleep for I'm going mad and I haven't a bed.' He gave me two tablets to make me sleep, put me into his bed which is just off the theatre, covered me up with his big military coat and went on operating again. Dr L. came in and sat on the bed for a while and talked to me till I fell asleep. The last I remember was Dr L. stroking my forehead. He and Dr D. saved my life that time. Since then I have worked without sleep until about six this morning. If I was well it would be OK, but I'm really quite ill and it takes all my nerve to stand these gastric pains which almost paralyse me every 5 to 10 minutes. All the food here is just swamped in olive oil and the meat full of garlic. I can eat nothing at all just now and luckily get lots of condensed milk. [...]

One of the men has just brought me a big mug of chocolate and some bread. What heaven! It is the loveliest chocolate I have ever tasted. [...]

1 May: Life is very nice just now for our battalion has just gone into rest. This place is all flowers and gaiety today, all ready for the May Day celebrations. [...] I just dashed out this morning in time to catch the procession as it left. I grabbed a bunch of May flowers and ran to join the girls. I walked with the Spanish girls I knew. There were about one hundred of us altogether dressed in snow white carrying a large bouquet of flowers. The procession consisted of about 1,000 people all told. First the military people with a band, then us, then the people of the village. We marched through the town, up and down and down and up every street and round the public square. As we went the air was rent with the singing of songs and shouting of greetings to the hundreds who swarmed the streets. [...]

Suddenly there was quietness and the laughter ceased. As we approached the hill which leads to the cemetery where our soldiers are buried the band played the 'International'. We sang it until we reached the gates where all music and singing ceased. I can assure you it was a solemn procession which entered those gates. When I walked in I gasped. Never have I seen such a scene. The whole cemetery was a blaze of blue flag lilies, all excepting the small, square area where the soldiers lie. We were told to wait on one side and it was a pretty sight to see. Close on 100 girls carrying large armfuls of multi-colored flowers standing perfectly still in a veritable field of blue flag lillies. We were given our orders for the ceremony and waited while the procession formed a square right round the plot where the graves were.

The 'International' was again played softly and we approached the graves in files of twos, on past them until we reached the square when we separated into single file and eventually just wandering anywhere sprinkling our flowers over the graves as we went. Most of the flowers were the white May flowers. Soon the whole area, pathways and all was a mass of them with hundreds of black crosses marking the resting places of all the men whom I have met, talked with, and in many cases attended in the theatre. [...]

It was well after lunch time so we grabbed some bread and cheese from the kitchen and a big drink of condensed milk and hurried to prepare for the next event. This was as follows: We girls carried a large tray strung round our necks with bits of ribbon (like the kids have for chocolates or ice cream in picture shows in Australia). On our trays were all sorts of cakes made by the village people, and other dainties for the patients.

We went through the wards distributing these and having a little chat with each patient. They had never seen me in anything but a white gown done up high to the neck, and to see me adorned like this with a wreath of flowers on my head was almost too much for them. '*Muy bien, muy bien Una*,' they shouted, and I forgot for the remainder of the day that there was such a place as a theatre. I became just a carefree girl like the others.

After distributing the dainties to the patients we entertained the children of the village giving them lollies, scrambles, etc. and playing to them. The afternoon ended with tunes from the band and then about 6.30 p.m. the village folk returned home and settled down to tea. After tea, what fun, gosh! some of the boys had got together a band composed of a mouth organ, an old piano from upstairs and a guitar, all out of tune, a kerosene tin and a couple of combs.

They dressed up in all kinds of mad costumes. Jerry, our theatre boy looked a scream. God knows what he was supposed to represent, but I fancy it was a duck, for all the time he insisted on making a noise like a duck drinking water. It was still quite light when suddenly we found a lorry load of flowers left over from the morning celebrations, among which were whole bunches of those white pom-poms. I snatched the pom-poms and then the battle began. The whole courtyard was soon a laughing mass of merry, fighting carefree boys and girls while the mad band played freakish tunes as an accompaniment. I hit Dr D. in the face with a pom-pom I had dipped in water, and Jerry squirted him at the same time with a syringe. He caught us both and threw us into a big tub of water which stood nearby. Consequently we had to change every stitch of clothing, and by the time we came down again the fun had ceased, and exhausted little groups either sat or lay about under the trees. [...]

18 March 1938

Dear Phil,

Have arrived in England at last. I was delayed a couple of days getting finger-prints, passports etc seen to. The last six months of my life has been nothing but suffering, & as for Teruel my God.

A hundred times I have just escaped by the skin of my teeth. We lived in a rain of shells, bombs & machine-gun fire. I have come to England for the purpose of writing my book & under no other conditions would they let me leave Spain. It has been a tremendous worry to me for I knew that I could not go much longer without being killed. [...] What I have seen & been through at Teruel simply must be published & then when I return to Spain it matters little what happens to me. I simply could not die not having made public what I have seen & been through. [...]

At Teruel I was almost captured by the Fascists. The whole Sanitary Service with whom we had been working were taken, on that occasion I was lost on the road to starve for 3 days & nights. Don't let this be known whatever you do, for apart from anything else it would be terrible for my people, but you can understand now the burning desire I have to write. [...]

A letter from you all will be a tremendous comfort. I am in an agony of mind at present because of the people of Spain. Surely help will come from somewhere. Also I let my surgeon go back to the front without me. We have worked together right through the war & I left him to that.[33] If the Fascists win, all our great leaders, wonderful men that we know so well will be shot. My heart is sick within me.

Una

Aragon
Agnes Hodgson

Agnes Hodgson *was born in Melbourne. After training as a nurse she worked in England and the USA, and at the Anglo-American Clinic in Rome. In 1935, when Mussolini invaded Abyssinia, she tried to volunteer to nurse for the Abyssinians. For a time she managed a farm in Tasmania. Agnes joined the group of Australian nurses going to Spain at the last moment. In Spain she was separated from the other three because of unjust suspicions about her Italian connections. She left Spain in poor health in October 1937. During the Second World War she organised the Women's Land Army in Tasmania.*

Here her story is told in extracts from her letters (published and unpublished) interspersed with extracts from her diary to keep the chronological order.

c/o British Medical Aid Unit,
Diagonal 428,
Barcelona.
30 December 1936

Dear Mr Thorne,
You know doubtless that I have been left here in Barcelona. The reason given to me was that I was to remain to work in a proposed hospital for the International Brigade in Barcelona. The arranging of these things takes time I know. *I'm very trusting but I have a feeling that my services are being shelved politely.* I hope this isn't so. [...] I came in all sincerity as you know – at the moment (and it may be that I'm developing flu) I feel I'm getting a raw deal. I didn't bargain for this mental worry. [...] 10.1.37. [...] Tonight I received word that I leave for Grañen early in the morning. *The British Medical Unit no longer run that hospital.* The Spanish doctors who were there before continue and some of the English nurses remain. [...]

* * *

2 January 1937 (Grañen): Spent the morning being shown about and getting organised – misty morning and cold – large rambling house, courtyard being filled with stones. We sleep in loft with wire mattresses on the floor. Two male members sleep on the other side partitioned by Union Jack. Spanish doctors and *practicantes* [nursing orderlies] sleep in another dormitory. Two theatres and common anaesthetics room, two largeish rooms adjoining each with two alcoves – serve as wards – the alcoves house women patients. Another room upstairs serves VD patients.

26 January: Went long walk towards Huesca or rather Huesca road – walked across fields, jumped ditches and channels – walked on the road to military headquarters – a hill between here and the range of hills. Huge lorry loads of oranges en route for the *frente* passed us – we were thrown a couple – other foodstuffs, bags of grain and various CNT and UGT officials passed us going and coming. Dentist fraternity came to live with us.

27 January: Went for walk alone – glorious warm sunny morning – snow thick on the higher peaks but no cold wind. Walked in breeches and sweater – burning off stubble – fields being ploughed, single disc ploughs two mules to each – three ploughs and teams closely following the other – another man ploughed with two oxen, black men clearing ditches and channels – carting manure. Vegetables and barley doing fairly well after the rain and soft warm days. Cart track ended in manure heap – nice stable smell – went on to high bank over looking the muddy river which takes up only half its bed! Lots of poplar and olive trees about. Remains of maize crops in low lying sunken paddocks or plots. Sat on riverbank in sun, chewed grass and thought of the lovely day – because of the fine day guns were a little more active. Incredible that war is just beyond those hills.

* * *

In February the weather was marvellous, with hot sunshine most of the day. Some of the staff swam in the river, but with snow on the mountains I, personally, did not venture. I was sick for a few days, and from my window could see the main road and the countryside, the earth, bare and cracked, stretching flatly to the mountains, and the lower Pyrenees.

At 9 o'clock each morning the goats and sheep, with little bells tinkling, came out along the road to pasture, then along the road came trucks laden with oranges – vitamins for the soldiers – driving furiously through the villages.

At the end of the day the mules and oxen trotted off to the lagoon to drink. There was endless activity on the road, small, covered carts and ancient ploughshares dragged by four mules, women with huge baskets of washing on their way to the river, and Pancho Villa's cavalry galloping off and home again. Pancho Villa, incidently, is our local headman.[34] [...]

Recently all hospitals have been apportioned to one or other division. We now belong to the Carlos Marx Column, connected with the PSUC, the Unified Socialist Party of Catalonia. We received orders to move to Poleñino, the better to serve our column. Later it was decided to use the hospital at Grañen for the Ascaso Division (FAI group, the Iberian Federation of Anarchists). The Spanish girls to whom we had given some training in nursing were left in charge, obviously thrilled with the responsibility. [...]

The local butcher and his wife gave us a grand breakfast of fried eggs, garlic sausage, wine and cognac. We had to leave Tom, the Alsatian dog, for while we were crossing the square after breakfast a woman claimed him. We were rather surprised, because Tom had always eaten and slept at the hospital since its foundation and we had been told that he was an 'ex-fascist' dog.

When we had said farewell to nearly the whole population we climbed into the ambulances, one of our surgeons nursing a priceless trophy, an angler's cap which the butcher's wife had filled with eggs for us. Some of us carried the blood transfusions and other precious things, and we took with us Alejandro and Pedro, two patients needing daily treatment, who insisted on coming. [...]

* * *

13 March (leaving Grañen for Poleñino): Atmosphere exceedingly hostile to us. Pancho stopped me on the stairs taking pillows, 'said nothing was to leave Grañen'. Ramón and Paolino were to be held for investigation – fled secretly in car. Aguilo left his hat at the butcher's, but we dared not go back for it.

* * *

Hospital de Sangre,
Poleñino,
Aragon
15 April 1937

Dear Mr Thorne,
[...] We had quite a number of fascist wounded here – they were treated exactly as the other patients and were amazed to receive such treatment from the Spanish doctors as well as nurses – also the officials who came to interview them treated them courteously as human beings. [...]

We are fairly well equipped as a hospital; lack of gasoline and lack of pillows in the ward makes me sad – one can't make three wounded comfortable with two pillows – one hopes they'll get more at the next hospital. Last night we got in a German, who'd been out in the Sierra for seven days without food – his leg was alive with maggots – it was amputated below the knee fortunately we may be able to save that much – he is a marvellous patient. [...]

About 120 fascist soldiers crossed to our lines from Huesca the other day – that's the largest number who have come over – it's not easy for them to escape as you may imagine.

I must go to sleep. Greetings. A.H.

* * *

9 June: Feeling bored and homesick. Hills look lovely – fresh breeze – just the atmosphere to make one long for peace and idle content. Don't really want to leave Spain but sick of nursing and hospitals.

* * *

Australian Bank
5 Gracechurch Street,
London E.C.3
23 October 1937

Dear Mr Thorne,
You'll have heard from my sister that I have left Spain – the reason being that I got sick again immediately on my return and as it seemed likely to recur with cold and stress of work I thought it better to leave. I regret having to retire so soon after my holiday and am very sorry by leaving Spain to disappoint the committee in Australia. My personal

regret leaving Spain at the moment when more than ever they need assistance you can imagine; but Spain is no place for people not thoroughly fit.[35] [...]

My division have moved and are fighting in the mountains above Boltaña in Alto Aragon on the road to Jaca ... We were a mobile ambulance unit but for the moment lived in tents by the roadside and operated in an ex-slaughter house – using two of the earth floored storehouses for the patients – we had about seven beds in each. We were about 4 kilometres from the front line. It was heart-breaking working under those conditions. I mean just receiving badly wounded men, all we had time to do was to operate on the most urgent cases, abdominal and head cases mainly – the others were sent to Boltaña – a three to four hour journey! We tried to keep the abdominal cases for a couple of days but sometimes it happened they had to be evacuated in under three hours after the operation. Some of the soldiers had been without food for three days – that didn't always happen, but advancing as they are and food having to be taken up on mules – I gather it isn't always easy to get it to them. And we hadn't much to give them, coffee and milk generally and not always milk. [...]

While I was in Barcelona it was bombed nightly between 7 and 11 p.m. The last night it lasted for two hours, the fascists making six attempts to fly over the city – the anti-aircraft guns kept up a barrage and they did practically no damage. I went over to Barceloneta one day and saw the havoc made of those houses, the school completely destroyed and 70 children killed – it seemed incredible the next night to be in France and not expecting to hear sirens.

Not Exactly Terrified

Isobel Dodds

Isobel Dodds, a New Zealand nurse, came 'from a background which believed in social justice'. Shortly after qualifying she volunteered for Spain. On her return home in January 1939 she lectured to raise money for Spanish refugee children. She trained as a midwife, married and brought up three children.

About January of 1937, I happened to be on night duty at the time, a friend saw it in the newspaper where they were asking for volunteers. She came up and said, 'Well, what about it?' and I said, 'OK, we'll volunteer.' So I wrote away, and about March-April it was decided that we'd go. [...] My parents agreed with me going, and Dad, I think, would have liked to have gone and joined the International Brigade if he'd had a chance. I think my father was really quite proud of me, and my mother was a devoted wife and she went along with anything father said.

The matron of the hospital thought I was misguided, but she did come along to say farewell at the reception that was given for me. The trade unionists all thought we were wonderful. The Catholic community were somewhat cool about it, and a lot of middle-class people thought we were going off to join the communists.

I suppose the best help and advice we had was from the doctor on the *Mooltan* when we were on our way over to Spain. He warned us to turn round and go back of course. But he said, 'Well, if you insist on going, and you avoid being collected by the white [slave] traders, well then you've got to have typhoid injections on board the ship.' He also told us to be very careful about drinking European water.

We got our passports and our visas without any trouble, but when we got up to Auckland we had a notice from the police, and we were told to report at a police station up in Auckland. They asked us for our passports and took them from us, with the intention, I think, of stopping us from going. Renee [Shadbolt], they asked if she had belonged to any political party or been the secretary of anything, Renee said 'No', she'd never even been a secretary of a tennis club. In my case they suggested very discreetly that I might have had an illegitimate baby somewhere or other, which they could have used as an excuse for stopping me. They didn't find anything really very much for Millicent. She was very romantic about the whole thing. The police told her that they thought she ought to just turn round and go home. [...]

We arrived just after there had been a lot of rioting in the streets of Barcelona between the Communists and the Anarchists.[36] There had apparently been some terrible shoot-ups in the streets. We didn't see any of it but we were very conscious of the fact that it had happened. [...]

The people living in Central Spain lived very hard, bleak lives; the countryside there is very unproductive. They used to say they had the most primitive forms of maintaining life and the most up-to-date means of destroying it. Agriculture was carried on there in the same way that it was carried on in the time of Christ, I'd say. Where we were it was a wheat-growing country. The countryside is very barren; it is very dry and bleak. The peasants who farm the land are very poor. You come to a village and you see, away in the distance, this huge big building which is the church and looks like a big clucking hen, and round it the little hovels where the people live. It's the same colour as the countryside because its made of the stone and rock from the same area. So you look across, and it's just part of the landscape, excepting that you see the big building which is the church and the small buildings around. But the people were very, very poor.

The peasants were all black. They had black kerchiefs over their heads, black shawls round their shoulders, canvas shoes with rope soles and black blouses and skirts with belts just tied round the middle. The men wore black trousers and black jackets and black caps. They lived in the village. They rode off to the fields to do their farming, to the fields beyond. They went with their donkeys, their mules. They carried on either side of them the animal skins that they brought back the water in. The men might ride, but the women always walked behind, but they were usually carrying skins of water as well. They were not the people that you heard laughing and singing. They were the people that toiled from sun-up to sun-down.

We finally got to a hospital near Madrid.[37][...] They weren't wards as we would have had them in New Zealand. Very much Crimean nursing, very short of supplies and very, very poor equipment, and no continuation of supplies. You could not count on anything. We had very primitive conditions for hygiene. We had to sterilise things by boiling them up on a primus stove, and if we ran out of petrol we had to con some from the drivers that were coming and going, because their petrol was scarce too. We flamed a lot of instruments, by burning alchohol over them. We did have one very small autoclave [steriliser] for the theatre, which when we were very busy was not very adequate.

When Franco was making his drive towards the Mediterranean which isolated Madrid [in the spring of 1938] the wounded started coming in in all sorts of vehicles, because communication started to break down. They came in in trucks and ambulances, anything on wheels that was coming in. They weren't on stretchers half the time, they were piled in the truck. When they were unloaded they usually had a blanket round them. This huge building we were in had a very large reception area on the ground floor, and they were brought in and they were just off-loaded on to the floor. […] To go into this place and see several hundred people just lying side by side moaning is just like a symphony of pain, the moans and the wailing, and they say '*Madre Mia*'. Its just something you never forget. We were able to do little for these people. We had limited staff, we had limited equipment. I walked along with a doctor. We stood by and looked each patient over, and he would say, 'All right, this one we can do nothing for,' and we passed on. Then we'd go to the next one, maybe you could do something for them; or if they weren't so badly injured we passed them by anyway. So there were only a very few we picked out and received treatment. Then when we got to work in the theatre it was absolutely chaotic. Limbs were amputated, one after the other, because it was the only thing we could do. I guess this is what happened at the Battle of Waterloo. There was nothing you could do about saving the limbs, because to save life you had to amputate. And in the end we ran out of sterile instruments. We ran out of spirit. We ran out of sterile water, because we didn't have time to boil up the instruments between operations. It was dreadful, because we didn't know what happened to these people. We never stayed there long enough to find out. We were playing God because you could not treat them all, and you had to choose them out, and you chose those most likely to survive. […]

You can have pity, but eventually exhaustion catches up on you and there's no more, you have to accept what you can do. There isn't much else you can do about it. […]

I've never been quite in the situation where death loses its meaning. Nursing training is such that you always hope to save the patient. All the time we were in Spain we were in danger, but we were never in battle, because we were nurses. When you're working and have something to do you're never exactly terrified. You may be fearful, and you're aware of things going on, but you're not exactly terrified, and its a great help to be part of the thing and feel you're helping.

We were evacuated after about two weeks. We went out at dead of night in trucks. Our belongings went on by one lot of trucks, and they went on by road, and we were supposed to be going to Valencia. But we never saw them again, because apparently the convoy was under shell fire, and they had been blown up and abandoned. We went by truck to a rendezvous where we got into a train. We spent three days and nights in this train, treking down to Barcelona. We were the last train to get over the bridge over the Ebro before it was blown up. And indeed the bridge was under artillery fire when we were hiding in a siding. We finally crept over at night-time; quite a traumatic experience because by this time all the way along the way you could see people on the move – refugees. We had very little water and very little food on the train, and it was pretty dramatic, because it was evident that the Republicans were in retreat. We did get through to Barcelona.

All the time we were in Spain Renee and I were determined that we weren't going to let our standards drop, and we used to wash down in a small basin – you know, Gracie Fields used to have a song, 'The Little Pudding Basin that belonged to Aunty Flo'. And we used to call this our 'little pudding basin'. We used to wash down in about a quart of water, and we washed from top to toe every day. We never got lousy in these places. We deloused the sheets in the wards, and we certainly deloused the sheets on our own beds before we got into them.

Once we got into Catalonia, and we were under conditions of being in transit camps virtually, we got body lice and we got head lice. We had lost all our belongings and we only had what we stood up in. It was very difficult to get even our clothes washed. We deloused each other's hair, and we did what we could with the body lice. We coped, but we were a bit inclined to realise that it was one of the casualties that we had to suffer. We were very concerned about the typhoid that broke out, and we blessed that doctor that we had on the *Mooltan* for giving us our typhoid injection. [...]

Snow and Springtime
Renee Shadbolt

Renee Shadbolt *was leader of the New Zealand group. She returned home early in 1939 and raised money for Spanish refugee children. Because Spanish Medical Aid was considered 'Red' she had difficulty in finding work – until the 1939 war. In 1949 she was appointed Matron of Rawene Hospital, Hokianga, in an isolated and depressed rural area of North Island. On retirement she was awarded the MBE, which she would have refused but for the expressed wishes of the people of Hokianga.*

28 January 1938

Dear Mr Jackson,[38]
[…] Am still at the original hospital I commenced in and we have been very busy for some time. We have had some very serious cases in. Have also been working with a very depleted staff and equipment – as the Spanish Medical Aid Committee London has withdrawn all support due to some internal strife. It has been a cold hard winter and food has been rather scarce and although of a fattening quality (due to so much bread) seems to leave the foreign inhabitants very anaemic. However the snow was very beautiful and we had such a fall of it on New Year's day. I was on night duty, and the sight in the courtyard with the pigeons fluttering around was like a fairyland. I struggled up to the top of the old fortress in the afternoon and the panorama was really marvellous. There are hundreds of acres of land in small holdings ploughed and the furrows covered with snow reminded me of pleating and the hills in Spain are so bold and bare standing like sentinels guarding the land.

The weather is much warmer now and I cannot say I am sorry as many of the children in the village do not appear to have sufficient clothing and looked so pale and forlorn. The sun and the spirit of the inhabitants here is very much in alliance as people seem to live so much out in the open, due I should think to the difficulty of firing the lack of sun assumes much more character than it would for instance in our country. […]

2 February 1938

Your Xmas parcels also arrived so you can imagine how excited Isobel [Dodds] and I were opening them and the things are really wonderful and have arrived in perfect condition. We have parcelled M[illicent] Sharples' share in a separate box to be taken to her so I hope they arrive quite safely and give her as much pleasure as they did us. We are giving a party tomorrow night so that some of the comrades here can share in the good things. Convey our thanks to everyone concerned as we know how busy you are and the work that goes into buying and packing these Xmas hampers is an addition to your manifold duties.
Yours fraternally
Renee Shadbolt

31 March 1938

Dear Mr Jackson,
This is just a short note to let you know that Isobel and I are still alive and kicking with the warm spring days and one feels that summer is not far off. [...]

The surrounding countryside is a beautiful sight with the trees just coming into flower. The Spanish agricultural workers have done marvellously considering their primitive implements and I should imagine that the best of the animals are used for war purposes. [...]

I am wondering if the Women's Committee in NZ would undertake the task of doing some knitting. Jackets, socks, baby clothes etc. These things are more than appreciated here and I know the women in New Zealand are excellent knitters. By the way I have a great longing for some NZ honey. We still have the remains of your Xmas parcel and I am sure Millicent Sharples will tell you how it was appreciated. We had a grand party with the rest of the English and Spanish comrades and the Personnel Staff. They toasted NZ liberally with *café con leche*. Cigarettes are of course as welcome as the sun in winter. By the way the cake that my Mother made and you so kindly sent on arrived in perfect condition three days ago. It must be a good 5-6 months old but does it taste good. [...]

With anti-fascist greetings
Renee Shadbolt

Six Inch Roses

Rose Freed

Rose Freed *was from a Jewish family from New York's East Side. She grew up in Ohio and became a laboratory technician in the Greenpoint Hospital. From there she joined the first American Hospital Unit for Spain in January 1937.*

Hotel Oriente,
Barcelona,

31 January 1937

Dear Lou,[39]

Left Paris with John Langdon Davies,[40] famous British author, who saw us off to Cerbère. We travelled all afternoon and night, arriving there in the morning. With the Pyrenees on one side and the blue Mediterranean on the other, it was really like entering paradise. There is no country in the world more beautiful than Spain. It is hard to imagine a heinous war in this idyllic country. We stayed at Cerbère until late afternoon, at which time Spanish soldiers came to escort us into Spain. We entered a large bus and started up the Pyrenees! The roads were perfect. For two hours we travelled up the mountain, and then to Port Bou. Radios installed in the trees shouted greetings to us. With our armed escorts and our uniforms the people were thrilled and cheered us wildly as the word got around as to who we were.

We were escorted to a very beautiful restaurant. My first meal in Spain was an experience in itself! First we were served with anchovies, then octopus and rice! Dr Barsky told us that we must eat everything we were served or the people would be offended.[41] I think now that Barsky was merely having some malicious joy. I don't think it necessary to describe the extreme uncomfort around the table. Of course they served beef steak too, but I think I shall never understand how octopus ever became Spain's favorite dish. I shudder at the thought that it may be placed before me again. […]

We have been in Barcelona for four days now, and on the go from

10 a.m. to 3 a.m. It is impossible to tell you how the Spanish people have catered to us. There is nothing we wish that is not granted to us. They look upon us almost as saviors. I feel embarrassed when I remember that ours is a common cause. What sufferings these poor people must have endured to display such gratefulness towards our puny aid! They cut their choicest flowers and bring them as their humble offerings to our feet. At times I feel moved to tears, and you know how hard boiled I am, don't you. My room is flooded with roses, hyacinths, narcissus, carnations, enormous violets and of course (conilliers!). Never in all my life have I ever seen such beautiful flowers. The roses measure 6'' in diameter. [...]

I have just come from the Palace of Luis Companys, President of Catalonia, where we were his guests. Movietone pictures were taken of us in the orange grove garden of the Palace. This palace was built in the thirteenth century. The beauty of Sert's murals, the gargoyles, the gold inlay ceilings and the huge crystal chandeliers were breath-taking. I left entranced. How bitter the thought that Franco and his Fascist horde is burning, plundering, destroying, yes, raping glorious Spain.

Well, I must dress to meet La Pasionaria tonight. I have been writing this letter in spasms for three days now, and have given up a theatre engagement to finish it, for we are leaving for Valencia Wednesday or Thursday. I'm anxious to get to work. From Valencia we are going to Madrid. The receptions are tiring, but the sight of the almond trees and olive trees in bloom now are never so. I love this velvet grass, these beautiful palms and huge cactus, the semi-tropical climate, this soft, melodious southern air. Although humanity is plentiful the humidity is negligible. Lovely Spain, cool breezes and warm suns – and Franco! A hard to imagine paradox ...

Have my friends write to me. We would all rather receive letters from home than sleep.

Lots of love to every one.

Rose

Tarancón
20 March 1937

Dear Lou,
[...] Last night it was Dr Goland's birthday. We made a party at the American Casa. I made rounds and came to see how things were going

at the party. We had just given Dr Goland his birthday present, which consisted of one dozen tooth brushes each in the center of a cup cake with bristles exposed and blue ribbon tied to each, when at twelve midnight the lights went out. We heard the roar of planes. There was a long silence in the room. I spoke. I said I was going to the hospital. Dr Bloom shouted, 'If you think anything of your life don't go.' Dr Barsky said he was going to the hospital. I ran to Hospital 3 on the Valencia Road, Dr Barsky went to Hospital 1, and Dr Odio to Hospital 2. I stayed outside the door of the hospital searching the brilliantly studded starry sky for a sight of the planes, but they were too high and had no lights. They circled overhead many times, they came lower and lower and the sound of the motors became louder and louder. I ran into the hospital only to find some of the Spanish *enfermeras* [nurses] in hysterics. They could not be blamed, they who so many times have been terrorized by the lousy tactics of the fascists, and whose minds reflected the fatalities of such terrorism, and whose fathers, brothers, sweethearts and husbands died on the battlefield singing as their last strength ebbed out for the cause of democracy and love for humanity – could they be blamed for hysteria when they realized what was coming. What right had I to be frightened, I who have just tasted what they have long lived through? With my heart pounding almost as loudly as the roar of the motors above, I spoke to them. I told them they must be brave. I told them that they must comfort their brothers of Spain who are lying in bed helpless, most of them unable to move. I felt strong and stern – what did it matter – our lives to be sacrificed for so many that they may continue to live in peace. They clung to me with an almost deadly grip, kissed me and dried their tears. The crash – you cannot – never can anyone realize the horror of what seems like the earth opening beneath you – the light of the magnesium flare bomb to see if they struck right – and then eight more crashes – then silence, too long, and shrapnel flying in all directions. I ran to Hospital 1, then to Hospital 2, then back to my post where I found all crying silently. I made them all go to sleep and stayed on alone. Later in the morning Dr Sorrel took the post with me. [...]

20 April 1937

Dear Lou,
[...] We have just opened a new base hospital – Villa Paz. Villa Paz was the home of a member of the royal family. It is a beautiful palace with

12 sq. miles of ground. There is a rapid brook with a most picturesque falls. The foliage is dense and looks more like a tropical country than the countryside of Valencia, which is quite tropical. On the outside of every door of the almost innumerable rooms is a small sign which reads that this house was taken over by the Republican Socialists. The owners's maid, who was so very haughty before the revolution, now must carry wood for all of the villagers. I understand that this palace, whose walls are adorned with priceless paintings and tapestries, was actually occupied for only two months during each year – just so the owner could collect taxes from the slaves, who tilled her soil from early dawn to late sundown merely for the compensation of dirty, sunless, cold and damp homes.

These very slaves are today sitting at our table, eating the same food we eat, and eating out of the finest china dishes, upon which the crown and the coat of arms of the king of Spain are engraved. And I have discovered, (much to my chagrin) that even though their stomachs are not lined with hereditary royalty, up to this very meal they have suffered no indigestion! Nor any ill effects from the wine (*vino*) which they drink out of crystal champagne glasses. Marvellous constitutions – *n'est ce pas?* [...]

Tonight, in the garden, where all the roses, lilies, violets, grapes, forgetmenots, irises, gladiolas, different varieties of ivy, cherry and almond blossoms are in bloom, around the swimming pool and under the huge pines, the nurses and doctors and patients and our Spanish friends are sitting and listening to the enticing music being played by Victor, our chauffeur, on his electric victrola. The entertainment is good and the moon is bright but treacherous. In our happiest moments we must fear a bright moonlight night. For it is then that we always fear and expect our uninvited guests to drop in from above. Who knows but that our expectations may come true and take form any moment or right now. For the past two days we have had a lone eagle observer. We haven't forgotten our horrible experience before. It burns in all our memories. [...]

Wearing Our Uniforms Proudly

Fredericka Martin

__Fredericka Martin__ was head nurse of the first American Hospital Unit to Spain. She has made her home in Mexico after living in the Bering Straits area of Alaska, where she compiled an Esquimo-Indian dictionary. In 1986 she was awarded a doctorate by the University of Alaska for her work with Aleut Esquimos on conservation and on Alaska native rights.

Anna dear:

The lovely blanket you contributed is warming such a splendid young Spanish boy right now. We are all cowering in the present rainy damp weather inside these stone walls, even in bed with hot water bottles, and we have to pile blankets on our poor patients until they are nearly worn out by the weight alone. Liss' blanket is helping Sally Kahn, Jack's aunt, right now. She is ill with the grippe, broken down from overwork. And we have her rolled in a blanket and hot water water bottles, trying to keep her warm.

We have been here three weeks this afternoon. We started to unload our furniture about four o'clock. Two days later we received patients and worked madly day and night. I wish I could convey my pride in my girls. They have been superhuman. They have never lost their cheerful spirit or quarreled with each other or grumbled. Not *once* has a nurse been for a stroll. You see, it is the nurse that oils the cogs of the hospital machinery. She prepares for the operations, and all the time when the floors were covered with wounded men on stretchers and borrowed mattresses, the patients here have had as good nursing care and better than many, as any ward patient in New York City.

We have thirteen Spanish girls whom we are trying to train but the results have been pretty hopeless up to now. Most of the actual work was done by our handful. When I tell you the girls had such swollen feet that some of them had to wear floppy patient's slippers in order to walk, it must sound unreal. But it is true. Running back and forth over these tiled floors is terrifically wearing. I had an old pair of white sandals that were still strong but stretched out because I wore them with woolen anklets. Well, wearing them one day without anklets, I burst the center strap of each one. I couldn't believe my own eyes, it was so bad.

When I cracked up a few days ago, I had a record of three sleepless nights and a maximum four-hour nap one night. And the first day I spent in bed I was delirious at times and issuing orders in English and in Spanish for every sort of job. The strain has been terrible for it was just one million times more difficult to do since I had only a few words of Spanish and signs to see that most of the work was done. I didn't crack from the strain but a patient walking from the ambulance fainted and there was only another girl there and we had to get him into the house. And lifting him I strained myself but after two days in bed I'm hale and hearty again. Only, once I was down, the nervous strain had a chance to express itself. [...]

I sleep in the linen room on the second floor where I can be reached at night by either a doctor, the American nurse or a Spanish aide if there is any emergency or crisis. The pharmacist also sleeps in the drug room on this floor – on call all night. One night, one of my sweet little Spanish aides woke me at 4 a.m. to ask if I would like hot milk. All I could do was laugh. I couldn't be cross at losing some sleep over such artless concern. I am '*muy simpática*' according to all of them but they jump when I speak just the same. When I was ill they massed around my door and created a traffic problem, cooks, scrub women, aides, stretcher bearers, all. But my discipline is so severe that the night cook was afraid to sit down to rest lest 'Martina' find her. [...]

The greatest tribulation of the nurses at present is the inability to keep neat and trim. The village laundresses cannot iron. Our uniforms come back a mess of wrinkles. Starch is hard to buy – so far we haven't found any. We have only one electric iron with us and the current is not strong enough to heat it. If we move on soon, we will always be in a village or the country; meeting the same conditions. We started out with starch but the box containing it was lost. We can make ourselves feel fairly clean with a sponge bath, but then we step into wrinkled uniforms and it is most depressing. Can the Women's Auxiliary take on the special task of helping the nurses and send them starch and irons, old-fashioned country ones for use on a stove, and since our uniforms will soon be in tatters because of the rigorous washing they get, these too. [...] We want to keep on with the same uniform which we all love and cherish and try to wear proudly. [...]

I had a small fruit cake and one day we had such a strain and a patient we all loved died, and I made tea and called them into my room and fed each one a tablespoon of fruit cake. We had no knives at the time – hence the tablespoon. The result was dynamic. Anne stopped shivering, Sally's lips got a bit of color in them, etc. And I wished I had brought a trunkful of fruitcake for them.

I am writing so hastily in an effort to utilize a free hour, never knowing when an ambulance will drive up and the mad rush begin again. All our lives we seem to have been running back and forth along these cold corridors. All our lives we have hated white moonlight because it means the birds of death are busy nearby, sometimes close to us, and we can never again consider moonlight beautiful or an aid to romance. All our lives we have been hating as we have learned to hate here, when we see the ravages of dum-dum bullets in the flesh and bones of the best youth of all the world. The other thing I wanted to mention is the special strain of this nursing. There is nothing impersonal about it. These patients are a part of us. When they suffer, we suffer and learn to hate more. There is a terrific emotional drain always. If you have any voice in the committee, beg them to send us more nurses and doctors. Don't let them forget us. They can never fill the need here but they must never stop trying.

My best to you.

Freddie

Strawberry Jam and Crackers

Ray Harris

Ray Harris *was the longest-serving American nurse in Spain. She arrived in Spain with the first American Hospital Unit in January 1937 and left on 31 December 1938. Before going to Spain she had worked at the Lebanon Polyclinic and the Bellvue Hospital in New York. On her return to the USA Ray worked as a nurse in the camp for migrant workers in California described by Steinbeck in* The Grapes of Wrath, *and in similar camps of Mexican migrant workers in Southern California.*

The Furriers Union gave each nurse a 'fur coat' before we left NY (Jan 1937). I was thrilled, never had a fur coat. It soon became apparent that they stole every cat and rabbit and made them into fur coats. Everyone on board ship had a small flurry of fur. Our coats rapidly disintegrated. Never knew what happened to them, probably flung in the ocean! [...]

The room was quite large, can't remember whether it was a school or meeting hall. It was ringed with white iron, old fashioned beds. They had large pillows and white bedspreads. The room appeared spotless and the beds all occupied. This was my introduction (as well as our unit) to the Australian and British units. They opened a hospital some time in late 1936 – vicinity of Madrid. We were asked to assist there, until we could locate our own hospital. We arrived late at nite – tired, ready for rest. Unfortunately bed space was limited. The nurses' quarters was a curtained area in the corner of this room. We would have to share beds. I shared a bed with an exhausted sleeping nurse. We woke up in the early a.m. ready for work. The nurse informed me she had head lice and nits! Luckily I never became infested. I do remember the lovely p.m. teas – strawberry jam and crackers etc. [...] Shall I tell you about the time Langston Hughes came to visit us.[42] How he ever got 'lost' in the nurses' bedroom I'll never know. We were four or five in the small dormitory in Villa Paz – ready to go for bed, discussing same day's events – when Salaria Kea suddenly screamed. There was Langston sitting in a corner, just watching us. He apologised, told us he was enjoying the talk etc.

Or the time when George Hirst, my English boyfriend, bedded down the linen room for a nite. What a nite that was. We were 'up' all nite – 12 for extra linen; 2am flash lite batteries for an ambulance accident on the road; 3.30-4 soap etc for the wash women who came in early to wash clothes; 5-6 again linen and towels; 7 I had to be on duty. I remember George bleary-eyed, head over the bed, making his morning tea on the primus stove with a dangling cigarette in his mouth. What a nite of love that was! [...]

It Isn't Romantic, But ...

Mildred Rackley

Mildred Rackley *went as secretary and interpreter with the first American Hospital Unit for Spain, and was later Director of the British Hospital at Huete. She grew up on a ranch in New Mexico and graduated from the University of Texas, later studying and teaching art in Germany, Italy and Spain. She edited* Fight, *the magazine of the League Against War and Fascism. During the 1939-45 war Mildred worked in Californian shipyards where she was an active union organiser.*

An administrator's job is a thankless task and it never stops. When the hospital is half empty and the doctors and nurses are strolling about the countryside, reading books or drinking tea to kill time, the administrator's job becomes harder than ever. It is when the personnel of the hospital have little work that their nerves become jumpy – always ready, and waiting. People with jumpy nerves are tough to deal with. They fret because they don't know what is happening at the front, because they don't know when the order will come to move the hospital to another front, because they don't get mail or packages from home, because one gets a leave and another doesn't, because somebody has got more stripes than somebody else, because the cook is dynamite and the food is bad, or because of almost anything.

In the early days before the personnel was developed, I used to be a combination quartermaster, hausfrau, secretary, straw-boss of plumbing installation, liaison officer, paymaster and interpreter. I used to go out combing the countryside for fields of cabbages and cauliflower. In one day I spent hours getting a permit for a thousand litres of gasoline and fifty litres of oil for the ambulances so that we would always be able to move. It took several more hours to find barrels and persuade the people that they ought to sell them to us. That same day while hunting barrels we stumbled onto an enormous stove which had been in a big hotel. They gave it to me as a present for the hospital. The truck broke down on the way back to the hospital, so I spent most of the night on the road.

In fact, I've spent a lot of nights out on the road. One afternoon Dr

Byrne and I set out to get a supply of food from a new commissary I had heard about. We were newcomers and they refused to give us anything. After pleading and threatening not to leave until we got food for our patients, I finally called up headquarters at the base and they gave us a truckload of food. About half way 'home' our old truck wheezed and died. It was late at night, and it was a deserted road. Dr Byrne set off walking toward the nearest town to phone for Carl, and I stood by the waggon. It was bitter cold and a stiff wind was blowing. I had to choose between sleeping among the soft crisp cold lettuces, and the cabin. I chose the cabin; it wasn't so draughty. Even then, it was so cold I got numb, and every half-hour or so, I would get out and run up and down the road to try to get up a little circulation. They picked me up at six o'clock the next morning

We had a Frenchman who won a sheep in the village lottery. He came back to the hospital rather late at night with his sheep, and somehow managed to get it up the stairs to his ward without being seen and tied it to the leg of his bed. That was before the days when we had guards. Streams of women with chickens or rabbits under their shawls used to try to slip past the guards to ask the storeroom man to exchange them for canned milk or sugar or soap. Finally we got the livestock coming around to the back gate. [...]

Little Josefina was a refugee from Córdoba. She had spent most of her life working in the fields. She was such a little thing we almost refused her work, but she told us she was very strong from her field work. Louise Jones, our head nurse, was her ideal. 'I don't ever want to go back to the fields again, I know what that means. I want to learn to be a nurse like Louisa. She is so good. I want to be like her.'

In the English Convalescent Hospital, we tried the most interesting experiment at collectivisation of the patients with the personnel in the work of developing the hospital. A patient chooses a piece of work which he thinks needs being done, consults the administration and gets full co-operation in realizing his work. The patients take care of the swimming pool and bath house and fire the boiler, Kuba repairs every watch, clock and machine in the hospital, Michel organized and catalogued the entire storeroom, Thompson organized the food stores, Wilson and Charlie Youngblood clean the patio and the walks daily, Ruperte Iglesias has classes for the illiterate Spanish patients and girls, Bart organized tremendous 'sings' in all languages, Ludwig Holl organized the material and built five kilometers of telephone line giving the hospital proper communication. The president of the popular front granted us a piece of land and in the spring we will have a real garden. We are raising pigs, chickens and rabbits, and have a small flock of sheep and milk goats.

It was a pleasure to work in the English hospitals because none of us ever allowed ourselves to forget that we were building the hospitals for the *patients* and not for the personnel, and that we would never allow any sort of personal or professional frictions to arise to disturb the well-being of the hospital. It is not a romantic job to have the responsibility for feeding, clothing and evacuating hundreds of patients with varying degrees of serious wounds, and I was able to carry on only through the wonderful cooperation I have always had in the English hospitals.

Crying Would Have to Come Later

Lini de Vries

Lini de Vries *was born of Dutch parents in New Jersey. At twelve she started work in a cotton mill and later graduated as a nurse. Left a widow with a small daughter, she completed a four-year high school course in one year and four months, and worked in the Public Health Nursing Service while studying at night in the Teachers' College of Columbia University. She joined the first American Hospital Unit for Spain, and in May 1937 was sent home on a speaking tour to raise money for the unit. She worked in public health in south-west USA and in Puerto Rico. During the McCarthy period she was hounded, so emigrated to Mexico to continue working and teaching in public health.*

Now it was February 1937, and we were to serve the Jarama battle on the Madrid front. [...] Within four hours after the battle had begun, we had 93 wounded. Our hospital was equipped for fifty. A little later, the same day, we had 200. I was on the first floor, where they came in. Those who had died en route to us were left in the bitter cold courtyard. Occasionally from among the dead we heard a moan and found life.

The wounded lay on the floor, and two or three lay on each bed. First we fought to keep them alive. Later we got their names, in order to list them as wounded. When we had time, we went through clothing matted with blood on cold, stiff, dead men to see if they had letters on them or any identifying information. I cut through clothing of boys I had danced with on our way to Spain. My eyes were heavy with lack of sleep and unshed tears. This was no time to cry! The crying would have to come later. [...]

Our fifty-bed hospital was jammed with hundreds of wounded, but it was easing up. The front had been held fast at the cost of thousands of lives. Now we took turns to go off-duty to get a few hours of sleep. When it was my turn, I walked past the operating room and heard Dr

Barskey ask for me, so I stepped in. A pallid, fair young lad lay on the operating table. Dr Barsky said, 'He is Dutch. He does not understand English. Please tell him that we are going to operate. Tell him we are going to give him a spinal anesthesia; then help him get into position for the anesthesia.'

The boy's eyes lit up as he heard my voice explain to him in his language what had to be done. His name was Peter. 'Stay with me. Don't leave me. I am dying, I know. Don't leave me,' he begged.

The doctor who was giving the spinal anesthesia said, 'Okay, Lini, you can leave now and get some sleep. You need it badly.'

Peter clasped my hand firmly as if he understood. 'Don't leave me. Don't let me die alone,' he whimpered.

I answered the doctor, 'Later. I must stay with this wounded man now.' Softly I spoke in Dutch to Peter about the streets of Amsterdam, about the beach at Scheveningen, as I watched his abdomen being opened, exposing a shattered spleen. I also knew it was hopeless now.

'Promise me before I die that you will keep on fighting for Spain and for what is right,' he said. I promised him. 'Sing me the cradle songs. Sing me the folk songs. Sing to me,' he begged.

With a pinched throat and unshed tears, I sang to Peter as softly as I could. I thought again of Till Eulenspiegel's wife as she placed the ashes on the hearts of her sons and daughters: 'As long as there is injustice in this world, you must fight against it.' Peter had heard these words; he had read them in school. I was hearing them through the din of the bombers overhead trying to locate our hospital. Dr Barskey finished operating by candlelight as our lights went out. Silent sobs caught in my throat as I felt Peter's pulse fading to nothingness, to death. [...]

Typhoid vaccine was to be delivered to be given to the front-line soldiers and to the staff at Colmenar. One of their nurses had typhoid, and some of the soldiers had it. I readily settled for a ride to Colmenar since I hoped to see the front-line Lincoln Battalion doctor who was quite special for me.

Fleecy white clouds drifted across a breathtakingly blue sky over a flattish landscape bordered by the purple mountains of Guadarrama as we traveled toward the front. It was hard to believe that a war was going on. When truckloads of children being evacuated from Madrid passed us, I was again aware of Moors on the front and Germans and Italians overhead. But those bomb craters at the entrance to the bridge reminded me again that it was best to enjoy the scenery while I lived. I relaxed with the clouds. Within no time we were at the hospital, in time for tea. The operating room table served as the tea table. I was graciously asked, 'Do you prefer lemon or milk in your tea?' This was a part of England running the hospital at Colmenar. They had had it worse than us during the Jarama battle, since they were within range of the battlefield. Of this the British did not talk as they served tea! They were more nonchalant and casual than we were. These British are amazing people, I thought. [...]

Near the top of the hill, sheltered by trees, we could see the headquarters of the Lincoln Battalion and the cookhouse. As we walked up the incline carrying the materials being delivered to the front, it still seemed peaceful, except for the occasional loud noises. I don't know who was more surprised, the men at headquarters or me, when I walked in. They had not been away from the front at Jarama since their arrival in early February, and they had not seen a woman in months. My favorite doctor scolded me for coming up to the front, but his eyes told me that he was glad to see me. One by one, men slipped out, and others took their places in the first aid station. They asked about their companions who had been in our hospitals, and they wanted other news. The few of the Lincolns who were left slipped out of the trenches to chat a bit with me.

Over a cup of muddy coffee, the doctor described a road that he had conceived and was helping to build. By using this road the stretcher-bearers would not have to walk so far and would not be in the sights of the snipers' guns. He was as enthusiastic as a newly diploma'd road engineer, to be building a road right under the noses of the fascist rebels. In his enthusiasm, before he realized it he was showing me the new road. We walked among the olive trees, and at irregular intervals I heard a ping and a zip with a bit of a whine close to us. 'What is that sound?'

He replied, 'That is the whine of a sniper's bullet. Here, take my helmet. Put it on.'

I did as I was told, but soon took it off. It was uncomfortable. I gave it back to him, and turned up my cape collar.

As the ping-zip-whines became more frequent, the doctor shouted, 'Drop!' We dropped and lay on the sun-warmed earth. I saw beauty over our heads where the sunlight filtered through the olive leaves and the yellow mimosa. The ping-zips played a minor note to the music of our whispered words and acts. We must have fallen asleep, both of us, the doctor and the nurse. Then the sun was less bright, and gone was the sound of the whining bullets. Maybe they thought us dead. We were very much alive, alive with the joy of two people who cared for one another. [...]

I was notified that Dr Barskey wished to see me in his office. I wondered what on earth the problem was. I had never been called to his office before. I soon found out. He told me to take Modesta – who had now joined us – and take over at Castillejo.[43] The hospital there had fifty patients and a Dutch doctor in charge.

'I want you to get Castillejo organized so that it can handle three hundred convalescent patients. Two hundred and fifty cots will be delivered soon. You will also get the needed hospital supplies. I am counting on you to handle all the rest – feeding, laundry, care, and so forth – for a potential three hundred patients,' Dr Barsky said very calmly. [...]

At first I didn't say a word about my being sent down from Villa Paz to administer the hospital at Castillejo. I felt I had to earn this right. I explained to Modesta that we must pitch in and work side by side with the six young girls who were already there. By seeing us working as hard or harder than them, they might gain confidence in us.

As their confidence in us increased, the complaints increased also. 'It is hard enough with fifty patients. How can we do the laundry, the cooking, the cleaning, and the nursing when the patient load increases? There are men who could help us carry the water, help us in the work, but they just walk around. They forget that today we are all equal according to our constitution,' they grumbled.

'Of course you are correct, girls, but you can't expect the men to change their Moorish, European attitudes overnight. However, I have an idea. Leave it to me,' I answered.

'What is your idea?' they asked.

'My idea is to call a meeting of the ambulatory patients, the whole staff, and just about everyone who can be walked or carried, to discuss how to run the hospital. I'll get the wounded Lincolns to help me by volunteering for chores,' I replied. This was a new lesson in co-operation for them. I hoped it would work!

The girls said, 'We want to learn to read and write. We are too tired at night and have no time in the day. The soldiers are learning in the trenches and in the hospitals. Why not us?'

'I think we will be able to do all of this. We will ask the men to help us,' I answered, hoping the Lincolns wouldn't let me down.

I knew that no Spaniard or other European of his own free will would scrub a floor, wash a dish, wring a sheet, peel a potato or do what they thought was 'women's work' in any way. I had to find a way. The Germans of the Thaelman Battalion might volunteer, but who wanted to listen to long speeches on women's rights with quotes from Engels, Marx, Lenin and Stalin? Neither I nor the others. We wanted helping hands and fewer words. I looked for the few Lincolns. One had a leg in a light cast; two had their arms in casts, and so forth; but they all were able to walk. I spoke to them and explained the need for them to volunteer at a general meeting that would be called. 'Please set an example. The Spaniards admire the Americans more than any other nationality group. Please volunteer for squads or committees of potato-peeling, washing in the brook, carrying water to the hospital, washing dishes, making your own beds. Please, won't you help?' I begged.

They griped, which I expected, but they said we could count on them to volunteer and to help get others to volunteer. I knew that with this, 90 per cent of the problem was over before we were loaded with 300 or more patients. [...]

We called the meeting for that night. The bed patients sent from each ward a delegate who could walk. I had interpreters ready: Greek, French, Italian, German, Spanish and English. Dr van Reemst opened the meeting, and then I presented the problem confronting the women nurses, of doing all the work for a hospital which now had fifty patients but might soon have 300 or more. I said that I knew there was great desire on the part of all of us to learn Spanish, and the Spaniards wanted to learn to read and write Spanish. If all able people helped, we might be able to have an efficient hospital and also an educational program. I called for discussion.

It came, but hot and heavy. Through many languages the gist was: They came to fight, not to do women's work. The men of the International Brigade here were of all political shades: anarchists, communists, socialists, democrats, monarchists who hated Franco, and so forth. One of the Americans asked, 'Don't you believe what you preach – the right of women to develop?' With that, bless their hearts, the Americans began volunteering for dish-washing, scrubbing, washing, digging latrines, and so on! The first Spaniard to follow was a replacement who was very proud to be in the Lincoln Battalion, now known as the Lincoln Brigade. Slowly other Spaniards volunteered, and a few from the other European groups followed suit. I was happy with the results, and the assistant nurses were beaming. For them, this was revolutionary. I preferred thinking it was evolutionary, but either way we were on the road toward progress in human relations right here at Castillejo. I had always felt that progress should begin in the situation in which one found oneself, and the less talking about it, the better. I had seen in New York and now in Spain that the more political or other discussion, the fewer the deeds!

President, secretary, treasurer, and other officers of the Hospital Volunteer Association of Castillejo were elected. We closed the meeting, setting the date for the next one within the same week.

The next morning, with some dirty sheets in a pillowcase, I walked down to the brook. I heard voices arguing and stood sheltered from their sight by the willows. I peeked through and saw the girls pounding the sheets on the flat rocks. Two of the Lincoln Brigade, with their fractured arms sticking out like angels' wings, were wringing sheets. They were Irish-Americans from Boston. One had his right arm in a cast, and the other, his left. 'The angels,' I thought fondly. Two Spaniards, who had been with them at the front, were pounding sheets along with the girls. A few Germans were stretching out the damp laundry on the grass to dry. A Spaniard leaned on his crutch and sneeringly said to the other Spaniards, '*Tú no eres macho. No eres hombre. Estás trabajando como mujer.*' ['You're not manly. You're not a man. You're doing women's work.'] The youngest Spaniard answered with anger, 'You sound just like one of those Hitler Germans or Franco Moors,' as he leaped up to attack him. The Lincoln men quickly handed him the end of a sheet to wring as the Germans began their political lecture to the protesting Spaniard leaning on his crutch. [...]

The Italians of the Garibaldi had not volunteered for any of the 'women's work', but they volunteered to help supply food. Chick-peas became boring meal after meal. They began bringing in fish from the stream. When they hobbled back on their crutches clasping live chickens, I didn't ask them where and how they got them. I hoped some day they might manage to bring back a whole pig. [...]

The people who lived in nearby caves asked permission to use the chapel for a meeting. 'Of course,' I replied. 'This is your building. We are only borrowing it for a while to use as a hospital.' They graciously invited us to sit in on the meeting. I wondered what it was all about. I hoped we had not offended them or stolen too many chickens. But no, the meeting was about the fertile land not in use around the two summer palaces, Villa Paz and Castillejo. It was almost painful to watch the careful articulation and slight fear with which they voiced their ideas. Then one voice timidly said, 'I have a plow.' Another offered seeds. The ambulatory wounded soldiers who had not offered help to the hospital suddenly were offering to help plow the earth and plant the seeds. A co-operative was being formed right here. I saw democracy aborning among the cave dwellers, former servants of the royalty. [...]

Perhaps never again in my life will I be with such idealistic, intelligent, gentle people from so many lands. This was a crusade for the freedom of man. Maybe you bickered once in awhile, gripe you certainly did, but you were all united toward one goal: man's right to be free! In 1937 I was seeing almost pure idealism. Yet I had a guilt complex for being here in Spain: I had left my young daughter in the States, even though I'd left her well cared for. The photos which came to me from New Hampshire showed her busy and happy. I was torn between my feeling of guilt and the love I had for service. Anything that I had ever learned, any skill I had, any belief I had in humanity was working here in Castillejo. I was seeing all the principles I believed in coming true in one spot. I was seeing men of all races and creeds working together. I was seeing democracy aborning in Castillejo. You, my fellow idealists, were teaching me. The illiterate peasant was teaching me.

If I learned nothing else, I learned something most important, proven over and over again by these 'teachers' – something which I had vaguely learned at Columbia University that I was witnessing here in real life: There is no direct correlation between intelligence and education. Here were illiterate farmers and soldiers whose social philosophy was superior, it seemed to me, to any I had seen before. War was being fought near them, around them, over them; but their most vital consideration was life with a future. Clinics sprang up where none had been. Trenches were dug with a special section for classroom work. Small theater groups performed to people who had never seen theater. Paintings, as in our hospital, were carefully cherished. The desire to increase knowledge was the most exciting force in Spain. [...]

Americans and British

Irene Goldin

Irene Goldin went as a nurse with the second American group and served with British and American Units in Spain. She later married an Austrian International Brigader. They worked in a home for German and Austrian refugee children in France. With the war of 1939 he was interned and Irene worked in the American Hospital in Paris. When the Germans took Paris they escaped to the south and later joined the Resistance. After the Liberation Irene worked in a US Army hospital, and then became head of the Unitarian Service Committee in Bouches du Rhône, helping refugees. Since 1950 she and her husband have lived in Vienna.

My group left New York on May 31, 1937, on the *Normandie*. The State Department was not at all keen about our going and we received our passports at the very last moment. Spain was off-limits for Americans at the time and special permission was necessary.

Esther Silverstein was in my group and we were together for almost ten months. Although we were Americans we were sent to the English base hospital at Huete, which was a small village not far away from the American base hospital at Villa Paz. Our group consisted of Esther, Mildred Rackley, who was to be the new Director of the hospital at Huete, and Stanislaus Rubint, a young Hungarian lad of sixteen whose parents lived in Madrid. He was very talented in languages and spoke English, French, German and Spanish fluently. He was later adopted by Dr Barsky, who took Stanislaus with him to the States when he returned there in June 1938.

Esther, Stanislaus and I were sent to the Brunete front in July 1937 and there we were assigned to Dr Broggi and his team.[44] We were glad to work with Dr Broggi. He was unassuming, calm and friendly. My knowledge of Spanish was negligible and Dr Broggi did his best to help. I had told him that I knew a bit of French. Whenever he ordered something for a patient, he would take a minature French dictionary out of his pocket – he always had it with him – and look up the essential words. Somehow or other, although it was so small, it always contained the very words he was looking for.

We drove to Brunete in one of the ambulances and we were always behind some lorry which was loaded with munitions or soldiers. At the time we were too inexperienced to be worried about the dangers we were exposed to. Our hospital was set up in a large building in the Escorial – it had formerly been a Catholic school for boys. The large dormitories were easily transformed into large wards for our wounded. The building was situated on a slightly elevated terrain and there was a large garden before it. In the evening, when we were off-duty, we would sit there and watch the different lights in the sky. They were caused by anti-aircraft or emanated from the different villages which had been set on fire. Our hospital was never bombed due to the historic importance of the Escorial.

Our ward was on the second floor, and the large room contained at least fifty cots. At one end of the ward there was a little room which was large enough to contain two cots. Here we took care of the severely wounded patients. One of them was Julian Bell, the nephew of Virginia Woolf. He had received a direct hit in the chest when a bomb exploded not far away from the ambulance which he and Dr Larry Collier were driving. The latter escaped unscathed. When Julian was admitted he was unconscious and he remained so until he died. Dr Collier was a medical student when he went to Spain.

Another ambulance driver who was wounded at Brunete was Max Cohen. He was also English and came from London. He had a serious head injury and could not move his arm. One morning, I had just sponged his arm and was getting ready to give him an intravenous injection when he suddenly raised his arm. He meant to surprise me and he succeeded. I nearly fell backwards. Max made a complete recovery.

Dr Broggi was a remarkable surgeon and he was very successful in treating the wounded with severe abdominal injuries. The mortality rate for injuries of this kind was very high. A high percentage of Dr Broggi's patients recovered.

After Brunete we were sent to the Aragon front; then we spent some time at Murcia in the south, in a large base hospital. In the late fall we left for the Teruel front in our new autochir which was actually a mobile operating room on wheels, with all the necessary sterilising equipment, etc. We stopped at Benicasim, which was on the coast not far away from Valencia. The weather was fine there – mild and generally sunny. And the food was good – lots of vegetables. There were stands where one could buy dried fruit, and we bought quite a lot for our trip. We also ate snails for the first time – they were fried and were delicious. Benicasim consisted of lovely villas and it was used as a convalescent centre for the wounded of the International Brigades. Dr Fritz Jensen, an Austrian doctor, was its director. In 1939 Dr Jensen went to China. There he worked for the Chinese People's Republic. He met and married Wu An, a charming Chinese woman.

There wasn't an empty bed in Benicasim when we got there but the chauffeurs (ambulance and lorry drivers) came to our rescue. They gave Esther and me one of their rooms in one of the villas they occupied. We had a large comfortable bed and we enjoyed the few days we spent there – our autochir was being serviced. By the time we reached our destination winter had set in – we were caught in a severe snow storm in the mountains but we arrived safely.

After Teruel I had had an accident. When Dr Broggi saw me, he said my injury was still serious and recommended rest and bed rest – my bed was a mattress on the floor. By this time our group was really divided. Esther had been sent to a convalescent hospital – she had been severely ill. I was left behind with Lillian [Urmston] a nurse who had joined us on the Aragon front and Keith Andrews. We were all waiting to be evacuated since the front was obviously very near. One day, Robert Merriman, the Commander of the Abraham Lincoln Battalion passed by in his car. I was outside the hospital trying out my legs and getting used to walking. When he saw me, he seemed so astonished that I knew something was wrong. I explained to him that I had hurt myself and had been left behind with Lillian and Andy. Merriman looked very grave. 'You can't remain here.' I explained that the three of us were waiting for orders from the Service Sanitaire. He was adamant. 'The three of you are requisitioned.' I never did find out just when the hospital was evacuated. But I couldn't walk quickly or run or swim the Ebro, and many had to do that.

A Special Privilege

Esther Silverstein

Esther Silverstein *nursed in the Public Health Hospital in San Francisco.*

In Spain she served with British and other US nurses. She was invalided home suffering from malaria, undulent fever and dysentry. Later she took a PhD in Medical History and became a lecturer and consultant in the University of California.

In retrospect I can say that even though my knowledge of English custom was derived from my readings in nineteenth-century English fiction I seemed to adapt well to the English members of the 35th International Division Sanitary Corps of the Spanish Republican Army.

One of the group, Keith Andrews, is memorable. He provided all the surgical teams with necessities for the maintainance of sterile technique and accomplished this by very hard work and the most constant attention to detail. Had he not done so we would all have been blown away.

He operated five or six primus stoves at once, all filled with gasoline, on top of these sat pressure cookers and in each pressure cooker lay a metal drum containing supplies being sterilized.

From this unit Keith Andrews supplied us with laparotomy sheets, sponges, towels, dressing, gloves, gowns and masks. He had one primus stove which always had a tea kettle 'on the boil', and from him I learned to drink strong tea with milk in it.

'Andy' was working whenever we were and if I came to get fresh supplies I was given tea and told, 'Sit down and have your tea, they can do without you for a few minutes.' He was a serious person and his work was of the greatest importance.

Dorothy Rutter was a 'trained nurse' as was I.[45] She worked in the ward. Her disposition was sunny and she was good at her work. The patients loved her, as well they might.

Someone gave her a very small, grey rabbit which she cared for tenderly and when she worked lived in her uniform pocket. Its head rested over the pocket's edge and the patients were made happy by it.

Dorothy explained that if the patient was busy looking at the rabbit perhaps changing his dressing was less painful. [...] We had black-out curtains and few lights. We carried flashlights. There was an endless coming and going of persons who were taking care of the wounded, but I gave injections, made rounds, kept intravenous infusions going and followed earnest messengers to various bedsides to give emergency care.

One of those working was Dr Saxton. We met and introduced ourselves. 'I do the blood transfusions,' he said. We became friends almost at once. Understated and laconic, he was open hearted, friendly and kind.

I could write about each and everyone of the British in our unit. It was a special privilege to work with them and with Irene Goldin, the other nurse from Hartford, Connecticut. The memory of all of them I shall hold in high regard, esteem, affection and respect until I die.

Doing Christ's Duty

Salaria Kea

Salaria Kea, *the black American nurse, was born in Georgia. Her father, an attendant at the Ohio State Hospital for the Insane, was stabbed to death. At the Harlem Hospital School of Nursing, she led successful action against racial segregation. In 1935, with other Harlem nurses and doctors, she raised a hospital for Ethiopia, then being invaded by Italy. In March 1937 she joined the American medical unit for Spain. There she married an International Brigader.*

I said I'm not just going to sit down and let this happen. I'm going out to help, even if it is my life! But I'm helping. This is my world, too! And I'm not going to sit down and just let people do what they want to do, when it's wrong. And I'm a nurse! Look at all those soldiers and all the people being hurt – look at all the people even in Spain, young children, being bombed. Not being taken care of, and all that. Women, men, everybody. And I was doing Christ's duty.

* * *

27 March 1937: I sailed from New York with the second American Medical Unit ... I was the lone representative of the Negro race. The doctor in charge of the group refused to sit at the same table with me in the dining room and demanded to see the Captain. The Captain moved me to his table where I remained throughout the voyage. [...]

Official instructions were to set up our hospital at Villa Paz near Madrid.

Villa Paz had been the summer palace of King Alfonso XIII, deserted since his abdication in 1931. The villa is set in a lavish garden. The peasants attached to the estate, impoverished and illiterate, still lived in the same cramped, poorly lit quarters they had before. In a corner of the usual one-room hut, on top of a tile they burned dried dung from the cattle. This was their only source of heat in rainy and cold weather. They had turned the villa itself over to the cattle. So accustomed had they become to hardship and poor living that, even with the king gone, they did not feel free to live in his beautiful palace.

This was my first concrete example of discrimination where race was not the basis ... The peasants believed that nothing could be done about their situation. Psychologically, they were just as imprisoned as the Harlem Hospital nurses who had accepted racial discrimination in their dining room. Like those Negro nurses, the peasants were now learning that something could be done about it: one could resist, one could fight – liberty could be a reality. There was nothing inviolable about old prejudices; they could be changed and justice established.

The Second American Medical Unit, authorized by the Republican Government of Spain, at once turned the cows out of Villa Paz, cleaned the building and set up the first American base hospital in Spain ...

The beds of Villa Paz were soon filled with soldiers of every degree of injury and ailment, every known race and tongue from every corner of the earth ... These divisions of race, creed and nationality lost significance when they met in a united effort to make Spain the tomb of Fascism ... I saw my fate, the fate of the Negro race, was inseparably tied up with their fate: the efforts of the Negroes must be allied with those of others as the only insurance against an uncertain future ...

The Negro men who fought for Loyalist Spain never tire of telling how they celebrated when they got news that the Second American Medical Unit included a Negro nurse. Their batallion had been in the trenches 120 days of continuous fighting. I am told that during the entire First World War a fighting unit was never required to be under fire longer than this. Their clothing was shabby and worn. Many had so little to wear they could not appear in public.

I was so excited over going to Spain I did not realize that many other negroes had already recognized Spain's fight for freedom and liberty as a part of our struggle too. I didn't know that almost a hundred young Negro men were already fighting Hitler's and Mussolini's forces there in Spain.

As soon as I had reached Spain many of these American boys began to ask: 'Have you met Oliver Law?' 'Do you know Doug Roach?' 'Aren't you Salaria Kea?' 'Garland sent you this note.' 'Oh Salaria, Milton Herndon said that he would like to meet you.' For two months messages and letters came to me from the Negro men I had never seen. The first Negro I saw was Douglas Roach who was sent by Oliver Law. Doug's conversation ran like this:

'So you're Salaria Kea. And you hail from Ohio. Well, I come from Boston. Do you know why I'm here? No, this is not my leave. I am not due for a leave yet because Law came over first. But he did not have any pants or shoes and mine were too small for him. So, he sent me to meet you for him. I won over the ten Negro boys in the game.'

'Game?' I asked.

'Well, you see when Oliver Law realized he couldn't come down to meet you in his underwear and asked who would like to sub for him, naturally, all of us wanted to. He suggested pulling straws, and the one pulling the shortest would go in his stead. I pulled that one so here I am. Oh, Salaria, I almost forgot something. Law sent you this letter and his picture with a machine gun.'

Doug spent two days with me. While he was there Harry Haywood joined us. In July I was pleased to see Carter, the first Negro ambulance driver to come to Spain. During the subsequent days Roach, Garland and other wounded Negro soldiers came under my care at Villa Paz. [...] When I first saw Pat I thought he was a very shy and business-like man. I wondered why he had come to Spain. Pat seldom seemed to notice anyone. He was known on the base as a 'loner'. He would sit at his desk every night for what seemed hours, writing. Ellen, a nurse who was on duty at that time, was curious about what he was writing. Often she would take a look only to see poems – some completed, others just a few lines. To her surprise all the poems were about me. Ellen and I were very good friends. She would slip me a poem in the morning and scold me for not speaking to Pat.

I put his poems in my pocket and, after my tour of duty, I read them during the long walks I took with the hospital's pet dog, Paz. One day I was reading some of the poems while sitting with Paz in the center of a poppy garden. Paz began to bark. I turned and saw Pat strolling toward me. When he came near I teasingly asked, 'Have you lost something?' and handed him one of the best poems. As he read the poem to himself he blushed deep red. I asked him to sit down and he sat beside me. He confessed, 'Since May I have liked you. But I know both of us came to Spain to do a job. Although we may be criticized by some if we fell in love with each other, we would feel ashamed of ourselves if we did not carry on our anti-fascist work.' Together we decided to be just good friends.

We discussed North America, Ireland, and all groups and races who were victims of fascism and other injustices and how we two could help to abolish the enemies of the human race. [...]

Pat and I had known each other for eight weeks on an evening a group of us went swimming. On the way back to the hospital, Pat and I were walking ahead of the others. We were climbing a hill where grew every kind of weed, grass and bush. Suddenly he popped the question, would I marry him. I plopped to the ground still wearing only my bathing suit. I did not realise I had fallen on a cactus plant until I reached my quarters and sat on the bed. My whole body seemed punctured by hundreds of tiny pins. I knew dear Ellen would help. When she arrived a few minutes later, I told her what had happened. She called Dr Mary Pearson, one of the female doctors in our unit. They soon went to work removing the cactus needles.

The next day when Pat and I met, he asked if I had an answer to his question. I gave several excuses as to why we should not marry, especially since he was white and I was black. I gave in when Pat asked me:

'Would you let the reactionaries take away the only thing a poor man deserved, and that thing is his right to marry the one he loved and believed loved him?'

After thinking about it, I realized I loved Pat. We were married October 2, 1937 at Villa Paz. We spent our honeymoon in Denia, Valencia and Alicante. After our honeymoon, Pat was sent away leaving me at the base hospital. [...]

Male Arrogance Defeated

Evelyn Hutchins

Evelyn Hutchins *was the only American woman to serve as a
truck- and ambulance-driver in Spain. Brought up by a 'Wobblie'
(IWW) step-father, Evelyn organised longshoremen and other
workers on the West Coast. Like her brother she volunteered to
fight in the International Brigade but was refused. Volunteering
as a driver she still faced male prejudice. After the war she
returned to union organising of office and shop workers and led
campaigns to save the lives of Spanish trade unionists in Franco's
prisons.*

When I first heard about Spain, they were bringing in education
for children, in the little villages and so on, that never had any
schools. And they were bringing in the vote. And women were voting
too, which – I thought that was really nice, here's a little country, and
they're bringing in the vote! And you say, 'Well, here it's going to
succeed, isn't that marvelous! At least everything isn't turning like in
Germany or like in Italy; I mean, here's another kind of country!'

And I went all over the city and collected tons and tons of clothing
[for Spain] and brought it back and put it in a bale; and I'd go right
out again, and collect some more, and collect some more, and collect
some more ...

I asked them if they knew how good I was at driving. And they
knew, because they were using me all the time. I asked them if they
would have allowed me to go if I had been a man. And they admitted
they would've. And even my size, as small as I am, 'cause – two of the
other ambulance drivers were my size. You know? So I told them, well,
if you don't let me go, then you're just a chauvinist, that's all. A male
chauvinist, you're just a chauvinist. And you're not supposed to be
because you're supposed to be a political person. What – uh! Then
they would say, 'I? I'm not like that! *I* would let you go! But it's the
others ...' So my attitude was, 'You let me take care of the others.'

It made me so mad. But I raised hell with them and finally shamed
them into allowing me to enlist. [...]

These are ideas that I went to Spain with. And when I was in Spain I talked about them all the time; I kept saying, 'Look. I don't want to swear. I don't want you to see me going around like this, like I'm a big tomboy.' We didn't use butch in those days, but tomboy. I wanted somebody to think of me as just me, and this big truck is not, is not formidable to me. I wanted them to know that I could do it, I could climb all over the truck. When I had something wrong with the truck I'd open up the hood and I'd get up on the fender, and I'd start working with it on the inside and so on. Women have worked hard for many many many many millenia. And people have to recognize that, including women! They have to know that – that women have always worked hard. And they should damn well be given the credit for that …

I could go anyplace I wanted to go. And I had a sense of real protection and real concern, wherever I went. For example, if I went there the second time, I would see them way down the road someplace, and they would be waving to me 'cause they'd recognize the truck, and so on. And I had to stop and I had to talk to them, and so on, and they were very excited about me and happy that I came by, and it made their day, and stuff like this – you think it didn't make mine? There's something very emotional, there's something very powerful, when you find a way to connect with people. With their concerns, with their needs, and you speak that common language. It is powerful! It's a reason for living.

Blood for the Front

Celia Seborer

Celia Seborer *was a trained clinical laboratory technician. In October 1936 she went to Spain with her journalist husband, George Marrion. At first she served as assistant to the Canadian surgeon Norman Bethune, who was in charge of the Madrid blood-transfusion-service. Later she worked as a nurse, and eventually practiced her own profession.*

Celia was made an honorary sergeant in the People's Army.

American Embassy, Madrid
Christmas Day 1936

I am a free woman again having obtained permission to leave the Embassy when I wish. I'm really looking forward to being able to work at the Blood Transfusion Lab. I hate to feel that I'm absolutely useless here and do nothing but eat up food that might be used by someone who really needs it. But when the service really gets going I think I'll be just busy enough. We hope, in addition to doing transfusions, to do a little research work on blood – also for transfusions – to see how long it can be kept and under what conditions. [...]

Prof. Haldane, the eminent British scientist, is here in Madrid.[46] He is engaged in making some simple gas masks – and showing how to make them. He is staying with Dr Bethune 'my Boss', so I had lunch with him yesterday.[47] He's a great big fellow – prominent features and tremendously bushy eyebrows. Had a sprained ankle, a bad cold, and an upset temper because he is unable, apparently, to obtain a gas in order to test his gas masks. Its quite unfair to make any judgment of him, but he seems to have all the necessary qualifications for a scientist.

Valencia
5 February 1937
c/o American Embassy.

I haven't written for quite some time, or so it seems to me. So much has been crowded into the last few weeks that I've lost all perspective of time and acts in time. Just about the time Marrie left Valencia, Dr. Bethune left for Barcelona leaving me in charge of the 'Blood Trust'. It proved to be a golden opportunity to get down to serious work and with the very able and cheerful assistance of two Spanish doctors – Antonio and Vicento, who were to do the actual extractions and transfusions; we established real order, got the work systematized, got ourselves some publicity and began to do transfusion on an increasing scale.

Many times I accompanied one or other of the doctors to the hospital and actually assisted. Never having worked with wounded people before, I was appalled at the sight of so much blood and such bloodless faces. Their cries and groans haunted me for days. But to be able to call up the hospital the day following the transfusion and to find out that the wounded man had come through quite nicely thanks to the transfusions was comforting knowledge and it helped me to go on with the work. It was hard but very satisfying work.

After Dr Bethune came back, things didn't go quite so well. He is too restless but I refused to be budged as far as our routine went – so he immediately turned to thoughts of enlarging the scope of the work. Fortunately Antonio and Vicento were interested and immediately began to plan for it in a realistic fashion and make sure that the work will grow in importance to the army in Spain ...

Life here in Valencia is totally different from that in Madrid. One is hard put to it to realize that these people are engaged in war. The shops here have good supplies of food – particularly of sweets and pastries which just don't exist in Madrid. Streets are jammed with idle strollers until one gets furious at all these able-bodied people doing nothing. Cafés, movie theaters – all crowded. It's quite distressing and in spite of the greater luxury here, I prefer Madrid. In Madrid too, cafés, are crowded, but with a different group of people. One sees truly proletarian faces there – here: a type of petty, bureaucratic bourgeosie. There the air radiates a feeling of determination and confidence having to do with winning the war. Here are languor and disinterestedness. It's quite distressing.

The first unit of the American Medical group arrived yesterday. How good it was to hear American voices again and know that there will be Americans actually working here. Up to now we've really been ashamed of ourselves as Americans. Best of all, they brought regards and letters from many people we know and we've discovered many mutual friends. If I could, I should be more than happy to connect up with them, but right now they are quite unsettled, heading for Madrid in a day or so and then, when I know where they are going to be, I shall see what I shall see.

Ceil

Valencia
22 February 1937

A few days ago I went to a big meeting held here by the CP. As they have no Madison Square Garden the size of meeting is limited to the size of the theatre. This one was jammed full – people standing in the aisles and the back of the orchestra and in the balcony – probably about 2,000 people. What they lacked in numbers, they made up for in enthusiasm and responsiveness. Dolores Ibarruri – 'Pasionaria' spoke. I knew that she was a dramatic and inspiring speaker, but was quite unprepared for the beauty and warmth of her voice. It has a rich, enveloping quality that makes one feel that her arm is about one's shoulder, and she is talking directly to one. Her gestures are few, simple and direct, but her spirit, courage and human warmth are contagious.

Ceil

Murcia
2 April 1937

Dear Family:
An unexpected opportunity to get a letter off.

The evolution of a trained nurse as I can tell you, tho I could hardly be called a trained nurse, is a long and difficult process, very wearing physically and spiritually – but I'm glad to report that I seem to have arrived at some sort of a goal and breathing space. I'm getting quite good at dressing even big and very nasty looking and swelling wounds, and quite hardened to all sorts of groans, grunts, shrieks and moans – and I've found that a thoroughly cleaned wound progresses much better, even tho the cleaning is painful, than one too gently treated.

The organization of the hospital is progressing, and we have more nurses and therefore a little less work, for which a chorus of thanks. I must say tho, that I pretty nearly had to collapse before my load was reduced to a point where I could see a way of carrying it. So now I have 24 beds instead of 44 or 59 as I had at first. Which, after all, makes a difference …

It's difficult to find anything to write about from here. We live in such a terribly confined world. One's life here is completely concerned with the aches, pains and progress of one's patients and I don't imagine you'd find it terribly interesting to know that the little Spaniard in bed 8, Room 13, had a pain in his back last nite and why.

If I ever started writing about the men, I'd first have to have more time to talk to them and then I'd never finish my letter. But one is constantly amazed at the difference in men – their capacities to resist pain, or their weakness. I have a French boy with a badly wounded and fractured leg which is in a plaster cast, and the other morning when I was making out the laundry list for the day and asking who needed a clean shirt or a handkerchief, he asked for a new leg – one that would be the right size and better than the one he has now, and so on and on.

So all is well here and don't worry if you don't get mail – no time, energy or ambition to write.

Ceil

Murcia
30 May 1937

Life here goes on as usual, I have my microscope and very slowly (oh-so slowly) the lab is beginning to take shape. My time is well taken up with various tasks but it is not exhausting and I can do pretty much as I like.

Many of the things we looked forward to in the first days are now realities. The best Spanish girls go to school every afternoon for classes in nursing. We get lectures twice a week. There is a class in Spanish and gymnastics in the morning for those who are ambitious enough to get up in time. The medical equipment and treatment get steadily better. We now have a very fine Spanish nerve specialist and a nose and throat specialist. An American orthopedic specialist has also been sent down to us – so, you see we are developing.

Ceil

Murcia,
11 July 1937

Probably the most vital parts of our work and one that till now we have underestimated and neglected is our work with the Spanish girls and women here in the hospital. They are of all types, generally uprooted from homes and families, refugees from Madrid, many of them with all sorts of background. Here they are, most of them working for the first time in their lives, outside of their homes. Some have lost their fathers, husbands, brothers – others have their menfolk at the fronts, and all their love and affection is transferred to the wounded. They may not know exactly how to do some task, but there really is nothing they won't do for the men. Wash, scrub and fix the beds and go out and shop for the men, and try to make little delicacies, and run and fetch and bring and carry till they are all worn out. Each one fights for her particular man, and if we have a fiesta of some sort in the canteen, they get together and carry out all the men who can be transported. One night we had a garden party. They got all the extra mattresses down and carried out, with the help of the stretcher bearers, every wounded man who couldn't walk but could be gotten out of bed.

They need political education and they are getting it, too. Many are members of the CP and nearly all belong to their trade union. They have their troubles and are gradually learning how to conduct their affairs for the benefit of all. It's interesting to watch their leaders develop. The ones who are best at their work, who learn the most rapidly and work with the most thoughtfulness and care are the ones who are developing most rapidly, politically. I get on very well with them, and have made friends with them. We manage, in spite of the language difficulty. I only wish I had more time to be with them.
Ceil

A School for Nurses

Ruth Waller

Ruth Waller *served as a nurse with the American medical units in Spain, helped to set up a nursing school for Spanish women and broadcast from Madrid Radio.*

Our particular base is a large town in Southern Spain. And the south of Spain, by the way, does not enjoy the ideal climate in winter that many Americans imagine; it is rainy, cold, and damp. Central heating, of course, is unheard of. Last year at about this time, and in just such weather, the work of creating a hospital base was begun. To those pioneers it must have appeared a formidable undertaking. Apart from the inevitable lack of physical equipment and the absence of suitable buildings, they themselves must have seemed pathetically few to hope ever to accomplish such a gigantic task; and they did not accomplish it alone. At every step of the way, they were aided by the eager, if untrained, co-operation of the Spanish women. Our base, as it exists today, would have been impossible without the aid of these refugees – for most of them had either fled from the cities occupied by Franco or had been driven from the burning villages in the war area. The story of their effort and the knowledge of how much more useful to their brothers at the front these chicas could be, gave me the idea for the school.

Interestingly enough, the hospital in which I began my work in Spain last May had formerly been a university and it was there that we created the first nursing school in the province. At first it was a very simple affair. We improvised a class room. There we brought the girls in groups of five or ten and showed them how to do such things as the taking of a temperature, recording it, how to count the pulse, respiration, and the significance of these observations.

Then we took them into the wards and showed them how to make a bed, and later how to make the bed with the patient lying in it. At first they thought it would be necessary to have the patient get up and sit in a chair while the bed was being made. All of these, to us, simple procedures had to be carefully demonstrated, explained and taught. In the course of time they learned to recognize symptoms of shock, of hemorrhage, the need for emergency treatment, how to help with the surgical dressings; even how to give a hypodermic.

I had expected them to be enthusiastic – and I was not disappointed – but what pleases me most is the seriousness of their continued interest. The novelty of the class has surely worn off for the older pupils, but I know that it is not a chore for them; it is the major interest of their day. You could easily understand why this is. If you could see them at their usual work; on their knees scrubbing the cold marble of the long halls with colder water. The school is for these Spanish girls an assurance that life can hold something more for them than the scrubbing brush and pail. We, at home, are apt to take such an assurance as everyone's birthright; however, in Spain it is a new idea – the new idea that we are all working to see realized in the coming life of this people.

At first the teaching was entirely practical but as the technique was learned they wished to know more about the *why* of everything. At this stage we called upon the doctors for help and together planned a course of lectures to be given by the different doctors, and designed to teach the girls something of anatomy, physiology, the cause of disease, general principles of treatment, drugs, diet and so forth. The course is still in progress and now we are beginning a second course of practical instruction, a course more advanced than the first. In this we hope to correlate what they are learning in the theoretical lectures with their practical problems. This course is very elementary and not be compared with the three year's course of instruction given in America but the girls are learning enough of the fundamentals to make of them competent and responsible nurses' aids. [...]

In addition to the nursing school the girls have organized a collective, which meets in each hospital once a week. At these meetings various problems are discussed and there is usually a lecture by one of the doctors on some subject related to nursing. These collectives also edit a nursing journal twice a month. [...]

I think that none of us working here can doubt the importance of the educational side of our jobs. We soon found out that the fight against illiteracy was a strong factor in the fight against fascism; that women and men alike, in throwing off their political fetters, were stirred also to overcome the old ignorance of which those fetters were the symbol. Men from the trenches, women from the devastated towns and villages, know today that education is one of their strongest weapons. That is our reward for our work here; to see, and to be able to guide, a spirit of such intensity.

So Personal, the War …

Marion Merriman

Marion Merriman *was the only woman to be a full member of the Abraham Lincoln Battalion of the International Brigades. Her husband Robert Hale Merriman was the first Commander of the Lincolns. She served as an administrative officer. In November 1937 she was sent home on a speaking tour. Robert was killed during Franco's breakthrough in Aragon in March 1938. Marion later had an administrative career at Stanford University.*

As the training continued. Bob received a letter from headquarters advising him to proceed to Madrid to represent the American volunteers in a broadcast planned by a number of American writers. They were gathering at the Hotel Florida in Ernest Hemingway's rooms.

Madrid was under bombardment every day. Bob said to me. There most likely would be sniper fire. Did I want to go with him? It could be dangerous.

I wouldn't miss it, I said. I was in the war with Bob for keeps, I thought to myself. But I was scared – for Bob, for me, for all of us.

I wondered what it would be like if the bombs should fall while we were in Madrid. But I was curious about Hemingway. Bob said he heard John Dos Passos would be there too. [...]

As we drove into Madrid, the first thing we saw was the big bullring – the Moorish architecture, arch upon arch, dusky brown with beautiful coloring in the tiles, the columns. It was magnificent, I thought. Entering Madrid was like entering any big city's industrial section. We drove through a ring of factories, then into the nicer part of the city.

'Even under bombardment, Madrid is marvelous!' I said to Bob. The wide tree-lined boulevards and modern buildings had an air of dignity that even blocks of bombed-out ruins could not dispel. [...]

But the scene changed, quickly. As we walked down a broad boulevard, we heard the crack of rifle fire. Then the tempo picked up. 'That's machine gun fire,' Bob said. The machine-guns rattled in the distance, perhaps a few blocks away, I couldn't be sure. Then we heard the boom of artillery and the reality of Madrid at war returned deeply to me. The artillery shell landed some distance away, collapsing part of a building, which fell into a rubble of dust. We dashed down the street, staying close to the buildings. The horror of war was driven home to me. I was terrified.

I was shaking badly when we entered the Hotel Florida and went directly up the stairs to Hemingway's room. Bob steadied me, then knocked on the door.

'Hello, I'm Merriman,' Bob said as Hemingway, looking intense but friendly, opened the door.

'I know,' Hemingway said. Bob introduced me, and the writer greeted me warmly.

Then Hemingway and Bob fell into conversation about the war and the broadcast they planned.[48] They were joined by John Dos Passos, Josephine Herbst, and a scattering of American volunteers and correspondents who sipped Hemingway's scotch and compared notes and stories. I slipped into an old chair, still quite shaken by the action outside.

I studied Bob and Hemingway. They got along. Each talked for a moment, then listened to the other. How different they were, I thought, Bob at twenty-eight, Hemingway at least a good ten years older. Hemingway seemed complex. He was big and bluff and macho. He didn't appear to be a braggart but he got across the message, through an air of self-assurance, that he could handle what he took on.

Bob was taller than Hemingway by several inches. They looked at each other through the same kind of round glasses, Bob's frames of tortoise shell, Hemingway's of steel.

Hemingway was animated, gesturing as he asked questions, scratching his scalp through thick dark hair, perplexed, then scowling, then, something setting him off, laughing from deep down. He wore a sweater, buttoned high on his chest, and a dark tie, loosened at the neck.

Bob was clean shaven. Hemingway needed a shave. He didn't appear to be growing a beard, he just seemed to need a shave, the scrubble roughing his cheeks and chin. He looked like he had had a hard night. He had a knot on his forehead, probably suffered in some roustabout skirmish.

Hemingway sipped a scotch, as did Bob. Someone offered me a drink, and I thought I'd never been as happy in my life to get a drink of whiskey. Even in the relatively safe room I remained frightened. The sheer madness of the war would not leave my mind. [...]

As Bob and Hemingway talked, the contrast between them struck me time and again. Bob was an intellectual, and he looked like one. Hemingway was an intellectual, but he looked more like an adventurer. Bob looked like an observer. Hemingway looked like a man of action.

I was fascinated by Dos Passos, whom I had always thought was a better writer than Hemingway. John Dos Passos was, without question, a seasoned writer of the prose of war. But as a man, he didn't impress me. I thought he was wishy-washy. I couldn't make out everything he was saying, but his message was clear – for whatever reasons, he wanted out of there, out of Hemingway's room, out of bomb-shaken Madrid.

I was scared too, with good reason. But somehow Dos Passos acted more than scared. I guessed it was his uncertainty, his facial expressions, his general attitude that this was a lost cause, given the superior strength of the Franco forces. Dos Passos criticized the Spanish Republic, for which Americans were fighting and dying.

Hemingway, on the other hand, let you know by his presence and through his writing exactly where he stood. Hemingway had told the world of the murder in Madrid, including the murder of children by fascist bombing. He had told about 'the noises kids make when they are hit ... There is a sort of foretaste of that when the child sees the planes coming and yells *"Aviación!"* Then, too, some kids are very quiet when they are hit – until you move them.' [...]

The following day things got more harrowing. About four o'clock in the afternoon, we were pulling out of a gas station near the post office and we heard a dull, vibrating thud and saw a puff of smoke and dust go up from the bank down the street. People scattered like leaves in a storm, and our bewildered chauffeur stopped in the middle of the open square, but not for long.

We raced up a side street and parked the car on the sheltered side of the narrow street. Fortunately, I thought, the shells from artillery can't come straight down between the buildings! Bob and others calmly joined a larger crowd out on the nearby boulevard, around the corner, to see what was happening. I decided to stay in the car. But, a moment later, the shelling began again. I was frightened into a cold sweat of terror.

At first there was a moment of what seemed like dead silence. A hushed, all-pervading sound suddenly filled everything around me like the mighty sigh of a sudden wind in the forest. Then the noise of the shelling exploded, the burst of the artillery surrounding every part of me. My mind, my head, my eyes, my shoulders, my entire body was immersed in the horrible sound.

I jumped from the car and ran down the street. My God! My God! This sucks up all the air into silence and then the explosion bursts and the air is gone and the silence is overwhelming again. My screams froze in my throat. I ran to Bob, who made me stand quietly against a wall until I got over my terror. I wasn't as much hysterical as I was angry. All I could think was, 'the bastards, the bastards, the bastards'. I couldn't say a thing. [...]

Because Bob was the commander, journalists as well as political observers and the soldiers wanted to know more about him. They sought him out for interviews, but for personal information about him, inquirers had to go to others. 'He's vibrant,' Ed Bender told an interviewer. 'He's very interested in things. He isn't too emotional, doesn't carry on about things. He's vibrant in the intellectual sense, not the emotional sense. And he's very curious about everything. He's not one-sided or dogmatic. He's not a real radical, not a Communist, though he does have leftist sympathies, which made him go to Spain.'

Ed, who was a Communist, could recognize that Bob was not one, that he was among the many Americans who were there not to fight for communism but to fight against fascism. That, Ed thought, gave Bob credibility among the non-Communists who needed politically independent leadership. Such men saw Bob as an intellectual with a social conscience rather than a cause. It was important how the men in the training camps read their officers. Everyone at Tarazona was sizing up everyone else.

'These soldiers,' Ed recalled, 'felt this was a democratic army and that they had a say in what went on. To a degree it was a different kind of army, they [the soldiers] were more politically conscious of what they were there for. If someone was dissatisfied, he felt he had a right to complain.

'Bob Merriman understood this. But he knew discipline was necessary to have these troops be able to fight effectively so he was a disciplinarian in the training.'

Of my presence, Ed noted: 'I never heard any expression of resentment that Merriman had his wife around, because she was a person in her own right. She was doing something there herself. She wasn't just tagging along. She also established good relationships with many of the other Americans. They didn't see her simply as the commander's wife but also as a nice person. She was accepted on her own.'

Sometimes I was accepted a little too much. Occasionally, the men made advances. I put them off quickly and, whenever I could, with kindness. The ones who really exasperated me were those with the political arguments: 'Now, comrade, it says on page such and such about sharing ...' I told one such enterprising young man that such sharing really wouldn't work, that if I slept with him as he suggested I'd have to sleep with the other two thousand men to be fair and that I wasn't up to it.

These things were bound to happen, Bob and I realized. Men at war are lonely and, by and large, celibate. There were few women around in the smaller towns. The Spanish women were quite guarded by their families. If an American was able to get a date with a young Spanish woman, her mother and sister would esort her. The commanders discouraged the men from going to brothels.

Because we could see their loneliness, Bob and I encouraged the men to gather in our room in Albacete's Regina Hotel for conversation and coffee and what cakes and sweets we could buy in the market. Our room became a gathering place, both when Bob was there and when he was not. The men talked of home and of the war, and they usually all left together.

I thought nothing of it when the men continued to come to the room when Bob was away at the front or on a training mission or dispatched to Madrid or Valencia. But the Spaniards were shocked to see so many men trooping to the room of the commander's wife. And on occasion I had to keep things from getting out of hand. One night a Yugoslav tried to get romantic and pressed me to sleep with him. When I declined, he asked if I would sleep with his commander who he said was so lonely. I declined that, too, bursting out laughing. I'd been propositioned before, but never by a surrogate! [...]

The other incident, which I did not share with Bob, nor with anyone else, was much worse.

Rumors reached Albacete that two Englishwomen were in Murcia creating trouble among the American volunteers. Bob was approached by brigade officials with word that the women were visiting the hospitals and encouraging the Americans to quit the Spanish Republican effort, telling them that they were not getting a fair deal. Because the matter involved women, there was a feeling I should go to Murcia to learn what I could about them. So Bob assigned me, along with two officers, to the mission.

Bob stayed in town with me that night because I was to be off on the special business the next day. At eight o'clock in the morning on May 30, I left for Murcia with two pleasant Slav officers. As we drove through the barren lands, I caught up on my diary, writing entries as we motored along. We reached Murcia about noon, went on to Orihuela for lunch, then went for a swim, my first in the Mediterranean. Later I jotted in my diary: 'A sandy beach, warm caressing water. Hold life, hold life so close.'

We had dinner, the two officers and I, on a terrace overlooking a sleepy village caught in the arm of a cove. We marveled at the rosy gray of the sea dotted with slow-moving fishing boats. And, during dinner, I noted that the atmosphere, the swim, the moonlight, the pure beauty of where we were, seemed to give one of my companions romantic ideas. In woman-less war, I'd seen the look before, I dismissed it.

That evening we checked into the hospital at Socorro Rojo.[49] Weary from the long, if enjoyable, day, I fell quickly to sleep. But, suddenly and sharply, I was wide awake. The man whose 'look' I'd noted at dinner was holding me down, one hand clamped over my mouth. I fought him, clawing, kicking. I couldn't scream. He raped me. I kicked him away. He fled the room.

I was stunned. I sobbed, terrified. I climbed from the bed, slowly, and pulled the blankets around me. I ran down the hall to the bathroom. There was no warm water. I filled the bathtub with icy water. I scrubbed and scrubbed, shivering from the cold and the fright. Crying, shivering, I scrubbed for hours. I couldn't cleanse myself, however hard I tried. I felt filthy, thoroughly filthy. I washed and washed, and I cried into the cold, early morning darkness.

The next morning I didn't know what to do. What could I do? Should I try to find a way back to Albacete? Should I somehow get hold of Bob? Should I try to reach Ed Bender? What should I do? I had to calm myself. This is a war, I told myself. Men are dying and maimed. This is my burden. As horrible as the rape was, the worst that could happen would be a pregnancy. If that happened, I steeled myself, I would go to the hospital's doctors or to Paris and have an abortion.

But should I tell Bob? I asked myself, over and over. I searched and searched for the answer and finally concluded: I must not hurt Bob with this. If I tell him, I reasoned, Bob might kill the man. Or one of the other Americans would, for sure. There would be great trouble. No, this must be my secret burden. I cannot tell anyone – ever. What has been done cannot be undone.

I went down to the commissary where the two officers were eating breakfast. One was, as always, cheerful and friendly. He seemed confused when I didn't sit with him. The rapist was brazen, arrogant. We continued the mission. I ignored the rapist, but I could not get the rape off my mind. But I went on with my work. I interviewed the Englishwomen. I memorized impressions and wrote notes. When we returned to Albacete three days later, I reported to Bob about the Englishwomen's efforts to distract the Americans. I said nothing about the rape. The war filled Bob's mind. I could not trouble him further, and I did not.

Nor was I pregnant. [...]

[After the Republican victory at Quinto and Belchite in Aragon, Marion joined Bob at Belchite.]

As Bob explained the battle to me, walking through the town's ruins, the shadows lengthened across the empty fields nearby. Here one of our best machine-gunners fell, beside that wall Burt was killed, there was Danny's grave, here Sidney fell, a sniper's bullet between his eyes, there Steve Nelson was wounded. Our losses were actually very low, but they included some of the best and most loved of our men.

As we passed a little factory, huge sewer rats scurried into a drain beside the road. They were as large as cats. Even though it was two weeks later, the smell of burned flesh still hung faint and nauseating in the cool dusk. Their forces far outnumbered ours, but the fascists had not even attempted to dispose of their dead. They had left hundreds of decaying corpses stacked in various buildings. [...]

As we passed through the debris-filled streets, the air of desolation and death deepened. Homeless cats scuttled about, hungry, and dogs howled and fought bitterly down the blackness of narrow streets. The full moon was bright by the time we reached the cathedral in the center. Across its worn stone steps limply lay a purple and white Falangist banner. Further down was a priest's cassock, perhaps shed in flight.

Only the square admitted enough light for Bob and me to read the fascist posters still stuck to broken walls, posters depicting the horrors of Marxism rather than the horrors of the war that a small group of fascists had started. I noticed there were posted rules for the modesty of young women, rules requiring long skirts and long sleeves, saying sin is woman's because she tempts man. There were no posters promising a government for all of the people.

As we walked, the thought of Sidney Shosteck, so young and sincere and intelligent, who should have walked beside us, heightened my sense of tragedy of the ruined city. Bob told me again how he had sent Sid into Belchite on a mission after most of the fighting was over, not believing his aide to be in any real danger.

'Sidney was killed outright,' Bob said. 'I feel his loss more than any other person I've known here.' Bob had kept Sid out of the street fighting as much as possible. Then, in a crucial moment, he had sent him to direct a tank with a prisoner to show them where the military headquarters of the fascists were. The prisoner went in front of the tank and Sidney behind. But a second-storey sniper shot Sid in the forehead. He never knew what hit him, Bob said, shaking his head as we walked. He added, quietly, 'Sidney's loss here is great. It will really be felt by all of us.'

As Bob talked, I held his arm. I felt I had to support him. He seldom showed his needs to others, but, from our college days until that day in Bechite, I had always known when he needed me, and he needed me then more than ever. Yet I could hardly stifle my own desire to run away from the very smell of death that had reached so deeply into my lungs. I wanted to get away from every reminder I saw around me of that barbarism.

The clear memory of Sidney's soft, dark eyes and crisp black curls over his forehead was almost too sharp for me to bear. He was like a dear, slightly bewildered but happy boy the night he left with Bob. Except for Bob, he was the only one I kissed goodbye, simply because I loved him as a true friend.

As we hurried away, past guards who had been posted near the cathedral, the moon strong and full on our faces, I was filled with a weariness and a heartsickness that only the warmth of the living could relieve. Suddenly, we heard piano music.

'Look,' Bob said, quietly, hushing me before I could respond. There, across a street in half a house, the front walls blown away, the inside looking like a stage, sat a Spanish soldier at a grand piano, playing Beethoven. We stood there in the moonlight, amid the rubble, and listened. The sight of that soldier playing that piano in that perfect little parlor etched itself into my mind.

But Bob had asked me to accompany him to Belchite not simply to show me what had happened but because there was work to do there. I was to gather a first-hand report for the ministry of war. Families of American wounded and killed there would need information to satisfy insurance companies who required facts. We verified deaths as best we could, talking with the soldiers who could give eyewitness accounts of the fighting at Belchite. [...]

Notes

1. The Jarama front, February-May 1937. Franco was trying to surround Madrid and cut the Madrid-Valencia road.
2. Penelope Phelps: see her contribution, 'English Penny', pp.78-80.

3. In March 1938 Franco's armies, with German tanks rehearsing 'blitzkrieg' tactics, broke through the Aragon front and cut Republican Spain in two. Aileen's unit had retreated across the Ebro into Catalonia.

4. In July 1938 a major Republican offensive recrossed the River Ebro.

5. In December 1937 a Republican offensive took the city of Teruel.

6. Ruth Ormesby, fell to her death escaping from a fire in Barcelona in April 1938.

7. George Jeger, secretary of the SMAC in London.

8. The writer George Orwell (Eric Blair) was in Spain from January to June 1937. He joined a group from the Independent Labour Party serving with the POUM militia.

9. British personnel were back at Grañen for the Republican Aragon offensive, August-October 1937.

10. Aurora Fernández: see her contribution, 'Enfermera', pp.73-7.

11. Benicasim was a convalescent centre for Internationals.

12. Dr Leonard Crome; Deputy Chief (later Chief) Medical Officer 35th Division; Chief MO of 4th Army at the Crossing of the Ebro. Awarded Military Cross serving with the RAMC in the Second World War.

13. La Granja Republican offensive, 50 miles north of Madrid, May 1937.

14. For the Republican offensive in Aragon, August 1937.

15. Christina, Viscountess Hastings, Marchioness of Huntingdon, a left-wing, Italian-born aristocrat; treasurer of the SMAC.

16. The Arganda bridge on the Madrid-Valencia road was heavily contested during the Jarama fighting.

17. For the Republican Brunete offensive, July 1937, aimed at ending the Nationalist threat to Madrid.

18. Sir Richard Rees, editor of *Adelphi* literary magazine, ambulance driver for SMAC, later Quaker relief worker; Julian Bell, nephew of Virginia Woolf; John Cornford, poet; John Boulting, later distinguished film producer; Molly Murphy, nurse (her husband J.T. Murphy, was a leading socialist). Portia is correct about Rees, Murphy and Boulting. But Cornford was an advocate of the International Brigade, and had been killed six months earlier. Bell had returned from China specifically to join the International Brigades.

19. Triage (from the French for 'sorting'), where wounded were sorted according to the degree of treatment necessary. Now general, triage was first practiced in Spain.

20. 'Andy' was Keith Andrews, an ex-soldier in the Royal Army Medical Corps who was in charge of sterilisation work for the British medical team wth 13th Brigade throughout the war. Dr Reginald Saxton came from Reading. In charge of blood transfusion services in 13th Brigade, he was one of the first to use stored blood for transfusions, a technique developed during the Spanish war. Saxton helped to introduce this technique into Britain. He served in the RAMC during the 1939-45 war.

21. During Aragon retreat, spring 1938; see above.

22. Huete is 145 kilometres south-east of Madrid.

23. Valdeganga is 50 kilometres east of Uclés and 50 kilometres south-east of Huete.

24. In fact he reformed the hospital which was used until the end of the war,

25. *Practicantes* were second-year medical students acting as assistants.

26. Dr Nathan Malimson, Chairman, North Manchester SMAC.

27. Flit: pre-war fly-spray.

28. Dr Douglas Jolly, New Zealand Christian Socialist, was one of best surgeons in Spain. During the Second World War he was a distinguished Divisional Surgeon in North Africa and Italy.

29. Rosita Davson, translator and SMAC administrator in Barcelona. 'Winifred' is Bates.

30. Colmenar de Oreja, is 35 kilometres south-east of Madrid, behind the Jarama front.

31. Phil Thorne, Secretary Australian Spanish Relief Committee.

32. Max Langer, Austrian refugee doctor; René Dumont, Belgian surgeon.

33. Dumont, with whom Una was in love.

34. 'Pancho Villa', anarchist *alcalde* (mayor) of Grañen; hostile to SMAC unit. Agnes's diary suggests a more distressing departure from Grañen than does her letter.

35. Agnes had been unwell and was working under very difficult conditions in the hospital she describes in this letter. Under stress she walked out of the hospital after a row about nurses' sleeping arrangements. In Barcelona she was offered a post at the new British hospital

near Madrid, presumably Uclés, but hearing of intrigues there (see 'Small Beer' by Nan Green, pp.87-92) decided to leave Spain.

36. The May 1937 conflict in Barcelona between anarchists and POUM and government forces, see the contributions to this volume by Helen Grant (pp.180-7), Mary Low (pp.257-61), Ethel MacDonald (pp.274-5), Jane Patrick (pp.276-7) and Mary Lowson (pp.278-80) and Emma Goldman, (pp.299-303).

37. Huete.

38. George Jackson was Secretary of the New Zealand SMAC.

39. Rose is writing to her brother.

40. John Langdon Davies, scientist and writer was science editor of the Liberal *News Chronicle*.

41. Dr Edward Barksy headed first the American Hospital Unit.

42. Langston Hughes, the black American poet, was a leading figure in the 'Harlem Renaissance' of the 1920s.

43. Castillejo del Romeral is 15 kilometres east of Huete and 100 kilometres south-east of Madrid.

44. Moises Broggi-Valles; leading Catalan surgeon. In 1985 he was elected for the second time as President of Barcelona Royal Academy of Medicine.

45. Dorothy Rutter, an English nurse from Bournemouth. She was killed while serving with the RAMC, when the British Expeditionary Force was evacuated from Dunkirk during the Second World War.

46. J.B.S. Haldane, Professor of Biometry, University College, London, was in Spain to advise the government on defence from gas warfare; on his return he campaigned in Britain for deep air-raid shelters.

47. Norman Bethune, the distinguished Canadian surgeon, was head of the Madrid Blood Transfusion Institute. In 1938 he went to China where he organised medical services in Mao's guerrilla army fighting the Japanese; Bethune died in China.

48. Hemingway based Robert Jordan, the hero of *For Whom the Bell Tolls*, on Merriman.

49. Soccoro Rojo Internacional was the Spanish branch of International Red Aid, a Communist-inspired organisation which gave help to the victims of fascist and other right-wing governments. In Spain it was supported by Socialists, Communists and liberal intellectuals such as the poet Federico Garcia Lorca.

Part 3

WITH THE REARGUARD

Fear is a Serious Thing

Lydia Ellicott Morris

Lydia Ellicott Morris *was an American Quaker who went to Spain in the autumn of 1936 to explore the possibilities for relief work by the American Friends' Service Council (AFSC).*

9, rue Guy de la Brosse,
Paris V
22 October 1936

Dear Mahlon,

[...] I will not make a long report of my time at Barcelona. As thee knows it was just a sort of Quaker impulse that took me there, in spite of having no letter from the Embassy in Paris. They wished to give such letters only to those claiming membership in some anti-fascist club or association, and I think Friends are not in the least a partisan group, but believe in serving the government they live under.

At the border the Red Committee were about to refuse admission, but I had letters from Clarence E. Picket, the Council for International Service of London Yearly Meeting, and Bertram Pickard, and by happy co-incidence if not Divine plan, there arrived on my train a young man named Müller Lehning who knew all these people, as well as about Friends' works of various kinds. As he was coming to help the Government now in charge at Barcelona they allowed me to come in with him, promising every co-operation in any work we felt called to do.

As they know we are a religious group, and they do not countenance any other religious group in this way, it made me feel very responsible to be just and loyal to them as far as possible. [...]

Our friend Müller Lehning gave us a good *chain* of introductions and we soon met some of the CNT officers and through them the two ladies (formerly teachers) who are in charge of the refugee work, and Dr Ibañez Inspector General of Health.

Mr and Mrs Russel Eckroyd also turned up about the work they wished started at their home at Castellón.[1] They had a letter to

President Companys and took us with them to talk to him. He also wished to give us every assistance and altogether we saw what we wished of the admirable social service work being done there at Barcelona and in the suburbs. We saw the regular fine standard work in caring for poor and children, and then the work of 'poor houses' etc, taken over from the Catholic Church in July last, where both sexes and all ages are cared for adequately. Then day nurseries were shown to us, of very modern and excellent planning. Then the villages where refugee children were put in every home, having been brought from Madrid schools with their teachers. Then the home (Red Cross) where refugee children are cleaned up and put in order to stay in individual families.

They have taken over many large houses for these groups, and classes can thus go on regularly. [...]

The house chosen for us by the Red authorities is a large residence near a wonderful little children's hospital in the suburbs. This they said they would furnish, and give us any class of children, sick, well, any age, or social group. It would hold 30 children comfortably and fifty could be put there. The garden was very large and practical. [...]

As I could not get about owing to lumbago, and I guess inactivity and perhaps even fear I got my passport put in order, and waiting till the fear had subsided for I do not mean to be ruled by that, I took the urging of the Consul to 'go on the early train tomorrow please' for permits have to be done again if you do not use them.

Now the truth is that fear is a serious thing alone in this work, and two people are much better for this reason. I was surprised to find how idleness, lonliness and nothing to read nor people who spoke one's language, gave me moments of cold feet. Tell the truth and shame the devil is a good old saying ...

The fact that Quakers are the only people standing for God who are wanted, urged, and invited to come in there now is just a very heavy responsibility. [...]

There is an immense place out in the country toward the front – a huge residence capable of holding 50 children, but I would favour it as a country day place for all these crowded families, and have a canteen connected with it that all sorts of town people would like to come out to for waffles etc. – a nice drive from town. Little children of ten or twelve could do the waiting. We could put a team of eight WIL women there and trades union women, to live but the children should not sleep there with a danger of surprise. I would have this place so organised that if a sudden retreat began we could at quick notice have immense quantities of food ready, doughnuts and coffee or something to distract the men from their sworn duty to lay waste and kill. [...]

The school people say, 'There is no political party for children, they are just children', and they mean to see that they are kept out of parties and politics. [...] I told them frankly we were of neither party, but wanted to keep safe these children if we could. [...]

From a Spanish Diary

Helen Grant

Helen Grant *was an assistant lecturer in the Spanish Department
of Birmingham University. She had spent much time in Spain,
was the friend of Spanish intellectuals, and was interested in
Spanish movements in drama and education. In the spring of
1937 she went with Francesca Wilson and her friend Muriel
Davies to see what the Spanish government was doing for refugees
and to explore the possibilities for relief work.*

Saturday 27 March 1937: Travelled third class to Barcelona. Train
crowded with people, mostly peasants. Travelling was much easier
than in England as everybody insisted on helping us with our luggage.
The usual Spanish habit of asking you to share their food. Great
delight of the carriage when we upset the wine all over ourselves
trying to drink from the *bota* [skin drinking bottle]. [...] Arrived at
Barcelona in just over two hours. Took a taxi, which surprised me as I
hadn't realised they were running. The taxis are all painted red and
black with the initials CNT (the anarchist trade union). No tips –
everyone very polite and efficient. [...]

Notices on the outside doors in our block said, 'This business is
under the workers' control' followed by the initials CNT and UGT
(anarchist and socialist unions). On one floor there was a notice on a
door saying, 'Swiss interests are involved in this business. It must be
respected.' The only sign of abnormality – dark streets at night. Cafés
full of people – trams running normally – buses and taxis – cinemas
open. [...]

Monday 29 March: Went to visit an anarchist school '*Instituto Libre*'
under the auspices of the '*Juventudes Libertarias*' (Young Anarchists).
The house was formerly a convent and was in the process of being
done up. A young man of about 25 welcomed us and showed us over
the place. He was very good looking indeed and talked good Castilian.
He told me he was, by profession, an electrical engineer. He told me
that he and a group of young men had decided when the revolution

broke out to save works of art and books from the ignorant masses. They took possession of the convent and saved it from being burned. The nuns had left four days before the military revolt broke out. He was very insistent that *even* religious pictures and books should be saved if they had artistic or literary value. He showed us pictures on the walls dealing with religious subjects which he said were valuable. In the library he pointed out the works of Balmes (nineteenth-century religious writer) Santa Teresa and St John of the Cross. He said that the aim of this school was to give free education in all senses of the word. Not more than twenty-five children in a class – quality not quantity. They aimed at having four hundred children. There was to be no headmaster but a committee of parents, staff and children. He was the founder, he said, of this school. It was hoped to set up similar schools in each district of Barcelona. He was very idealistic. Said English people thought anarchists ate children but he asked us to remember that there were always two sides to a revolution – a good and a bad side. Most people thought only of the bad.

There seems to be no money behind the school except the rent from some of the convent flats. He and his friends had made, themselves, a good deal of the equipment of the school. Showed us, with great pride, the shower baths for the children to have when they had played games. Not very clear whether the teachers were to be paid or not.

Tuesday 30 March: Paid our call, as requested, at the British Consulate. After waiting for a long time were summoned to The Presence. […]

King regarded us with intense suspicion but was conscientiously trying to make us see the light. For a whole hour he told us atrocity stories, his idea being, presumably, 'I'll show these silly women!' I think on the whole we won, because we put him on the defensive. I changed my tactics from being rather aggressive to asking innocent questions. After half an hour of raped nuns, murdered priests, burnt churches, I asked him if he could explain why it was that the people of Spain disliked the church so much. He replied that that was too long a story but when pushed said, of course, there had been the Inquisition and every revolution in Spain had been followed by attacks on the church. For example fifteen years ago in Barcelona they had exposed nun's coffins on the steps of the churches. It was like a kind of superstition reversed. […]

He admitted that many anarchists were fine chaps and that most of the atrocities had been committed by common criminals. He struck me as a coarse man – astute, even intelligent but with no understanding of conditions. For example, when we asked him whether people were still being shot he admitted that they weren't, but said that was because they had all been killed or had fled. He made great efforts to show us that he was a person of culture with a real knowledge of Spain but it took him aback rather when I told him I had been coming to Spain regularly for many years. He showed a complete indifference to the sufferings of nuns and monks etc., and merely seemed to speak of their murders because it was useful propaganda. He disclaimed, however, any attempt to put propaganda over on us. He said that the Spaniards were backward, hot-blooded and cruel and that they had not altered for centuries. 'Winston Churchill said to me, the other day, that he didn't want things to change either.' There also seems to have been a British admiral who said the same thing. The Spaniards, he said, could not be reached by books. He thought it was odd, however, that they were showing a sudden enthusiasm for reading. 'My guards downstairs, for example, spend all their day reading but this is just a passing fad.'

He shook us warmly by the hand and asked us to call and see him again. A nasty man but quite unaware that he is nasty. [...]

Wednesday 31 March: About 12 o'clock we went to Pedralbes to see a refugee home. We were taken there by Señor Esteva, head of another refugee home. The 'colony' in Pedralbes is in a wonderful position in the house of a former banker, right up on the hill overlooking Barcelona and the Mediterranean. The children were from Madrid. There were 90 children in all and the majority were the children of the employees of a Madrid brewery. The owner of the brewery was a kind man who always sent these children away for the summer. In November he sent them with his son (Mahu) to Barcelona to be out of the air raids. The son, a very charming young man dressed in blue overalls, was still helping to manage the colony. [...]

The rooms in this colony were airy and light and the furniture simple and cheerful. The bedrooms of the children were particularly attractive – the covers on the beds being in good modern designs and the beds painted gay colours. In the girls' bedrooms were dolls and pictures and books – in the boys' posters, detective stories and model aeroplanes. There was a very interesting wall newspaper edited by the children containing both cuttings from newspapers and original work. The children share in the organisation of the colony throughout, on a

self-government basis. Everything was brilliantly clean. The girls help
with the house work and the boys and girls worked in the gardens.
The gardens, about four acres or more, were beautiful and part of
them given over to growing vegetables. The little boys showed us over
them with great pride. They told us they were growing vegetables to
send to their parents in Madrid. One small boy told me that 'the little
ones' had had their piece of ground taken away from them because
they had neglected it and that they had been given a less productive
part of the garden. I was particularly struck by the fact that none of
the children were in any kind of uniform and there seemed to be no
obvious supervision in the garden at all. It was taken for granted that
they would behave properly. They were all extremely fit and brown
and the walls in the house were so clean that one would have never
imagined that ninety poor children from the Madrid streets had been
living there since November. We had lunch there and found it a very
sensibly thought out meal. [...]

Saturday 3 April: O'Donnell also told me that the situation in
Barcelona was ticklish.[2] This confirmed my own impression. Since
Thursday I had noticed a change of temperature. (Rica had told me
that while at the police station the police were rushing in all night
taking arms out of lockers.) O'Donnell said that he had been up until
five o'clock in the morning, armed, waiting in case of a raid. The
Anarchist papers, moreover, had begun to attack the government
violently, demanding the dissolution of the Shock Police (*Cuerpos
Uniformados*). They had also begun urging that the revolution should
not be lost sight of in the civil war and posters had appeared all over
the town saying; 'The Anarchists have sacrificed part of their ideology
by taking office. What are the Marxists doing? It is time they carried
out their side of the pact by socialising.' Another point made by
Anarchist papers was that mobilisation should not be carried out too
rapidly. I was told that one of the main causes for the crises was that
Anarchist leaders in the government signed decrees with the other
members of the Cabinet but that the rank and file refused to carry out
the decrees. This, of course, is understandable since the basis of
Anarchist theory is contrary to government from above and
delegation of authority. The Socialists, however, were anxious to win
the war and realised that the small farmer peasant and trader must be
encouraged and not frightened. [...]
  For the first time since I had been in Barcelona, I was conscious of

uneasiness. Both Francesca and I could not sleep. Cars were dashing through the streets all night. We would hear cars stop suddenly then a bang on a door. Moreover, I heard an outburst of shots. It was very uncanny.

Sunday 4 April: Had tea with Xirau and Margarita Comas. Xirau shut all the doors and windows and told us what had caused the government crises. Valencia had demanded the setting up of a supreme war council – the immediate appointment of a general from Valencia to conduct the campaign on the Catalonian fronts and an immediate offensive by Catalonia. The Socialists and Catalan Left supported Valencia's demand. The Anarchists objected. His view was that the Anarchists would lose – as popular opinion was disgusted by the failure of Catalonia to play an active part in the defeat of Franco. Many soldiers from the front had enlisted in the regular army disgusted by the disorganisation in the Anarchist controlled units. [3][...]

Valencia, Sunday 11 April: We set off at 9:30 in the War Office car. Cuthbert Wigham saw us off and shook his finger at the chauffeur saying in English 'Take care of them. Good ladies.' Our chauffeur understood no English but replied 'I will take care of them.' Our chauffeur, Antonio Carrasca, was one of the finest men I have met in Spain. We all felt we could trust him to the end of the world. He was a short, stocky man with an open determined face. He had been a foreman in a motor works and had an immense love for his work and the men who had worked under him. He was longing to get back to his job and become a 'Stakhanovite'. The works where he had been had been destroyed by shell fire. Since the 'Movement' he had been driving cars for generals and colonels but told us that he had been in the taking of the Montaña Barracks. He was a very simple type of man but extremely intelligent. [...]

Antonio seemed to admire Anarchists although he was a Communist. He said that the trouble about Anarchism was that it was impracticable at the moment. He was full of enthusiasm. [...]

We stopped for lunch at a small village called Olivares and had lunch with a peasant family. Excellent meal of eggs and meat, oranges, bread and wine. They cooked the food over a straw fire. They were very interested in us. Antonio was charming with the children. An old woman said that she was not shocked by our smoking because they now knew that it was only the church which had pretended that sort of thing was wicked. Then someone said, 'Yes, the priests told us it was wicked for women to smoke but it did not stop them from seducing the prettiest girls in the vestry.' The old woman talked to me for a long time. She wanted to know about England. She was very surprised when I told her that England was smaller than Spain and said, 'I always thought Spain was the smallest, poorest country in the world.' Then she turned to the other people and said, 'That just shows they never taught us anything.'

Antonio pointed out that it would all be different now that the children would have a better chance. A young girl was very excited by Miss Davies's scarf. Miss Davies very sweetly gave it to her. Antonio was very impressed by this and said that the girl would keep it for years and probably hand it on to her children. She did not want to accept it at first but we pointed out that it was to show that English people liked Spaniards.

Tuesday 13 April: We talked to Enrique Jiménez, the head of the evacuation committee. He told us that 300,000 children have left Madrid. He also told us that pregnant women were being evacuated as fast as possible. Three thousand were in a home at Villagordo de Jucar. Four hundred and fifty children had already been born there. He was immensely thrilled about this and seemed to find the idea of pregnancy very funny. He showed us a picture of two very pregnant women laughing at each other. We asked him whether there were people still living in the metro and refuges. He said, no, that they had cleared all these out and evacuated the majority. Some, however, had been transferred to empty flats in the well-to-do quarters. He emphasised that the greatest difficulty which they were up against was that the people preferred to remain in Madrid. They felt they were, in some way, helping by staying and it was difficult to get this idea out of their heads. They were using every propaganda device possible to make people evacuation-minded.

Francesca, Muriel Davies and I went to see the Casa Cuña, a children's home. [...] The Casa Cuña was rather different from anything we had seen before. The head of it was out but a large blowsy but good nature working woman said that she would be pleased to show us round. A colleague of hers, who looked as though she had been knitting beneath the guillotine and a toothless elderly workman also seemed to be part of the management. Their appearance was deceptive. They started by showing us a very efficient card index of the children evacuated by them. They told us that the Casa Cuña had originally been founded in August to take charge of the children of the men (and women) who were at the front. It was run, as she said, by militant Communist women. She herself had been in the militia. However, after a short time the Communist Party had ordered the women to withdraw from the front lines. They had at first been paid 10 pesetas a day like the men whether at the front or in the rear guard. Since January 30th, the militia women had been dissolved and no longer received 10 pesetas. I asked her whether the wives of the soldiers were paid a separation allowance. She said, no, they relied on their husbands sending the money or were authorised by them to collect their pay. 'You see,' she said, 'women still in Spain have no legal position.' [...]

I asked her how she collected children for evacuation. She said this was largely organised by the Anti-Fascist Women's Society. [...] She showed us round the house and we were impressed by the excellent arrangements – the cheerful decorations and the cleanliness. In one room were six very small babies. Two were toddlers and the rest infants. They were beautifully kept. The babies were asleep in pretty cots. Three women dressed in white overalls were in charge. Most of the babies were orphans. One had lost its father at the front and its mother in an air raid. It was hoped to evacuate these babies as soon as foster mothers could be found. [...] Casa Cuña was particularly impressive because it was run by real working people. [...]

Thursday 15 April: We left at seven o'clock. We were in great disgrace because we kept Garratt waiting.[4] Drove round to the Refugee Centre and collected our load of children. Two of the National Joint Committee buses were to start off with 60 children between them. It was rather a tragic sight. Parents obviously trying to keep cheerful and the children too. One little girl in our bus dried her eyes before turning round to say goodbye to her mother. Her mother was crying and trying to look as if she wasn't. One baby of four cried continuously for her mother. The school masters in charge of our group good humouredly said, 'We don't mind songs but we don't like tears.' I noticed that the majority of the mothers looked extremely anaemic and worn. This bore out what we had been told that the women were giving, as usual, most of the food to the children. There was one small girl of about fifteen very made up. She was very pretty but not so pretty as several of the others but our driver – Muggeridge, known as Enrique – made a great fuss of this child who was called Dolores. Before we reached the main Valenica road all the children were let out for a run. 'Very necessary,' Garratt explained, 'I have learned by long experience.' He explained further that this has to be done at an early stage in the journey. The journey was without incident. The children were remarkably good. A few small boys were sick. Garratt said that he was going to call the lorry 'Gloria mundi' because there was so much 'sic transit'. I was very impressed with the way the older boys and girls about eleven looked after the younger children. One little girl nursed a child of four the whole way. A little boy of about twelve had another small girl on his knee most of the journey.

We arrived at Valencia in just about eleven hours. The car went marvellously. [...]

The Margins of Chaos

Francesca Wilson

Francesca Wilson served with refugees in France, Corsica, North Africa, Serbia and Vienna, during and after the First World War and in Russia during the famine which followed the civil war. In Spain she inaugurated work in the south, returning to England to teach during term-time. During the 1939-45 war she worked with Spanish refugees in France, and after that war with the UN relief organisation in Yugoslavia and Germany. In the spring of 1937 she visited children's colonies with Helen Grant and Muriel Davies. When the others left Spain, Francesca headed for Murcia to begin relief work.

It was April, and though the weather was already hot, it had not lost its freshness. The journey passed like a dream. […]

Then the dream was over and we were in a nightmare. We were on the outskirts of Murcia in a vast, unfinished building of apartment flats, nine stories high, pushing our way through crowds of ragged, wild-eyed refugees. There were no windows or doors in the building: the floors had not yet been divided into rooms and formed huge corridors, which swarmed with men, women and children of all sizes and ages. There was no furniture, except a few straw mattresses. The noise was terrific: babies crying, boys rushing madly from floor to floor, sick people groaning, women shouting. There were said to be four thousand in the building, though I doubt if anyone had counted them. They surged round us, telling us their stories, clinging to us like people drowning in a bog. They were part of the hundred thousand who had fled from Málaga just before it fell to Franco's Italian army. This happened on February 8th. For four days and nights they had trekked along the coast road to Almería, picked out by searchlight and shelled by rebel warships at night, machine-gunned from the air by day. […]

The first breakfast was a great success. The children came in relays to a small room near the kitchen. They ate their biscuits and licked the chocolate out of their soup plates with enormous relish. Now and again there were scuffles, and I discovered that some enterprising youngster was being ejected from his third bout. There were also some outsizes in school children who had managed to get in – but I explained that though big, they were hungry, and they were allowed to finish their meal. [...]

But the next morning when I turned up to help with breakfast at the Casa Pablo Iglesias I felt something odd about the place. It was like an anthill that has been stirred up – the whole building was alive. I could scarcely get up the stairs for the press. We had to lock and bar the kitchen door and bear the smoke from the stove as well as we could. When we tried to let in the children in relays to their breakfast, we were stormed out and had to give up the attempt. [...]

We cleared a landing and put up doors and made it into a dining room. We would give breakfast, not only to the children, I said, but to the 'embarrassed' and 'creating' women too, as Spaniards call the pregnant and nursing mothers. There were men and women among the refugees whom I could buy at the price of a cup of cocoa to help with order. All the same, the first days were a bear-garden. It was easy to control the children, but the embarrassed and creating mothers were like wild animals. They broke down the doors, they flung down the sentries, they surged into the room, dipped their tin mugs into the scalding vats, fought with each other, tearing each other's hair and the clothes off each other's backs. They shrieked and gesticulated. It was not a breakfast – it was hell. They couldn't believe that there would be enough to go round. [...]

Where have I heard before of five thousand being fed, I thought? Of course, I remembered. But then it was a miracle. I understood it now – it was a miracle, not so much because there was enough food, but because they all sat quietly on the grass, waiting for it. The more I thought of it, the more I was amazed and determined that we must make the same miracle work here. [...]

In the end the breakfasts at Pablo Iglesias were like Sunday school treats followed by a mothers' meeting tea – or very nearly. And for weeks we gave bread and bully beef to the wretches who lived in the limbo where there was no second meal.

*   *   *

The most distressing thing to me all this time was the number of sick and dying children in all the refuges. The Murcia doctors visited them occasionally, but in such circumstances could do little for them, and they and the refugee authorities were very worried about them and the risk of spreading infection. A Children's Hospital was exceedingly urgent, so I asked Sir George Young on one of his passing visits to Murcia if he would support one. He agreed to do so if I could make the arrangements. This was not very easy, but eventually a very beautiful modern villa was assigned to us. In a week we equipped it with thirty beds, mosquito nets and the minimum of medical necessities. Sir George sent out an English nurse and the authorities assigned a visiting Spanish doctor.

The children poured in. I never had more hectic weeks than those first. Not being a nurse – my task was interpreting and administration – the children I admitted seemed to my unmedical eye nearly all to be dying, and when with proper treatment they began to grow better it was to me a miracle. At first there were sick babies and pneumonia cases, but very soon they were nearly all typhoid fever. [...]

I returned to Spain at the end of July, feeling like a millionaire with £250 that Friends and friends had given me. I was determined this time to give the younger refugees some occupation. The listless misery of multitudes of people with nothing to do weighed me down. In a factory in Barcelona I bought thousands of yards of material. I had already got one sewing workshop going in Murcia and I now set one up in Alicante. I found an excellent dressmaker evacuated from Madrid, bought two second-hand sewing machines and the Committee gave me a very pleasant room with an open-air balcony. Very soon thirty girls between the ages of twelve and twenty-one were busily sewing every day. Refugees poured in to be measured and fitted and every week they turned out dozens of garments.

Murcia still had my heart and I soon found myself back. Soon every refuge there had a workshop and more than a hundred girls were learning to sew and to embroider and even to cut out. The sewing class became the most cheerful place in the building, with girls chatting and singing at their work and sometimes reading aloud. I thought the workshops might be turned into clubs in the evening and brought along armfuls of books and games, and was astonished at the eager cries of 'Now we shall be able to study.' I discovered that most of the girls could not read or write. The Director of Education helped me to find masters, who at great sacrifice after a hard day's work came and gave night-classes in the refuges.

In Southern Spain people wear *alpargatas* [rope-soled sandals] summer and winter. The hemp and esparto grass from which the ropes are made grow in the district, so that it was not too complicated to set up *alpargata* workshops and get refugees provided with footwear and, incidentally, some men and women learning a useful trade. A cobbler's outfit and a couple of shoemakers helped those who wore leather. [...]

All this time nothing had been done for the boys. There were crowds of them, too old at fourteen or fifteen for the Government Colonies, hanging round the refuges and getting into mischief. This is what led me, with the half of my money still unspent, to start a Farm Colony in Crevillente in the Province of Alicante. It is in a delightful spot in the mountains safe from air-raids. [...]

We were lucky to find the buildings of an old flour-mill which, because of the springs in the mountains behind, had been run by waterpower. These buildings 'Rubio' [Blondie], a German engineer whom I found in Valencia, converted into living-quarters for sixty people – fifty boys and ten staff. All round the mill up and down the hillside there are terraces of land still carefully ploughed by the peasants, but because of the inaccessibility of the place most of them are uncultivated except for a few trees. The carob, whose pod-like fruit gives food for mules, is the most frequent, but there are occasional fruit-trees such as the pomegranate, the apricot and the almond, and a few date palms. In the old days when the mill was working this land was irrigated and planted with vegetables and cattle feed, and this is what our boys are doing now. [...]

In our farm the only animals we can keep are goats, rabbits and hens. Pigs are impossible at the moment because of the problems of animal-fodder at a time when food for human beings is so scarce. Even hens are a difficulty, but two ships brought out chicken-mash from England along with the peas, lentils, beans, flour, rice, cocoa, herrings and bacon necessary for the boys. For a farm of our kind is a long way from being self-supporting. The goats give some milk, the chickens provide eggs for omelettes, the rabbits in time will give meat, but the first substantial crop of food will be when the potatoes are lifted. When I was there in April we had our own radishes, lettuces and spinach, but only in the late summer and autumn will there be anything substantial. In the meantime the boys are kept continually at work, digging, weeding, sowing, transplanting and above all, watering and irrigating.

Irrigation has always been an enigma to me. Camping in Greece I have heard the calls of irrigators through the moonlit night – I have seen fields turned suddenly and inexplicably into lakes. I have found my walks cut off by rushing streams, where yesterday were dry channels, but I have never understood how it was done. Now at last I was initiated into its mystery. I took part in a ritual, unchanged from the days of the Moorish occupation.

First of all we had to go down, Rubio and I, to the Farmers' Syndicate in the village of Crevillente. About thirty peasants all dressed in black smocks, with serious, weather-worn faces, were assembled in a small room at the other end of which sat the auctioneer and a bell-ringer, at a little table. The next twenty-four hours were now put up for sale. The proceedings were conducted in the Valencian dialect and the bids, starting at 5 or 6 pesetas, went up by 10 centimes. The auctioneer went so fast and the peasants got in their bids so quickly that I was afraid we would remain without water and I kept poking Rubio in great agitation till at last he went up to 20 pesetas an hour and the bell rang for us. He demanded four hours and we were told that the water would come at 7.25 the next day.

That morning the whole Colony got up before dawn (the Spanish have pushed their time on two hours) and quickly swallowed cocoa and biscuits, for the business of irrigation is serious and exacting. I climbed up with Rubio and two of our boys to the tableland above the mill and watched while with wooden boards and earth they stopped up the outlets in the neatly cemented channels, down which the water would have gone briskly enough to a neighbouring farm if we had not prevented it. In the meantime other boys were working with feverish activity stopping up gaps and preparing new ones in the earth ridges of the terraces, so that when the water came it would inundate first the lettuces and then the potatoes and onions. In the meantime on the terraces below, with the same feverish haste, other boys were transplanting tomatoes and pimentoes from the frames and putting in seeds of maize, melons and the soya bean. Then at last Pepe, the small black-eyed boy who had been posted as sentinel on the top of the hill, announced the water's coming, and there it was – a yellow, foaming stream rushing through cemented channels and dashing in cataracts over rocks until it came to us. Someone was pumping it from the springs, and at 7.25 punctually it arrived. All were too much occupied for thanksgiving: there were no sounds but Rubio shouting directions on one terrace and Don Mariano, our schoolmaster, on the other. At last it was all over. The cataracts on the hillsides, the pools in the furrows of the potato field and round the pomegranate trees disappeared as mysteriously as they had come. Exhausted, we sat under a carob tree while Rubio read aloud to us the Spanish version of *Emile and the Detectives*.

A farm in wartime Spain, where very little can be bought ready-made, would be seriously handicapped if it had not workshops attached. Fortunately I have an active little sewing-class of refugee girls in the village of Crevillente. They make the mattress-covers, sheets, pillow-cases for our beds; the shirts, shorts and dungarees and knitted jersies for our boys – all without payment, for the 'cause', and because they know they are learning to sew and it will be useful to them later. In the farm itself we have a carpentry workshop in which twelve boys every day take part under the direction of the disabled soldier Polycarp. They make rabbit-hutches, chicken-houses, beds, tables, benches, cupboards and shelves, and do endless repairs. There is also a small engineering shop under Rubio which has done useful work though handicapped for lack of tools.

As the boys are refugees from all parts of Spain, they are at very different stages of culture and development. Some of them have little or no schooling, so there are short classes every day. The atmosphere of the place is one of happy and ceaseless activity. […]

On the dark background of the Spanish Civil War the Farm Colony at Crevillente shines out like a lantern in a stormy night.

Christian Insights

Elizabeth Burchill

Elizabeth Burchill was a Melbourne-trained Australian nursing sister, living in England by relief nursing. She volunteered for nursing with Sir George Young's Southern Spanish Hospitals. During the 1939-45 war Elizabeth nursed with Australian troops in the Middle East.

Intrigued to read in a current issue of the English *Nursing Journal*, 'Wanted: Nurses for Spain. Apply Southern Spanish Relief Committee', I answered the advertisement, and [...] went ahead with plans to leave England because it seemed to me at the time the logical step to take in my quest for adventurous nursing with Christian insights. And contrary to the Matron's well-meaning assertion that 'I would be sorry', I did not live to regret the immediate decision to involve myself in the closing phases of a civil war in a foreign country. This was nursing with a real difference. [...]

Guarded day and night by government soldiers our hospital was a two storey brick building set high in an enclosed garden. It was protected by high brick walls, framed by tawny mountains and overlooked the old Moorish city of Almería. The government also took over the monastery next door, transforming it into a 600-bed hospital for the care of sick and wounded soldiers. Patients were accommodated in dormitories, small rooms, cubicles and even in the ornate chapel. Nursing was done by a band of untrained civilian women who had replaced the nursing nuns who 'disappeared' during the early days of the war and uprising of rebellion against the church. [...]

Like myself, Marguerite was a new recruit to Spain.[5] A tall, slim brunette in her late twenties she had serious ways, the deep religious faith of a nun-like identity, and a delicate sensitivity which made her feel very deeply for the plight of the refugees. Marguerite accepted Spain as a challenge to her faith and discipleship and I soon learnt to admire her infinite capacity for sympathy and compassion. She was orphaned at an early age and became deeply attached to the nuns who raised her in the English convent of an Anglo-Saxon order.

Marguerite grew up to train as a nurse and to become a Christian idealist dedicated to an altruistic way of life. Distressed by demonstrations of man's inhumanity to man during the Civil War, she applied for service at the Southern Spanish Relief Headquarters, convinced she was doing the right thing. [...]

Our patients were innocent victims of the infamous 'Retreat from Málaga',[6] a disastrous war-time event that became destined for history; an extraordinary exodus described at the time as 'the greatest evacuation of a city in modern times'. It began when the lovely seaport of Málaga was invaded by victorious German and Italian forces aided by anti-government Moors. The brutal murder of prominent government supporters and other atrocities led two-thirds of the population to evacuate rather than live in a Franco-held city. Carrying what possessions they could manage on the sixty-mile trek to government-held Almería, a straggling procession of families set out on foot or rode donkeys in their attempt to reach their goal and haven of safety. During the retreat many were mowed down by merciless machine gunfire, attacked from the air, or killed by terrorist tactics. This slaughter of defenceless civilians shocked the civilised world and inspired volunteers from other countries to enlist in the government cause.

We were daily confronted with the drama of suffering, deprivations, tragedy and emotional trauma experienced by these helpless refugees. In the emergencies of war, only those children requiring the most skilled treatment could be admitted to our fifty bed hospital. With no formal system of nursing in Spain and no title for a trained nurse we were addressed simply as Señorita Marguerite and Señorita Elizabeth. Our favourite 'nursing aide' was a twenty-year-old girl named Concha who gained a working knowledge of English as an aid to better communication. She was eager to learn of medical requirements, followed us around the wards, performed basic nursing tasks with intelligence and compassion and although she had never heard of the heroine of the Crimean War, displayed many qualities of the true nurse. We were thrilled when Concha expressed a wish to go to England after the war to undertake formal nursing training and return to her own country qualified to teach others what she had learnt and practised. We even envisaged her as 'Patron Saint of Spain' in the nursing world! Wishful thinking, indeed. When I returned to England I wrote encouraging letters to Concha and was saddened to receive no replies or ever learn of her whereabouts. [...]

Marguerite and I found it difficult to relate to the Spanish doctor in charge of our hospital, mainly because of his severe reticence which was probably due to the language barrier. A short, swarthy complexioned man, educated in Madrid, he had never been outside his own country, had no knowledge of Nurse Training Schools and spoke no words of English. Although different in culture, knowledge and medical understanding, Marguerite and I set out to achieve a working harmony through diplomacy, tact, respect for the doctor's points of view and obedience to his orders. However, throughout our stay, the doctor maintained a cloak of professional reserve, expressed surprise that we were able to perform certain skilled, technical tasks and held to an unbounded faith in the administration of medicine and drugs by hypodermic injection. A serious man in our presence, his manner changed dramatically as he smiled and chattered to mothers who brought their children to Out-patients. I was often curious to know what he was saying to those of his own race. For our part, we increasingly found the doctor's technique, diagnosis and professional practice questionable to say the least. We really could not help deploring his scant regard for hygienic practices and ethical standards. We were quite unconvinced of the efficacy of the hypodermic injection method he frequently ordered to be carried out; especially in the treatment of childish ailments which only required tender loving care and simple treatment. Nevertheless, we sought to avoid direct confrontation with our appointed medical superior.

Malnutrition was seen in varying stages and because of it, many a child suffered the risk of infection, and many developed painful body abscesses at muscular sites through repeated hypodermic injections. Such was the pitiful case of a four-year-old boy brought to Out-patients in an advanced stage of malnutrition; a pathetic case, his arms and legs were no bigger than those of a six month old baby. Yet, in spite of his skeleton-like frame, no semblance of muscle, and abscesses, the doctor ordered us to give daily injections of a soluble glucose fluid for quick absorption into the deprived little body. We could not do it. It was an ill-considered order for the child had no muscles. I did not feel guilty of insubordination in abandoning the order and encouraged the little patient to take small, frequent quantities of vitamised fluid, a safer, but slower method that lessened the risk of the awful infective abscesses.

Day and night the routine, bustling atmosphere of our hospital could be interrupted by the noisy, ominous sound of the '*peto*', the air-raid siren. Its screeching tones caused sick children, denied the warm security of family life, to leap from their beds in terror and run to us for protection, clutching at our uniforms and exclaiming, with fear in their eyes, 'Franco, Franco, *Señorita!*', as if living again the horrible experience of the 'Retreat from Málaga'. [...]

In quiet times, the traditional practice of *siesta* was a rejuvenating experience if all was quiet. Even in war-time Almería, it could be observed with totality. During this welcome two-hour afternoon period shops closed, blinds were drawn, and people rested and slept as if there was no war on. In our upstairs living quarters it was always a treat to snatch a brief respite from nursing, remove our uniforms and lie supine on inflated rubber mattresses on the flat roof during siesta time. It was a wonderful experience to relax in this way, feeling the southern sun gently tanning our skin and to unconsciously absorb the cloudless blue of the sky and watch the fleeting shadows created by the dark green leaves of nearby trees. [...]

It was very cheap to obtain a professional hair shampoo and set in Almería – a luxury service costing only a few pesetas in a hairdressing salon. One associates upper-class Señoritas with sleek, black coiffures, traditionally adorned with decorative combs and soft, lacy mantillas, although in parts of Spain natural fair hair, without these adornments was not unusual. In fact, fair hair was coveted by some Spanish women who resorted to the use of a variety of bleaches to achieve the desired result. 'Many women would like your hair,' I was told, and one day, walking down the street with Marguerite, an incident occurred for which I could be forgiven for suggesting that 'gentlemen prefer blondes'.

Although not a gentleman in the accepted sense of the word, a strange man suddenly approached from the opposite direction and when he came close to me exclaimed excitedly, '*Rubia, Englaishia, rubia, señorita*' ['Blonde, English, blonde, *señorita*'] with all the exuberance of an ardent admirer. I felt flattered, the centre of attention for one brief moment, and as the stranger walked past, Marguerite explained quietly, 'He is just a poor Spaniard admiring your fair hair which is not often seen in Almería.'

No woman was allowed in the streets of Almería after dark. There was no real night life in the town anyway; the police enforced a strict curfew after sundown and places of trading closed; there was absence of public entertainment, the street lights were extinguished and people remained behind closed doors. [...]

The local cinema was open every day, including Sunday, from 4 p.m. to 6 p.m. There was a surprisingly frequent change of programmes with American and English full-length films captioned in Spanish. Sometimes the original title would be changed, as instanced in the *Barretts of Wimpole Street* which was altered to the whimsical title the *Virgins of Wimpole Street*. Most Spanish patrons arrived early at the cinema and when their number swelled to a crowd they participated in incredible scenes, calling loudly to friends a few rows away, gesticulating and holding loud conversations with nearby patrons. During the showing of the film these loquacious Spaniards registered approval or disapproval of scenes by hissing or loud applause, and right through the show made audible sounds by cracking nuts with their teeth. [...]

Never will I forget the unexpected, exhilarating visit of a gypsy troupe which comprised six lovely teenage girls who lived with their tribe in rock caves north of Almería. They came shyly to our quarters one siesta time and offered to dance for the English *señoritas*. And what a treat we were in for! They wore the traditional gypsy costume of red, swinging skirt, white blouse, black velvet bodice, red head scarf, dangling earrings and soft black shoes; the epitome of grace and Latin beauty as they treated us to a private exhibition of graceful, rhythmic dancing that enthralled us. For brief, precious moments we entered into an avenue of 'escape' where these modern exponents of a centuries-old art moved with lightning speed and appealing lithesomeness; their black eyes flashing with the swishing of their billowing skirts and the haunting sound of hand castanets keeping pace with the swift movements of light feet. The gypsies' visit appeared like a good omen and we interpreted their happy performance as a demonstration of goodwill towards the foreigners who came to help their country in its hour of need.

On another occasion we were honoured by the friendly gesture of the good-natured, laughing mayor of Almería. He gave a formal dinner party for the British nurses and an elite number of guests who included the British Consul, the Chief of Police and a few sophisticated couples. There seemed to be no shortage of food, with the menu offering various kinds of cooked fish, potatoes, pimentoes, fruit salad and an abundance of native wines. [...] From the head of a long table surrounded by his guests, the mayor rose frequently to propose various toasts, and singled me out for one. The incident was memorable because it had never happened to me before. Amid the sound of chattering and eating, the mayor invited the guests to stand and raise their glasses to the 'Australian, the blonde *señorita* in our midst,' and sitting there alone in the unusual scene I imbibed the experience with relish! [...] Another highlight of the occasion was the unchildlike performance of the mayor's eight-year-old son. A diminutive figure, with amazing confidence for so young a child, the boy stood upright on the chair beside his father and quite unabashed, entered into a brief moment of glory. Proposing the toast to the 'brave men of the International Brigade', the child raised high his glass and drank the wine without drawing breath as all joined in the popular toast. [...]

As in other government cities during the war, churches were closed to worship in Almería and it was hard that devout souls were denied that comforting source of 'escape' when they needed it most in their daily lives. All public display of religious symbols was forbidden and Spaniards were well aware that such display could mean death in those days of bitter conflict.

Spiritually, Marguerite was more sensitive to the needs of the people than I was and one day she participated in a compassionate act of religious freedom by which I most fondly remember her. Even perpetuated within the comparatively safe confines of our non-political hospital, what she did that day was brave and she revealed her spirituality in a rare incident. Seven-year-old Pepy was dying of an obscure disease which had developed in his malnourished body and his widowed mother sat disconsolately at his bedside, oblivious of all around her. On this particular day, as the unconscious child's brief life was drawing to a close, Marguerite saw the bowed form of the woman as a prototype of sorrowing Spanish womanhood in war-time, and in reaching out to help her, ignored the risk involved, doing a lovely thing in meeting, in what seemed to her, the mother's immediate need. She quietly left the sick room, went upstairs, took her black and silver crucifix from its secret hiding place, concealed it in her uniform and returned to the bedside vigil. Responding to a light touch on the shoulder the bowed figure looked up as with one swift movement Marguerite held aloft the sacred symbol. Oh! the radiant expression which transformed that tear-stained face is unforgettable. With urgent, shaking hands she reached for the cross and kissed it passionately, an act expressive of love and devotion that spoke louder than words. Deeply moved, I left the silent room feeling that I had been on holy ground.

Saving the Children

Dorothy Davies

Dorothy Davies was Matron of the Friends' Hospital in the Lebanon for five and a half years. At the end of 1937, while engaged in private maternity nursing she read of the need for nurses in Spain. She wrote to the Friends' Service Council and was asked to go to Murcia at once. Throughout the Second World War she nursed in Iraq.

It was just getting light as we drove out to the aerodrome, and the distant Pyrenees were rosy in the sunrise light. Flying was a new experience for me and I was thrilled at viewing the world from this angle. Going through the Pyrenees was awe-inspiring; at one time as we were flying through a pass there was a road above us on the mountain side. As we have heard this winter [1938-39] of the refugees struggling over the snowy passes into France I have thought of how grim the mountains looked even on a summer day. They must have been desolate indeed in mid-winter.

As we approached Barcelona I was so occupied in trying to see as much as possible of the famous cathedral that I did not speculate on the reason for the clouds of dust and stones rising into the air from the city. The noise of the Air France plane excluded all other noises and it was not until we had landed at Barcelona airport that I realised from the conversation of those on the ground that I had watched my first air raid.

Between Barcelona and Alicante we flew over the sea to avoid the Teruel fronts, and the first indication of the results of modern warfare was the sight of five half-sunk vessels in Alicante harbour and another that had been burning for several days. It was heartbreaking to think of the wastage of food and supplies so surely needed by the people.

The shattered houses and bomb craters along the quayside and the notices on every street corner directing passers-by to the nearest *refugio* [underground shelter] gave me a slight idea of the uncertainty of life in Alicante.

It was little wonder that after the intensive raiding at the end of May

[1938] it had been found necessary to move the hospital equipment to a safer spot. This was found at Polop – about thirty miles north of Alicante and in the mountains a few miles inland. The *finca* [estate] was the home of a wealthy merchant and had been unoccupied since the war started. With a little ingenuity it made a very satisfactory hospital, and as the children could be out of doors the whole day a little overcrowding was not serious. [...]

The children who had been brought up from Alicante were mostly convalescent but terribly pale and weak, and it was a joy to see them improving day by day with the sunshine and invigorating mountain air and freedom from anxiety. All had been through repeated air-raids and some had begun to look haggard and old. Some of the new cases who came to us were very, very ill, others were mainly in need of good food and normal healthy life. [...]

We had two small boys who had been found wandering about near the front who were too young to know their names or anything about themselves. One, Tato, was quite well and the pet of the hospital; the other, Raphaelito, was admitted soon after I arrived and was my special charge. He was very poorly with scurvy and painfully thin and so weak that he could not walk. When he improved a bit we put him at table with the others but he had evidently never fed himself with a spoon before, and when he did get something in it he always tipped it out before it reached his mouth! It was surprising how quickly he learned to eat without losing his food on the way.

We also had a number of older boys who had been evacuated from an orthopaedic hospital in Madrid. Some of these were enthusiastic gardeners and planted beds of beans as soon as they reached Polop – in two months the beans were ready to pick. The ground is very fertile where there is water for irrigation. The hospital had two large *balsas* or tanks for irrigation, and when these were filled we used to have them for bathing. I used to take in such of the children as were well enough for a good swill before they went to bed – some loved it, others were a bit scared. The land belonging to the house had been divided between five peasants who worked it for themselves. Here in the mountains seed-time and harvest and the routine of agriculture seemed to go on undisturbed – true it was old men and women and boys who worked in the fields but there was little to remind us of war except that for weeks together we were without bread or flour or potatoes. It was difficult to provide enough filling food to satisfy the children's appetites without these staples but we were able to buy some fruit and vegetables from the villages round about.

One early morning I went to market with Juan, a refugee from

Málaga and our general factotum and a great stand-by. We walked along behind a borrowed donkey whose capacious panniers we hoped to fill with supplies for the hospital. They were filled with large tins which had held Force [wheat flakes], chocolate etc, which we were taking to the tinsmith to be made into buckets as there were none to be bought.

There was a large market place but there were only two short rows of women with anything to sell, and they had eggplant, green peppers and cucumbers and grapes, a few bananas and lemons and some apricots, but the last all had grubs in. Next week when we came there were no vegetables to be bought as the government had fixed the price too low and those who had fruit and vegetables would not sell.

When I left Spain in January [1939] the only things for sale in the market were radishes, everlasting spinach, occasionally a few oranges and snails.

Life passed fairly quietly at Polop, we used to hear the bombs falling on the coastal towns when the wind was in that direction and occasionally we saw the raiders on their way back to Majorca. The main events were the visits of the American *camionetta* from Murcia with stores. One day after two months at Polop they brought an SOS from Murcia for me to go and relieve there as in the meantime a new nurse had come out to Polop.

On the journey we spent a few hours at the seaside holiday camp which Francesca Wilson had established for refugee children on the sea shore. They ran entirely wild and enjoyed themselves immensely. [...]

We heard that there was a lot of illness amongst the children in the Casa Pablo Iglesias. This *refugio* was for transient refugees and was a terribly depressing place. It was an enormous block of flats created before the war and for some reason condemned before it was ever finished. The windows had no glass in them and neither walls nor floors were finished. It was a wet December evening and nearly everyone was in bed to keep warm – lying on the floor, children and grown-ups huddled together under what cover they had collected. We arranged for several of the most ill to come into hospital next day, and I carried a baby with chicken-pox back in my arms. Her mother had typhoid and the baby was in bed beside her. It was from the *refugios* that most of the patients in the Murcia hospital were drawn. [...] Most were acutely ill with typhoid, pneumonia, TB, measles, diphtheria, whooping cough etc. We had a ward of babies whose main trouble was malnutrition. These feeding cases took much patience in nursing and had many set-backs. It was impossible to feed them on a normal diet as they had never had it and their little tummies could not stand it. They came out in spots or got diarrhoea, and we had to keep them in a long time and increase their diet very slowly. Some of the babies were like little skeletons. […]

Refugee children going out of hospital were able to spend a month at a convalescent home which the government had founded in the mountains on the edge of the Murcia plain. Others who did not go here came back to hospital for a midday meal for a week after they were discharged. We had a school for all the children who were up in both hospitals and any who liked could come to school after they had left the hospital. I regret to say that not many came after their week of dinners was over.

At Christmas under the guidance of the *maestra* [teacher] they prepared an entertainment for the children who were in bed. That and the Christmas trees proved a wonderful thrill, and every child had a present from toys sent by the children of America.

Food was very short though we were privileged in being able to import supplies from England. We used to have great crises when ships were delayed, but never actually had no food to give the children. […] We had corned beef until it ran out. When we opened our last case we found that the top layer was tins of beef, and underneath the box had been filled up with bricks! We hoped that the pilferer was hungrier than we were. Fresh meat was almost unknown, once I saw and smelt something savoury frying on a little charcoal stove in the street. It looked like rabbit but was probably cat!

We did have turkey for Christmas but you should have seen it – the moment it was plucked it was chopped into tiny pieces and quite unidentifiable. In Spain birds are never roasted whole. With the addition of a couple of rabbits also chopped up small there was enough for a tiny piece of fresh meat for all who were well enough and (for) maids and nurses, and I think that was the biggest treat of all – the Christmas food.

The Stricken South

Esther Farquhar

Esther Farquhar *from Wilmington, Ohio, was the first relief worker to represent the AFSC in Spain. Esther had graduated at Wilmington College and in social service work in Cleveland. She had taught in Cuba and was Professor of Spanish at Wilmington College and High School. In Murcia she took over relief work started by Francesa Wilson.*

Hotel Victoria, Murcia,
Spain

1 June 1937

The American Friends Service Com.
20 South 12th St.
Philadelphia, Pa.
EUA

Dear Friends:
I finally seem to be settled enough to have a few moments in which to tell you where I am and why [...]

On May the 29th we came to Murcia, driven in a lovely big car belonging to the Ministerio de Asistencia Social y Trabajo, which is a more or less new set-up since the new government came in on the 15th of May.[7] [...]

Murcia is in the midst of rich farm land but its people have always been very poor. The wealth of the landlords has been confiscated by the government but the people are still poor, and the local government has very little. They were literally swamped with refuges, having to use any building available regardless of its fitness. They say the population has about trebled but income and food have not. They have been putting their greatest efforts into trying to get the refuges scattered in the surrounding villages and the children into colonies, and they have sent out thousands, but the conditions under which the remainder are living must be improved, and they are very grateful for any assistance which can be brought from outside.

We were very much delighted when the physician's first statement was that they would like to set up a milk station for the babies and do the thing scientifically. He thought we should start with the babies under one year of age. Calculations were made and it seemed wise to start with one hundred babies, since we have only one hundred cases of milk in Spain and when the other two hundred ordered will reach us is so uncertain, this will give us about a month without danger of having to change the kind of milk. The orange juice will be furnished locally for it is abundant, but the flour which is to be toasted and added in small quantities will have to be furnished from outside. [...]

The only thing that seemed to be lacking then was bottles and the nipples, five a day for each baby. They thought that a supply that would carry us for more than a month would cost about 1,500 pesetas. [...]

This morning Eleanor Imbelli and I accompanied Sr Montalbán to Cartagena to get the bottles from a glass factory there. We had a very delightful drive and enjoyed seeing old Carthage, but the glass factory was closed for lack of raw materials. We were told that there were factories running in Barcelona and Valencia. [...]

It may sound extravagant to you to try to supply each mother with each bottle all prepared, but if you could see the conditions in which they are living you would understand. They plan to begin by weighing and examining all the babies, and making records for each, and those hundred that we shall feed will be weighed every day, and examined once a week by the physician. The sick ones will be sent immediately to the new hospital which is being opened today. Surely we can thus lower the death rate which has been about 50% for this age among the refugees here. [...]

2 December 1938

[...] I found that the relations of the [Almería] hospital staff and the two men who had been the back bone of the hospital, were very strained indeed, and it may have been due to that, and to the tactlessness of Aguilera in some matters, but from the point of our decision [to move them to Murcia] the English people were extremely unco-operative. The Spaniards resented their attitude and so expressed themselves to me rather freely.

I think I shall tell what the doctor said, because he expressed a feeling which has been manifest in the other hospitals also. He said he never felt at home in the English Hospital. They served him tea and said 'thank you – thank you – thank you', but he never felt that his orders were being obeyed. He had not been on the job very many days, but he found that the doctors that had gone before him either had not known what they were doing or did not care, for the children were not receiving the right treatment, and the whole situation had made him feel very badly. He hopes that now with the hospital entirely under his personal supervision, that it will be a real hospital where scientific work will be done. The difficulty has been that the English nurses feel themselves far above the Spanish doctors in their knowledge of hygiene at least, and are very much opposed to the use of so many injections,[8] and you can easily understand that this attitude on their part has made it very difficult for the Spanish doctors who are giving their time and services to our hospitals.

In passing let me say that Don Amalio in the Murcia hospital finally told us that he would have to resign if the nurses did not have confidence in him. After a rather difficult session of the doctor with the nurses, he decided that he could continue. Three of those four nurses have gone home, and I am very happy to say that the new administrator, Dorothy Morris, has worked with the Spanish doctors in the hospitals at the front enough to realise that even though their methods are different, they are good doctors and she thinks the English nurses should adapt themselves to the physician under whom they work. I believe that Mary Elmes also has more of this attitude, and so feel easy about our future relationships.

There were two tuberculous children whom they [the English nurses] wanted to bring to Murcia, but which I could not allow, since our hospital is not adapted to sanatorium purposes. It was arranged to give the families beds and to take food to these children every day in their own homes, and the nurse promised to keep in touch with them. Incidently the problem of the tuberculous children is one which is very pressing, and I hope that we may help to meet it soon.

There was also a probable syphilitic boy whom the English girls had grown very fond of, and wanted to take to Murcia. Don Carlos felt that he should be taken to the Provincial Hospital where they could test his blood and give the proper treatment, which our hospitals are not equipped to do. The nurses were extremely unhappy about my decisions in these cases.

Está la Guerra!

Emily Parker

Emily Parker, from Richmond, Indiana, went to Spain in February 1938 and worked in Murcia with British and American personnel. She was the former secretary of the Young Friends Movement, the Quaker youth organisation, and had been involved in relief work in the depressed coalfields of West Virginia and Kentucky.

Monday morning came and with it the thrill of crossing a new frontier. First we came to the French police and then a little further along to the Spanish guards. I shall never forget the soldier who came out and asked for my passport and papers. He read the letter written by Fred Tritton which said I had come to help the children, and he stood there a minute and tears came to his eyes and, without looking at any other of my papers he said, 'Pase, Camarada.'

It is impossible to describe the beauty of the view as we came down from the frontier. The great high mountains covered with snow and the blue of the sea … The houses are all of stone or mortar and all built together and on a curve, if that gives you any picture. It takes slow driving and a continual blowing of the horn. When the front wheels are around one curve the back ones are still rounding the last. It is easy to see why the people would be completely lost if these little villages were bombed because there are no open spaces and the streets besides being so crooked are also very narrow … Well, so much for traffic. Anyway it is different from the Skyline Highway from New York, I am not saying worse and I am not saying better, just Diff. […]

In Barcelona I stayed at the English Friends Center … It was a beautiful place. (Large central hallway with fountain, etc.) It was, however, bitterly cold when I was there because all of these houses are made of stone and have nothing in them but tile floors and when they have had no heat in them for a couple of years they do get chilly. […]

It snowed for three days while I was in Barcelona, a thing never heard of before. It was really beautiful until you remembered that it only increased and intensified the already too great suffering. Watching people shivering in the cold I am sure I was more uncomfortable with a heavy coat than I could possibly have been without one. And one feels disgustingly healthy somehow. [...]

We came on to Murcia and arrived just in time to eat supper with Mr Lantz (Mennonite worker) at the hospital. This hospital was less adapted for this use though it really is excellent. (English head nurse, two other English nurses, 9 Spanish nurses.) Most of the children are typhus cases here – refugees from Madrid in the main – a few from Málaga. Some of them are sorry sights. But some are up at least part of the time and have had great fun with the games I've shown them. They have organised a school here in the afternoon. Two young teachers come after they finish with their school. I gave them the peg board for the little ones to teach counting and color. It was a thrill to watch them. There is one poor little thing four months old just brought in. It looks like a dead rat. I don't see how it can live. It's hard to wish it would because its chance for even food is so slight – even if it should live – but when you see its mother hovering over its little bed you have to hope for her sake.

There is one baby about two that is a perfect example of what war does. In the first place he is the queerest looking piece you could ever imagine – absolutely pathetic – so ugly! But I've grown fond of him – he seemed so sad. I took him in the brightly colored ball and it was the first time I ever saw anything like light on his face. He caught on pretty quickly to the way it worked. Poor little thing, nothing to do but sit in bed all day. I think this hospital work as it is carried on here is one of the best pieces of work we do. The nurses were also all refugees – so are all the others who work about the place. Francesca Wilson (English worker) saw to it a garden was started here so now they have vegetables from it. Many people have given them chickens because they couldn't feed them any more so they are developing a poultry yard ...

The little baby just died. It's the war! When one sees so many cold, ragged, dirty homeless orphans one realizes that there are many things worse than death. But ... I keep saying, What if it were Ann or Freddie or Louis? It seems very different when you do that.

Last night the stars were very bright. They seemed closer and brighter than I'd ever known them, even more so than at Winni tho it is hard to believe. We have a wonderful roof here. I went up and saw the light on a far mountain. It's amazing the way light can pick out definite objects. I now understand, 'There's a light upon the mountains'. [...]

Plans were laid for going off at nine this morning with clothing, food, etc. to a place which is about 125 or more kilometres from here.

It was really beautiful. In some ways it is like a great desert. The mountains rise like sudden surprises out of the most unexpected places and are more like great piles of soft dusty earth than anything else. Some places must have a great deal of mineral deposit for some of the mountains have much color … All in all it seems as if once there must have been a terrific eruption and a huge pre-historic volcano had belched up this section of the country and then disappeared …

At last we arrived at our final destination about one o'clock. We went first to the home of the woman who has charge of the Evangelical Mission. She is an English woman and very definitely that – the good strong husky beef-eater kind. She has been in this place for fourteen years. Since her Sunday School was waiting I said we should go there first. So we went and would you believe it there were well over 200 there. I had a good surprise when I went in for here was this good solid Britisher up in front with a great LONG stick which she used for a wand and on her head a black lace veil. I could have easily pictured a Spanish lady in it but not this English costume with the good strong shoes. Well, she waved the wand and they sang such things as are NOT sung in the Arch Street meeting house and she would say 'God is love' and then lean over and crack some *chico* [lad] on the head with her wand because he was whispering and so it went – love spoken but the rod practised. However I am sure she had a good heart and the children all probably love her.

We had a very nice meal of bread and wine and goat. Whenever I get a small-boned animal I always try to believe it is goat or rabbit and not cat but these are no days to be fussy. Also we had tea. Although the lady said she had been in Spain so long she had forgotten how to speak English I noticed she made tea after the English way. […]

We left the clothing and food to be distributed by these people among the refugees and brought back a sweet little brown kid with us who is I am afraid destined for one of the *meriendas* [snacks] which we have in the afternoon for the children here from the *refugios*. I don't think I shall go that afternoon for I grew attached to the little thing on the way home. Dear, dear, *está la guerra*!

Before it was completely dark the new moon showed itself over the hill and last and best of all the evening star. Another day of fighting was over. Another day of trying to help in a small way these people. […]

P.S. The Baby Died

Florence Conard

Florence Conard *served in Spain and France for the AFSC from July 1938 until December 1939.*

[July 1938]

In many ways, Murcia seems to be an oasis of quiet. But certain things keep reminding us of what is happening outside. The soldiers, for instance, both wounded and well, the military trucks, the posters, the refuges and underground protections which have been built 'in case of accident', all these are convincing us of the reality which exists just beyond. One of the most appalling things to me is the fact that so many of the most terrible conditions here are not just war conditions, but are pre-war conditions. As someone has said, its very hard to discriminate between what should be done as an emergency program to meet suffering caused by the war, and what should be left until later for a more permanent social program. Yet the very apathy of the people towards these conditions is a blessing, considering the added misery that would exist if the people had had a background of education and hygiene. […]

27 July 1938

Just around the corner from the house where we eat lives a gypsy family. Lives? Well, they may call it that. Actually I have no idea where they sleep, but I do know that when I come past there after breakfast they are sitting there, mother, grandmother and several wee, naked children; and at night when I go past again they are still there, At meal-time they are working at some dark brew which is probably their whole meal, and this morning the mother had just finished punishing the little girl for breaking a bottle. All out on the street. There is nothing colorful or dramatic about them, except perhaps their faces, which show immediately that they are neither of Spanish nor Moorish blood, but of some dark race that came out years ago from the mysterious central regions of Europe. Gypsy faces are marvelous …

Dark, somewhat heavy, with prominent strong jaw-lines, deep eyes slanted just a little, and straight black hair worn almost always directly back from the face. Their bodies are wiry and slim, all too often covered with clothing so ragged and grimy that their native beauty is completely hidden. [...]

27 September 1938

Some time ago I was at the hospital for supper with the English nurses. After the meal, they slipped into the babies' room to see a little tyke that they didn't think would last the night. The child was supposed to be suffering from kidney trouble, but was actually an excellent example of a typical 'war baby'. It was about six months old, its head one third of all its tiny body. Its arms, I'm not exaggerating, were no bigger around than my forefinger and its loosely-covered fingers just hung from the wrists. Its eyes and cheeks were sunken and its jaw and cheek bones were so prominent as to seem completely naked of skin. Already it had begun to gasp a bit for breath, moving its head back and forth on the pillow as though the very motion would give it more air. Calcium was lacking in its body among other things. No bomb holes, or refugees, or women's tears and sob stories can move me so much as that struggling little life, so helpless against external diabolical forces. Just a PS, the baby died.

6 October 1938

About noon we drove out in the car and happened to have a puncture. The driver took the car to the garage, but it did not return until almost seven thirty that evening and we still had to make Murcia. So we started out. Five miles from Almería we stopped at a vineyard to pick a few grapes. I kept wishing that I could put up a tent in the vineyard under these vines that grow just above my head so that all I had to do to eat grapes was to open my mouth! The grapes were warm and sun sweet and the bunches were twice as large as my head in some cases. Our pause was very dear, however, for the driver discovered that another tyre was rapidly losing air, so he turned around and sailed back to town leaving us in the vineyard. He did not return for several hours, and the kind-hearted *cortijera* [farmer's wife] offered us dinner which included some homemade bread made of the whole wheat!! Our car returned at last and we again started out. We arrived in Lorca, where we were expected early that evening, at three o'clock in the morning. We stopped in front of the doctor's house, but though we had the expert knocking of our *carabinero* friend, the driver, we could waken no one. However, we did disturb some police guards who came around to find out what we wanted.

We explained that I was supposed to stay in Lorca to help start a canteen for the children and that my friends had to go right on, so we started out to find a room for me. We tried various hotels, but they were all full and at last we found one in a rooming house. Can you see us, walking down twisted, cobbled streets with only a narrow strip of star-pricked heaven above us, lighted only by the glow of two cigarettes? Tired as I was, the stillness of that Spanish town crept into me and rested there. So, I bade my friends goodnight and went up to my dimly lighted room to bed. I noticed that I had no top sheet or blanket, so I put on a sweater and lay down. Several hours later I woke up long enough to see a small dark shadow scamper across my pillow, but I was still weary enough to do no more than brush it off and return to my broken sleep. The moral of his experience and others is 'When about to sleep in a strange bed, do not investigate and you will rest more happily'. I never could have enjoyed a second night in that bed, but the first one was not a problem. [...]

Of Houses and Horses

Ruth Cope

Ruth Cope, *an American Quaker from Chicago, served from July 1938 until June 1939, in Spain and with Spanish refugees in France. She was accompanied by her husband who was Secretary of the AFSC in Chicago.*

Calle de San Nicolas 25
Murcia, Spain
21 September 1938

Dear Family:

We have at last a house. This is a great pleasure to all of us as it is a commodious sunny house, and very clean with a great deal of white tile and plaster. The owner of the house lives below so everything is tended to very well. It is built along the lines described in our first Latin book, that is the rear of the house is built around a court. This court is open to the basement and must be used in getting from one room to another (except for the rooms in the front of the house). This is a very sociable arrangement as whenever you carry a dish from the kitchen to the dining room you can just look over the little iron railing and see what the maid below is carrying from her kitchen to her dining room. The babies in the house find it a particularly companionable arrangement and call up to us whenever they see us around. There is a glass roof over the court now which keeps out rain and wind. Below with the babies are three bird cages which house an extensive collection of canaries and finches.

While on domestic matters, it tickles me just a little to be using two of Mrs Krauel's dish towels, which I providently brought with me, in this little tile kitchen with the tile stove built for little fires of charcoal and the hand-moulded ledge above the stove for pots and pans. Above the stone sink, in which are cut two circular wells for washing dishes which drain into each other (the usual method), is the inevitable wooden plate rack. I always thought a plate rack was the ideal way to keep odd plates and now I have one. Gee. We also have another

— 213 —

wooden rack for pans and dippers, etc. There are cupboards under the stove for wood or charcoal and a rather dank cupboard under the sink. All possible surfaces have the usual tile about six inches square with which all Spain seems to be made. They come mainly in red and white and gray, and often with all over designs. Some times vivid blue is used for wall tiles. We have also a table and two chairs and a big earthenware jar big enough for Lowell Cox to hide in (any four year old). Our particular kitchen is fitted with a portable gas stove but this is quite a flourish. [...]

14 October 1938

Dear Mother

[...] You can never tell just when you have gotten to the bottom or the top of a Spanish house as they have outdoor porches and rear chickens and rabbits at all possible sublevels and elevations. In addition to our ground floor where the washing of clothes takes place and which seems to have once had a corner for a *burro* [donkey] there are two other levels for chicken culture on porches or the roof and the floor we live on, devoted only to humans, as yet.

The roofs here take pretty much the place of a front yard and practically every house in the block has a little whitewashed penthouse and flourishing cactus and other plants. Most of the plants are familiar to the sight, but I am not much of a botanist. I wonder if Dr Allee knows if the flies and mosquitoes here are the same as those at home. They are the most persistently international thing I have struck so far. Leather lumberjackets and Listerine tooth paste are two other notably international features. The tooth paste is quite a scarcity and tooth brushes are already luxuries, nay, are even in the heirloom stage as they cannot be bought. [...]

You doubtless read of the bombings of Cartagena on the night of the 10th. We could see the strings of red flares rising over the mountains that lie between us and hear the detonations. As a spectacle it was quite similar to watching the 4th of July rockets from the porch at Bowling Green. We were up on the roof in the brilliant moonlight watching the southern sky while in the streets below the children were playing and screaming uproariously as children always do when allowed to play late at night on a warm evening. [...]

13 November 1938

Dear Family,
I ought to start burbling 'Noel', 'Happy New Year' etc, as this will have to be the Christmas letter. Armistice Day came and passed in gloomy oblivion, and I suppose Christmas, too, will be received with mixed feelings.

I am still content to leave the mechanism of war to those who enjoy the art, but the psychologies of war that were always an unknown quantity to me are becoming clearer. Always a mixed picture. The woman who has lost most of her property rises above it, almost. Another is completely crushed by his change in fortune and we can hardly draw him away from the miseries he nurses. Some seem truly oblivious of property loss and throw themselves into the work at hand. And with the poor, mentioned you remember in the Bible, the line between Greed and Need is hard to draw. As for the underlying conditions of the war itself, everybody has a totally different notion. [...] Our best friends here, of course, enjoy much the same political inclination that we allow ourselves, although there is much we do not agree with, and stay silent about. [...]

6 December 1938

To finish up with the horses, as I said the horses are congenitally international and move along to the tune of Whoa! and a kind of cluck, similar to the sound used at home. Not the 'giddap' of fiction. Sylvester reports seeing horses tandem. This tandem business is hitching up one animal in front of the other, so close that if the front animal does not keep on the move he will be given a nudge from his friend in the rear usually about 12 inches behind him. They are very clever, these front animals, at keeping just out of kissing distance in the rear withut pulling any of the weight. The only clear reason I can see for hitching up so many animals this way is to exercise the whole stable at once. From two to five animals are seen. They are never all the same sort. The lead is usually a donkey, the rear ones are larger donkeys, mules and horses. The big teams are most frequently seen with the great wine barrels which are slung, by the aid of a chain and pulley arrangement, between two big wheels. They get it just off the ground and then start off with little clearance. Sometimes these big barrels will be slung one below the cart and one in it. They just have to have the horses one in front of the other or they would *never* pass each other in the street. The miraculous part of the whole business is that the reins are fastened to the top of the cart (when the high carts are used) and the driver doesn't get within six feet of them but walks at the *rear* of the cart. Indeed, often only the first horse has reins at all, the donkeys, etc. up in front are led by an inner light, if at all. The idea of walking in the rear is to apply the great complicated brake to the wheels when necessary. He will yell at the horses and then heave on to the brake. You can imagine the tug of war that takes place when the lead horses are a bit confused. These Spaniards are some people! Another advantage of walking in the rear, especially when there is only one *burro*, is that all carts have just one big wheel on each side and by pushing heavily on the tail end of the cart you can spin it around a little and poke one of the shafts into the *burro*'s soft tummy. This usually conveys quite a definite idea to the *burro* and he will turn aside. You will see that getting one of these carts to change its direction involves considerable strength and powers of suggestion. It certainly involves much higher powers of cooperation between man and beast than just pulling at a bit in a tender mouth. The only difficulty is that the drivers are most obliging and will usually shift to the proper side of the road when a *camion* [truck] approaches, but as the shift involves quite a lot of readjustment in the minds of *burros* 1, 2, 3, 4, and 5, it takes quite a while, and the *camion* driver who has been sliding over the good Spanish roads at 40 or 50 miles an hour, has difficulty in choosing between the right or left ditch or the middle of the caravan. I shall certainly miss these carts at home.

Christmas – Once a Year

Martha Rupel

Martha Rupel *was a nurse who went to Murcia with the
American Quaker group. She represented the Church of the
Bretheren, a sect whose members had emigrated from Germany to
the USA in the nineteenth century. They were known as Dunkers
or Dunkards because of their practice of annual ritual immersion.
Martha served from July 1938 until December 1939 in Spain
and France.*

Calle San Nicolas, 25
Murcia, Spain
8 January 1939

My dear Friends: [...] The Christmas season is over and I appreciate
your thoughts of me at that time as you expressed, so feel I must tell
you of my Christmas here. We had a very enjoyable season
considering all the grief and sadness that is all around us all the time.
On Sat. four of us 'young' girls, or shall I say spinsters? went to Polop
where we have a small Children's Hospital. It is about 75 miles from
here, up along the Mediterranean sea coast, then back a few miles into
the mountains. It has a beautiful location and away from town, so it
was a delightful rest to be in the country away from the crowds and
where there was peace and quiet. It was very cold, but there was a
fireplace before which we could toast our shins and we did plenty of
this too. After three days of this mountain air we dreaded to return to
Murcia and to the realities of life and to the struggles before us.

On Christmas Eve we were all invited out to a Spanish home to
celebrate. At about 9 o'clock we sat down to a feast of artichokes and
kid which was very tasty, considering the amount of garlic used. We
then sat around the open fireplace, watching the flames flare up with
each gust of wind which was whistling and whirling around the house
outside, while the Spanish people sang their songs and danced some
of their provincial dances. Each province has its own typical songs and
dances and as all these were refugees we had quite a variety of these.

They love to dress up in their typical costumes and perform in them, but now they have so little with which to do it. The evening was very quiet and peaceful and quite informal. When anyone felt like singing they just sang, and surprisingly so most of the songs were solos, although the Spanish people love group singing.

Christmas day was ideal, bright and clear, altho cold enough to have ice over the swimming pool. The morning was spent in taking a walk in the hills and overlooking the blue, blue sea, wrapping gifts and decorating the Christmas tree. The decorations consisted mainly of articles made by Pepe, the boy of 12 who has been in the hospital for nearly a year. These articles were made of paper, cardboard, tinfoil, and tin cut in various shapes, and a few balloons which added color. It really looked lovely when finished. In the afternoon the children gave a program of songs, dances and recitations, and the older girls gave a little play which Pepe had written, directed, and for which he had made the costumes. It was all very well done as the children love to perform and were not at all self-conscious. The toys were then given out to the little tots and the older ones each got one of the Friendship suitcases. I wish you could see all the joy that these suitcases bring. They were so happy with everything, and especially with the dolls as many of them had never had more than a few stones and sticks for a doll before. Paper, pencils and crayons were also prized very highly as none of these articles are to be had. Refreshments were then served to the crowd which included the mayor, a few other officials and several interested people from the villages nearby. After supper the evening was spent around the fireplace talking. It was a delightful day and one in which it was hard to realise our purpose in being here – very different from Madrid which was shelled heavily that day. When, Oh when, will peace and good-will come into the hearts of men!

Monday was another delightful day. After a leisurely eaten breakfast, which in itself was a treat as we rush around so here, an English nurse and I climbed one of the mountains back of the house. We went clear around it, got into snow and crawled over snow banks etc. Snow is rather unusual (they have unusual things here too) for this part of Spain. Coming down the other side we ran into so many goat tracks or trails, that we soon lost our own, so we just kept coming down, climbing over rocks on our hands and knees, jumping ravines, and always wondering if we would have to climb all the way back to get out. We also got into mud which clung to our shoes, just as what I always thought, only Iowa and West Virginia mud could do. We arrived safely after five hours of hiking. [...]

New Year's Eve we Americans were out to a German home for

supper where we again had kid. After supper we all went to our hospital here in Murcia to be with the Eng[lish] nurses to see the New Year come in. This group was made up of Eng[lish], Swiss, Irish, American, and one from New Zealand and one from So[uth] America. It is a Spanish custom to eat grapes as the clock strikes midnight – one grape at the time of each strike and if you succeed in doing it you are supposed to have a successful year. I succeeded, but when No.12 had struck I found my mouth was full of hulls and seeds. I guess we did not have the right kind of grapes. We were listening on the radio to hear Big Ben from London, but when 12 came and we could hear nothing we supposed we had the wrong station and as the Cathedral clock began to strike we all hurriedly ate our grapes, then one bright chap remembered that we were one hour ahead of England as we have daylight saving time here, so we had to count out more grapes and wait until one o'clock for Big Ben and New Years (God's time). With all that my year ought to be successful.

New Year's day we were all invited out a few miles to a Swiss home for a turkey dinner. It was a community affair as a Swiss couple gave the turkey, the Quakers tried for several weeks to fatten it, and another Swiss family furnished the other part of the dinner. A good time was had by all. And yet these are not all the festivities. I had a birthday last week and the foreign staff came in for a surprise. Our German friend stirred up a cake and took it to the baker and implored him to bake it right away, but he put it in the oven three hours later so the cake was rather a flop but we ate it anyway as it was the only one we had had here and why should we fret about a little heavy food. He was very upset about it, but after being assured that his spirit and intentions were appreciated he ate more cheerfully. These sound like good times, and they were, but the good old days are gone. No more fresh meat, no more cake, Christmas comes but once a year.

The Beleaguered North

Bronwen Lloyd-Williams and *Lydia Mary Gee*

Bronwen Lloyd-Williams *and* **Mary Gee** *were sent by the Friends' Service Council to the north of Spain in the spring of 1937 to explore the possibilities for Quaker relief work in the area. They had previously been working in Barcelona and Southern Spain. As a result of their reports three cargoes of relief supplies were sent under the charge of Anne Caton. When Santander fell Anne escaped into the Bay of Biscay in a small open boat, as did thousands of others. Many were drowned but Anne's party reached France after sixteen hours.*

A sense of tragedy overhangs Bilbao. The streets are crowded with hungry, haggard looking people, the cafés with occupants who sit reading before bare tables, the only drinks available being camomile-tea and whisky. White bread and meat have not been seen for weeks, fruit and vegetables are a rarity, and the staple diet is beans and rice.

In Santander there is a slightly more cheerful air. Just before our arrival a ship had run the ineffective blockade, and there was rather more variety of food; but such relief is temporary, and the lack of all that is necessary to life is only too evident here too. In Asturias matters are even worse. Belarmino Tomás, the miners' leader, Governor of Gijón, told us that in the winter children walked barefoot and starving through the snowy mountains.

While their physique is undermined by lack of food, the people's nerves are strained to breaking-point by constant air-raids and bombardments from the sea. The sirens sound and the streets are suddenly dense with men, women and children running to the refuges, terrified, yet without showing panic, without disorder, laughing and joking till a silence falls broken by the drumming of the aeroplanes overhead which may discharge their deadly loads causing incalculable suffering and damage. Durango was attacked by General Mola's forces the day after our arrival, when more than a thousand of the civilian population, including nuns and priests, were killed and wounded either by bombs or by machine-gun fire directed at them from aeroplanes, and the town was left a heap of ruins and dead bodies. They are brave people these Spaniards of the North. [...]

There are great efforts at social reform in spite of the war, child-welfare and maternity services are established ... and we saw nuns, 'the little sisters of the poor', still in their habits, working among the old people in Santander, respected by all. They had refused all offers to take them away to France. 'We have known the boys of the Popular Front since they were babies,' they said to us, 'and while there is work for us to do we will do it.' Churches are open and regularly attended in the Basque country, and there is much practical Christianity shown in Santander, where the authorities took great interest in our accounts of Quaker work and asked many searching questions about it. They are proud, and did not willingly ask us for help, but here and everywhere else there was one poignant appeal – 'Take our children away. Save them at least from the horrors of this war.'

Basque Children for England

Leah Manning

Leah Manning, *of Spanish Medical Aid, and Edith Pye, of the Society of Friends, were sent by the National Joint Committee for Spanish Relief, in London, to Bilbao in April 1937 to arrange for the evacuation of 4,000 Basque children to England. Doctors Audrey Russell and Richard Ellis went to examine the children who were chosen.*

I had arrived in Bilbao on April 24 and on the next day had gone to Mass with the Foreign Secretary and his family, spending the rest of the day in his office. The morning of the 26th I spent quietly at the office of *Asistencia Social*, discussing in outline the plans for evacuation. In the afternoon I made my way down to *La Prensa* where a group of journalists had invited me for a drink, among them Philip Jordan and George Steer,[9] who during the next few weeks were to prove towers of strength and encouragement to me. A day begun so quietly was to end in indescribable horror and dismay.

'A raid's coming up,' said Jordan. 'Do you want to go down to the shelter?' I shook my head, so we went outside. Phil's ear had caught the sound of bombers in the air, although there had been no warning. Across the hills to the east the air was alive with Heinkels as wave after wave drove in from the sea. They were followed by Junkers. Horror-striken, the Basques amongst us shouted, 'Guernica! they're bombing Guernica!' It seemed incredible that such a monstrous thing could happen to this quiet little market town, renowned from time immemorial as the home of Basque liberation where, before the famous oak tree, rulers of Spain had traditionally sworn to observe Basque local rights. Helpless to do anything we watched from the hills. Until nearly eight in the evening, incendiary bombs and high explosives rained down every twenty minutes. The town was open and defenceless; it was crowded with market day visitors and as people fled from the destruction they were dive-bombed and machine-gunned from the air. The roads out of the town were jammed with dead and injured: 1,654 killed; 889 injured.

We drove over that night, to find such a scene of utter devastation as will be printed for ever on our minds. It cannot be described in words; only Picasso's 'Guernica' can depict its stark horror. If this raid was intended to destroy the morale of the people it utterly failed in its purpose. Bitter hatred against the Germans, who were responsible, and against non-intervention controls, which were to operate from the end of that month, filled the hearts of the people with a cold fury. [...]

After the evacuations of May 16, I began to feel anxious. It seemed as if we were never going to get away. I wasn't worried about my own safety, although the 'Radio General' was constantly making threats against me. I was afraid that the carefully built confidence would evaporate as it became known that there was a growing reluctance on the part of the British government to accept any of the plans so carefully detailed by the Basques. [...]

I began to send out imploring telegrams – to the Archbishop of Canterbury, to the Catholic Archbishop, to Lloyd George, to Citrine. The answers came back, helpful and encouraging. 'All right,' said the authorities, 'we'll leave it to the Consul to decide.' But Mr Stevenson was adamant. He could not advise His Majesty's Government to accept 4,000 children of all ages. I had played my last card. I thought of England en fête for the Coronation, and for the first time in all those weeks my nerve went. I trailed along to see Philip Jordan and broke into a fit of weeping on his shoulder.

'Please don't cry, chum, we'll think of something. Here I'll give you my beret!' – his beret with its Basque badge, given to him by a soldier long since dead! But he gave me more than a beret. In ten minutes flat, he evolved a complete plan for out-manoeuvring London and taking back with me 4,000 children in family groups with their escorts: just what I had set my mind on doing since I first talked to Aguirre.[10]

'This evening,' began the conspirator, 'we are going with Stevenson, by submarine, to St Jean, to celebrate the Coronation. With the Consul out of the way, your buddy the pro-consul is in charge. Get to work on him. Con him into sending a telegram in the name of the Consul agreeing to your arrangements.' I had no hesitation in doing all I could to persuade Señor Oganguerren to send that telegram. It went off that same night and the reply, in confirmation, came in the morning.[11] Mr Stevenson never knew what had hit him. [...]

At last the night of departure arrived. The quay was a thick, black mass of parents, defying bombs as the children, some happy and excited, some in tears, were taken aboard in orderly companies. Head to tail the señoritas laid out our precious cargo – on the bulkheads, in the swimming pool, in the state rooms and along the alley ways, for all the world like the little *sardinas* about which they were always singing; and out there, in the grey waters, two ships of the British Navy stood by to guard our going.

I don't know if sea-sickness can be brought on by mass hysteria; if so, that was what my children suffered from. For two dreadful days and nights Richard, Audrey and I slipped and slithered from one pool of diarrhoea and vomit to another, giving drinks of water and assuring them it wasn't the fascists who had stirred up the troubled waters against them.

We reached Southampton Water on a bright Sunday morning. Miraculously the señoritas had cleaned up the children and changed their clothes. Many of them had made their Confessions on the Saturday evening, and I was asked by the priest in charge if it would be possible to bring a priest from Southampton to celebrate the Mass. I sent a wireless message, and within the hour my request had been met. I shall never forget that picture – moving in its simple piety, the young kneeling figures with upturned faces – as the Celebrant raised the Host for adoration.

Colonia del Inglés

Esme Odgers

Esme Odgers, *the daughter of a coal miner, was secretary to the Central Committee of the Australian Communist Party and editor of the journal* Woman Today. *She sailed for England saying that she was going for the Coronation of George VI, and then volunteered for Spain. She was in charge of the first children's colony supported by the British National Joint Committee for Spanish Aid. When Catalonia fell she shepherded her charges over the Pyrenees and re-established the colony in France. She married a Spaniard and they lived in South America.*

Colonia Infantil,
Avenida de la Republica,
Puigcerda
30 June 1937

Dear Phil,[12]
We have just received another 68 children from Madrid. Barton Carter, an evacuation worker from the National Joint Committee for Spanish Relief, drove one of the lorries containing 32 children direct. It is good to have an American here.

He told me when they left Madrid the mothers who came to see their children off cried bitterly. But they realised the children had to go. They couldn't go on living in a city where shells were bursting daily in the streets, where bombing 'planes were a constant menace, where food was scarce. Only the day before 17 Italian 'planes had circled insolently over the city – no doubt taking pictures of the working-class quarters, their usual target, for future bombardment. Our group was made up of children who had lived in the working-class quarters.

Spanish children are vivacious, unself-conscious, generous, friendly and well behaved. I may add very demonstrative. I am literally swept off my feet at times and kissed in a most violent manner. Of course, our children had never left Madrid before, and I am told they talked about every curve and hill they passed. When on the second day they saw the beautiful Mediterranean (they were three days on the trip) their pleasure knew no bounds. One little girl in the front seat just stood up and clapped her hands for joy. A little boy kept shouting '*un rio, un rio*' (a river, a river). Barton said he tried to explain that it wasn't a river but a sea, but he paid no attention and kept on shouting '*un rio*'. Crossing the Pyrenees they were again thrilled and never tired of repeating over and over again, '*bonita, bonita*' (pretty).

Passing through the towns and villages, people of all sorts would gather around the lorry and talk to the children and give them sweets or peanuts. Everywhere the youngsters were greeted with friendliness and cheers. The Spanish people are extraordinarily kind to children and would give the shirt off their back to help them.

When they arrived in Barcelona, the Refugee Committees offered the use of a lovely house (the owner had fled the country) where the children could sleep. Most of them had never seen such a place before. I am told they gazed with awe in their eyes at the lovely things the house contained.

They arrived here about 10.30 p.m. We had been busy all day putting the house in order and because we expected them before this time, decided to do a bit of scouting. We arrived at the Plaza and could tell they were there. Excited shouts, '*Salud, niños!*' came from all directions. For children who had been exposed day and night to bombardments, they were astonishing. They stormed in the lorry and then clamored out of it. The noise was terrific. However, despite their excitement, they all looked indescribably poor and dirty. We hurried them off to the colony where we had a steaming hot supper prepared. Soon they were in bed sleeping soundly – a sleep that will no longer be disturbed by murderous fascist bombs.

The children have now been here for three days and it is astonishing to observe how quickly they adapted themselves to the new environment. Only a few days ago they were witnessing the tragic spectacle of war. Today they sing with great enthusiasm. At present they show little or no sign of nervous strain as a result of their experiences, but, of course, the effects may show themselves later in unexpected ways. All, however, miss their parents and are excited about the promise of a photograph to send home.

The 68 children who have arrived during the last three days have been placed in a fine villa called Torre Moner, now known to the local people as Colonia del Ingles. There is a shocking lack of equipment and adequate food. It must not be thought that the organisation is responsible. Ayuda Infantil is not in any way to blame.[13] Literally thousands of children are arriving daily and it is impossible to cope with the situation. We heard only last night that there are 50,000 waiting to be evacuated from Madrid, and that 5,000 children from the Basque country are on their way here through France. We are working furiously on the establishment of a milk canteen to enable the children to have some nourishment as soon as they arrive. A hundred times I think of Australia with its abundant supplies of fresh food. What are we doing out there to relieve the distress of these courageous people? I can only urge that you redouble your efforts.

A Black Cloud

Norma Jacob

*Norma Jacob, an English Quaker, and her American husband
Alfred decided in 1936 to take advantage of the greater religious
freedom in Spain under the Republic and develop a Quaker
Centre there. When the Friends' Service Council began relief work
with refugees Norma and Alfred were put in charge of the Spanish
end of the operation. After Franco's victory they remained in
Spain to continue Quaker work, but in June 1940 Alfred was
arrested and accused of spying. After intervention by the British
government they were expelled from Spain and left to farm in New
England.*

In spite of the brilliant and never failing sunshine, a black cloud
seemed to hang over Barcelona in the last few weeks before we left.
The gay and beautiful city was transformed. Out in the aristocratic
suburb of Saria we watched the agony from a fairly safe distance, but
we could not help sharing in the suffering of those brave people who
have become our friends. Relief workers cannot do much to mitigate
the affects of high explosive (though we were able on one occasion to
come to the rescue when a bomb totally destroyed the kitchen of an
infant welfare centre just at the moment when the day's milk ration
for several hundred delicate babies was being sterilised) but we can
make other burdens a little easier to bear.

From a beginning a little more than a year ago with eleven children,
we are now rapidly approaching the ten thousand mark, and are
struggling to keep pace with the new opportunities that open out
every day. [...]

The saddest cases are those of babies whose mothers are too
under-nourished to feed them, and the very old people who can digest
little but milk; the former get milk perhaps four days a week (what do
they do on the other three?) the latter never get any at all.

Relief work of this kind has results far exceeding the merely
physical improvements in the children's conditions. Her are some
reports from our feeding centres: [...]

The children didn't get any breakfast here before, and I am sure it makes a great difference to their whole life to get a nice warm meal in the morning. And they do like it! ... They were very dirty most of them during the first week, but you should see the change which has already taken place. There is hardly a child now who does not come stretching out his small hands so that we can see how clean they are. The children are neat and tidy too. it must make a difference to feel that someone is taking an interest in them. [...]

Almost the most painful impression one received when visiting refugee centres was of the absolute despair and sense of abandonment felt by the mothers. Even the best local efforts have proved utterly inadequate to deal with so gigantic a problem, and it is only outsiders like ourselves who can attack it at the point of most need by supplying the absolutely indispensible foods for the youngest children of all.

The sense that people in other countries care about what happens to their children and that something effective is being done, on however small a scale, does even more than the food itself to restore to these women hope and confidence and self-respect.

The Uprooted

Kanty Cooper

Kanty Cooper *was a sculptor who had been a pupil of Henry Moore, himself an active supporter of the Spanish Republic. When, in 1937, severe rheumatism prevented her from following her art, she applied to the Society of Friends to be sent to Spain. At the Quaker canteens for refugees in Barcelona she acted as an interpreter. Later she worked with Spanish refugees in France, and as a welfare worker in Greece and Jordan.*

The gravity of the food situation was not at once obvious, for while the people looked thin and ill, they endured uncomplaining. Their courage and grim humour rarely deserted them. 'We Spaniards die dancing,' my Spanish assistant told me, but it took time for me to see the truth of this statement. After waiting for hours in a queue which only produced one small onion, a woman could still joke, telling me it was not even big enough to make her cry. [...]

The crisis of the situation was brought home to me by two incidents. First, the charwoman's small daughter of eight fainted in the middle of a milk distribution. She had no more than a cup of milk for breakfast, I discovered, and the family nothing to eat the day before but boiled turnips for lunch and a lettuce with two tablespoons of rice among the four of them for supper. They finished their bread ration the previous day, 'Because,' the child explained, 'we were so hungry.'

A few days later a woman collecting her milk asked if she might speak to me in private. As soon as we moved away from the crowd she said, in a conspiratorial whisper, that she had heard there were mice in the store. It seemed a very odd remark and I could see no need for the secrecy. However, I told her we had set a trap and caught one.

'Next time you catch one do me a favour and let me buy it.'

'Buy it? Why?' I asked, still more puzzled.

'Naturally, to eat,' she said.

The staff enlightened me. Cats, rats and mice were eaten, but in Spain dogs were not considered fit for human consumption. If any could be found they were sent to the zoo.

'The zoo ought not to exist at a time like this,' I protested. 'You should be eating the animals not feeding them.'

'We have to think of the future,' a man replied, and to my astonishment everyone agreed with him. [...]

It was during this period of frequent raids that I noticed the child Marita. She attended a canteen housed under the glass-roofed courtyard of a municipal building. A huge canvas hung under the glass. Originally intended as protection against the sun, it was now considered an air-raid precaution to catch the glass should the roof be splintered by blast.

Despite my efforts to prevent queueing the people had acquired the habit. They would collect long before the doors were opened, and it was impossible to persuade them to come later when they could pass through without waiting. Several times I noticed a very fair-haired little girl who only appeared when we were due to start. She was never made to stand in line, and the women pushed her to the head of the queue although they would never allow anyone else to go out of turn. I was worried by this apparent favouritism and suspected that she must be a relation of one of our workers.

'Why do you allow the little girl to go in first?' I asked a woman who seemed to know her.

'She has much to do, poor little thing. She must get back to her children.'

'To her children?' I exclaimed incredulously. She could not have been more than twelve or thirteen at the most.

'Her little brothers and sisters,' explained the woman. 'Her mother died in childbirth a month ago and now she has to care for the family. It is for that we allow her to go in first. She can't leave the children for much time. She is afraid there will be a raid and she not there to look after them.'

Marita was self-possessed and businesslike. She would walk in, collect her milk, flash her wide smile at us and depart.

The small figure, dressed in the deepest mourning, was always neat and tidy. Her straight gold hair, scraped back severely from her high forehead and tied with a black bow behind, fell to her waist. Her skin was a rare golden-brown and her eyes large and green-grey. Her colouring was vivid against the dark simplicity of her dress. She was striking now. One day she would be beautiful.

We realized that, with Franco's advance towards Barcelona, air-raids would increase, and we tried desperately to find a safer building in which to house this canteen. In the meantime we had to carry on where we were. One night there were two raids during the hours of darkness, and another started as I was getting up. As soon as

the all-clear went I was driven down to the canteen and dropped off.
The streets were covered with shattered glass which crunched under
the tyres. Men searched for survivors in the ruins, ambulances dashed
past us with men clinging to their sides blowing whistles. I was in a
hurry to get the milk distribution finished during the lull which
usually followed a raid. We worked frantically, our eyes on the time.
Marita arrived late. She was pushing her way through the crowd,
which parted willingly to let her pass, when the first bomb fell. The
ground shook, it seemed dangerously near. Everyone panicked,
women fought to get under the table, surging backwards and
forwards across the yard and shrieking. Milk flew in every direction.
Marita dropped her jug, screaming, 'My children.' She made a dash
for the door where she was caught by the guard. Another bomb fell,
much nearer, twenty or thirty yards down the street. We listened to
falling masonry. Then the whole place shook violently. A bomb had
fallen in the square outside. The glass above our heads shattered and
tinkled down into the protective cloth. Slowly the dust descended,
thicker than a London fog.

The blast caught the guard. He reeled backwards, loosening his grip
on the squirming and kicking Marita. She shot through the door and
disappeared. We held our breath waiting, expecting that the next
minute would be our last. Little Marita would not stand a chance if the
deadly blast caught her in the street. Nothing happened. It took us
some minutes to realise the danger was over. Slowly we relaxed;
woman after woman broke down and wept.

I went out into the road, but Marita had disappeared. I must have
lost all sense of time since the last bomb fell for the ambulances had
already arrived. Two men bandaged a casualty with severe head
wounds. A dead horse lay at my feet, the cart, blown to smithereens,
scattered over the ground. Across the square trees had been mowed to
the ground and a house had one wall sliced off so that it appeared like
an open doll's house, beds, tables and chairs still in place. [...]

Some months later a woman, collecting her ration, was taken with
labour pains. I put her in my van and drove her through streets so
narrow that we had to back when we met a small car. We reached a
high block of tenement flats and parked with two wheels on the
pavement. The stairs were dark, dank and dirty, and we groped our
way up, clinging to the banisters. I saw the woman into her flat on the
sixth floor and was just turning to leave when the door on the opposite
side of the landing opened and Marita appeared. She stared at me in
astonishment.

'Señorita,' she said. 'You here! You must come and visit my family.'

I followed her into a small, unexpectedly light room. A door stood open onto a tiny balcony. Iron palings enclosed it; to each a pot was wired. Aspidistra, plants with variegated leaves and geraniums covered the fencing.

Across the end of the room a washing line was stretched. From it hung small garments and two dripping, spotlessly clean blankets. In the centre of the room five children were having breakfast: a small piece of bread and half a cup of milk. They were quiet and orderly, Marita, it seemed, being a strict disciplinarian. The boys' hair had been plastered down with water, the little girl wore hers in two pigtails which stood out on each side of her face. Although little more than a baby she, like Marita, was dressed in black. They all stopped eating and stared at me. Marita introduced them formally, starting with the eldest. Each got up, bowed, shook hands and said, 'Good morning, señorita,' sat down and remained silent. Marita beamed with pride. She was delighted to have her little family and her gay clean room admired. She had tried to keep everthing just as her mother had left it, she said, and took me to examine a darn she had made in a brother's shirt, the stitches so small they were almost invisible. I asked what the family did when a raid started. I had a vision of Marita marshalling the children down all those stairs to the basement in an orderly crocodile.

'We stay here,' she said, and added, with true Spanish fatalism, 'We can only die once, and if we are going to be killed by a bomb, we shall be killed wherever we are. [...]

As early as August 1938, 32,774 refugees had entered Barcelona, a city with a pre-war population of 1,062,157, and ever since had been pouring in in increasing numbers. They arrived in waves as fresh towns and villages became involved in the retreat of the government forces. They arrived by train or on foot, lugging their salvaged possessions in bursting suitcases or sacks tied with string. They came, blocking the street in carts piled high with bundles, mattresses, cooking pots and, on top, women, children and chickens. The horses and donkeys plodded with hanging heads, the men staggered with weariness. Uncertain what to do, they wandered aimlessly or sat on the pavement hoping to be picked up. Those who found no accommodation housed themselves in the metro.

The seminary was intended as a reception centre where the refugees could be sorted out and dispersed. The task was too great, the place hopelessly inadequate. The people slept in dormitories, men one side of the building, women and children the other. There were no beds, except for people who had brought their own. Mattresses were laid on the floor, one for two people.

Once I found an old woman, lying on one mattress and covered by another. She lay so still that at first I thought she was dead. Near her, on the concrete floor, were the remains of a fire, burnt twigs clustered round a blackened pot. The refugees had supplemented their rations with a cat the night before. The smoke must have drifted into the old lady's face. Ashes lay on her white hair and yellow skin.

The staff were desperately over-worked and the sanitary arrangements were appalling. Since people made use of the passages, the stink was nauseating, and pervaded the whole building. Lack of occupation was almost as demoralizing as the dirt and privation. The old sat listless, the young quarrelled and children swarmed everywhere, yet their spirit was never broken. They believed in their cause, were fighting for their ideals, for their rights and a better way of life. They now shared a common misfortune and this, perhaps even more than the common cause, brought out extremes of generosity and unselfishness. A woman would refuse our offer of clothes, saying she knew that our supplies were limited and others in greater need. We found poor labourers with hungry children of their own adopting those of a dead comrade and bringing them up as part of their family.

I soon discovered that I could rely on the people's co-operation. I would drive a loaded van to a canteen with the certainty that the milk boxes, too heavy for the staff to lift, would be unloaded by unknown, underfed men passing in the street. We were working for their children, they said, it was only right that they should help. No hand was ever stretched out for a tip, which even the poorest would have been too proud to accept. Adversity brings out unexpected virtues and strengths. I felt as if I were looking at the people through a magnifying glass, seeing them as I had never seen them before.

The Fall of Barcelona

Muriel McDiarmid

Muriel McDiarmid *was a civil servant doing voluntary work for Spanish aid committees in London who was seconded to the Quaker relief group in Barcelona in the autumn of 1938. She was one of the last of the group to leave Barcelona and kept a diary of the fall of the city. Afterwards she reported on the conditions of Spanish refugees in France. During the Second World War she was business manager of the journal* Labour Monthly, *and later worked in a US hospital.*

Wednesday 25 January 1939: We listened to the English news and the most absurd statements were made. […] Later we listened to the Spanish (Barcelona) news, which consisted solely of a passionate exhortation to the populace to resist, and to contest Barcelona street by street and house by house. It was magnificent, but tragic. That last day was the saddest I have ever lived through. No newspaper appeared, no cinemas or shops of any description were open, and it was deathly quiet, as there were no air raids after 3 p.m., only intermittent shelling. The telephone was not disconnected ... We spent the day burning all the literature which might have been considered unacceptable to Franco.

After 'the Burning of the Books' we turned our attention to the storehouses, which had been allowed to get into a disgraceful condition by those in charge. This occupied our minds and tired our bodies, and we were able to distribute quantities of food to large numbers of people who came from all parts to take their rations for a week, two weeks, a month. It seemed to us better to let the people have what they wanted then, rather than wait until the fascists arrived and probably took the stores away. […]

The departing government had appointed *carabineros* to guard some of our stores, and this saved some that might otherwise have been broken into by the terrified people, who seemed to think that they would not be allowed to leave their houses after the arrival of the fascist troops. This was, in fact, what happened at Tarragona, but not in Barcelona. Other soldiers of the retreating army just walked away when they reached Barcelona, and returned to their families, where they retired into private life and reappeared a week or two later. They stated they had no ammunition left. Certainly the firing was most sporadic all day.

Wednesday night. The end of the exhortation to 'resist to the end' was greeted by a burst of shelling, but strangely enough the rest of the night, with the exception of a terrible explosion at 11 p.m., was perfectly quiet. To me this was worse than the constant noise we had been hearing for so long, it was so uncanny, and I slept very badly. One develops the faculty of sleeping through at least some of the air raids, and this silence kept me awake. I thought perhaps there had been an ultimatum to expire at dawn. Dawn came and no sign. At 8 a.m. firing recommenced, however not very enthusiastically. We seemed to be completely surrounded, as whichever window we stood at, the firing seemed to come from that direction. It was impossible to know whether the firing came from government or fascist troops.

What was so uncanny was the calm between the bursts of firing. Six British subjects (four of whom could not speak English) slept at our house last night and went off in a lorry to the British Embassy at Caldetes this morning (*Thursday, 26th*) in a great state of panic. We learnt later that they had been evacuated on a battleship. I do not think many British subjects remained in Barcelona throughout the occupation. The Consul and his staff stayed, but the Embassy staff of course left long before. We ourselves kept all our things ready packed to leave at a moment's notice if necessary.

The English news (wrong again) stated that Franco's men started to occupy Barcelona at 12 noon, but we heard nothing of it until about 3. Even the *Hoja Oficial*, the official (fascist) statement on the subject, only states 2 p.m. We were exhausted by the constant noise of shelling and rifle fire and (what was far worse) the unending flights of dozens and dozens of planes around and around the city, flying low over the houses. They dropped no bombs but caused great terror among the people. Worn out, therefore, with strain and the really hard work of the day before, we had retired to our separate rooms for a rest not with any hope of sleeping but just for a little solitude. [...] I spent the rest period on the roof and was in time to see the first tanks entering down Bonanova. The men were seated on the tanks with guns pointed at the pavements, though I did not see them fire. They were all waving the red and yellow flag of Franco. There were very few people in the streets in this suburb of Barcelona (Saria), and even fewer cheered or gave the fascist salute. A friend of ours was in the street and saw (so he claims) the first Moor to enter Barcelona. The Moor had a flag in one hand and a hand grenade in the other. Raising the hand with the flag, he said, looking meaningfully at our friend: '*Viva Franco!*' Not knowing whether the Moor might throw the hand grenade if he did not answer, our friend said: '*Si, hombre, Viva Franco!*' without great enthusiasm. The Moors ran nervously one by one across streets, fearing an ambush. The number of people in the streets increased as the afternoon wore on and more and more troops went along the road. There seemed to be about an equal number of Moors and Spanish soldiers wearing the red beret of the *Requetés*, and leading mules. Later, we found that a Moor was spreading his blanket in our garden, but we could not ascertain who had posted him there. Doubtless an officer who had his eye on all the lorries parked there. The Moor was a young and inoffensive lad, who informed us that only the 'Reds' bombed open towns, the Nationalists never did! He was most incredulous when we informed him that the opposite was the case, but continued to hand out cigarettes generously, in return for which someone gave him a pair of socks. At that time, we also had two guards of the Republican regime guarding the house, so we rushed them into civilian clothes as soon as we could. A few days later they reported to the fascist authorities and we believe they were not interfered with. The Moor had walked all the way from the Ebro in the last fortnight.

The entry of the troops was going on at the same time by another road, Diagonal, and every five minutes or so there was a spatter of rifle or light gun fire, which we assumed was every time a tank passed a given spot.

Some people had already hung out the rebel flag of red and yellow, and I am convinced that many of the Spanish people who worked with us were delighted to see the fascists enter. At this time, however, all the Spanish workers had gone home except those who lived in the house.

On Thursday evening the British Consul called and asked us if we would give hospitality to an Englishman who had been in prison under the Republic for thirteen months, and had that morning, together with all the other prisoners, been released. It is to be carefully noted that these men were released by the Republicans, not by the fascists, as so frequently stated in the fascist newspapers. His story contained no hint of the atrocious tortures described every day by released prisoners.

There was no resistance to the entry of the troops as far as we could ascertain, except that we were told that a few shots were fired from the Anarchist headquarters in Durruti; but this was only hearsay. But at about 5 p.m. there came the loudest explosion I have ever heard, from close by apparently, as the windows of the house next door to us were broken. Later we learnt that it was a munition factory blown up by the retreating army and from the ruins the job had been well done, as hardly two bricks remained together of the white building. [...]

Friday morning, 27 January: I went out into the streets this morning to look at the new regime. The town looked like a scene from a Moorish film. Diagonal was completely full of troops. Moors and others, with their horses and mules, and their harness and weapons piled on the ground around them. I have never seen such wretched, thin, saddle-sore animals before. In the main street, Diagonal, Paseo de Gracia, there were masses of people, some of whom appeared to be quite pleased and were cheering and wearing red and yellow ribbons in their buttonholes, but many, many others did not either cheer or give the fascist salute. In the Plaza Catalunya a military parade was being held, the soldiers simply marching round and round, and a cine camera was making a news reel of it. The van on which it was mounted was marked 'Cine Company of Madrid'. The Hotel Colon was supposed to have been burnt down yesterday by the socialists before they left, but the building itself is intact, only internal damage being done.[14] At the present moment all its balconies are crowded with people (almost entirely girls and soldiers) cheering and throwing down leaflets, rather after the American or Russian style, into the square below. On examining these leaflets, they turned out to be socialist anti-fascist leaflets left behind by the socialists! Exhorting the population to resist, and defend Barcelona!

In the poorer streets of Barceloneta and near the Cathedral, the people did not look nearly so happy, and I was able to see the appalling damage that had been done by bombing during the last week. Bad as it had been before, this was far worse. In some streets it was difficult to pick one's way, but even here one could see an occasional (very occasional) red and yellow rag hanging from a house with probably no windows. But all were relieved that the danger of bombing was over, and many people were carrying large bags etc. of food that had been looted from the warehouses. Lentils and rice were spilled all over the streets, and on picking a few up I found they were of better quality than we had been getting.

One old woman was crying softly. From time to time bands of young women rushed hysterically down the wide streets singing and shouting and greeting the soldiers, and loud-speaker vans broadcasting military marches, songs and exhortations were going round. I also heard lorries full of soldiers singing the Horst Wessel song as well as the Spanish national hymn. […]

On returning to the house […] I found that there had been trouble at the storehouse nearest to us. A fascist commandant said we were a red organisation who fed red children. A. protested that we fed all children alike, and that anyway we did not consider children were of any particular colour.[15] 'Oh yes they are, they are red children, they raise their fists. We shall take all the food away from the red children and give it to the white children.' There were a number of small attaché cases which had been sent from children in the United States. In each one was a map of the US with a gold star showing the home town of the child who had sent it. The Commandant pounced on the star, and said: 'This is red.' His knowledge of geography probably did not enable him to recognise the contours of the United States, and seeing a star presumably he thought it must be Russian!

31 January: Our own observations this morning. The bread queues were the largest I have ever seen in my life. The soldiers were beating women with rifles and jabbing them with bayonets. A woman came into the canteen with a bloody face and said a soldier had done it to her. We were told that 80 were shot in the Bull Ring last night. P. (a very right-wing person in the last regime, but she came to no harm for all that) said: 'The Republic was intolerant, but these people are far worse.' The Ritz Hotel is full of German officers.

8 February: A. told P. that they were going to treat every one alike, Reds and all, feed them well, until they were tried and shot; afterwards their widows and orphans would still be treated well!

I saw the *Daily Mail* correspondent who let us read his message before sending it to London. It was interesting to note that all mention of German machine-guns was rigidly censored. By this time you would hardly think they'd mind details like that.

10 February: P. was told that a synagogue has been destroyed by the Germans in Barcelona and all the books burnt.

15 February: In spite of the promise that: 'All those who have not killed their brothers will be pardoned,' nevertheless there have been many decrees issued full of hate and threats of reprisals against the 'reds'. One is that anyone belonging to any one of about 30 organisations shall be considered to be an enemy of the Movement and have their goods confiscated. Also those who have in any way contributed to the funds of the 'Reds' in any way. Further, all heads of departments must make an enquiry into the conduct of their staffs during the 'red' domination, and all those that were friendly to it must be dismissed, and among the penalties are that they may not even apply for work for periods of from one to five years. Denunciations of all kind are asked for.

The police have adopted the German trick here of questioning separately two men seen talking in the streets, and if the answers as to their subject of conversation do not agree, then it is too bad. Today at the cinema a notice was actually flashed on the screen that the audience 'must' stand with raised right arms during the 'interpretation of the National Hymn'.

Report from a friend living in Pueblo Nuevo, that the FAI are still active and have issued a pamphlet stating that Barcelona will be liberated again shortly, all will be well, and that Madrid will be defended. A rather simple, foolish and insignificant young woman we know was arrested. The circumstances seem to be that under the 'Red' regime her husband was a fascist sympathiser, and sheltered in his house another fascist and two nuns. This was discovered by the authorities, and the two men were apparently shot, for they have not been heard of since. The nuns were set free. Here the stories vary. One is that D. was a notoriously light woman and had an affair with the husband's friend; one is that simply she did not get on well with her husband and disapproved of the presence of the other fascist and the nuns in the house; the third is that she actually denounced her husband and the other man to the police. In any case, she has now been denounced herself by the sister of the fascist, and I fear her chances are very small. It is all the more tragic in that no one was more pleased to see the fascists arrive than she was.

24 February: A friend of P's who went to denounce someone was told by the department concerned that they are deeply disappointed at the small number of denunciations to date.

The Last Day in Valencia

Barbara Wood

Barbara Wood *was in charge of shipping Quaker supplies from Valencia to the relief centres in southern Spain.*

'Madrid has surrendered – the war is over!'[16] This announcement, given out by the Nationalist authorities from Madrid radio station, finally confirmed the rumours which had been current the previous week. It was no surprise to many of the Republican leaders and sympathisers that they should have lost the war: it had long been patent to everyone that the odds against them were too heavy. But that the Republic should go under was a bitter blow to those who had spent a lifetime struggling to establish a democratic form of government.

In the general confusion and *débâcle* the uppermost question in everyone's mind was: Would *convivencia* – living together – indeed be possible, or was it better to leave the country while the going appeared to be good? Many, profoundly disturbed by the abrupt breaking off of peace negotiations which at least promised some hope of finding a common meeting ground for all Spaniards in the rebuilding of the country's economic life, decided on the latter course and hurriedly prepared for departure.

But alas! the boats which had confidently been expected at the various ports of Eastern Spain failed to materialise. An International Delegation whose object was to enquire into the distribution of gifts of foodstuffs in Republican Spain and to assist in evacuation, was in Valencia at the time, having arrived on a French cargo boat carrying a load of food. This Delegation, together with the authorities in Valencia, had arranged for about 200 refugees to be taken off on the same boat, which left during the night of Monday, March 27.

A British boat, the captain and crew of which flatly refused to carry refugees, having been seriously alarmed by a threat of bombing if they dared to do so, was unloading in Valencia port. For the first time in the two-and-a-half years during which Friends have been sending food to the children of Eastern Spain, their shipment was looted on the quay, and we were able to save only a few lorry-loads of milk.

By midday a Falangist rising within the town placed it in Nationalist hands, well before the Nationalist authorities were ready to take over. Soon lorries and cars, including the two cars used jointly for the work of Friends and the National Joint Committee for Spanish Relief, were commandeered by youngsters of 16 to 18 and draped in Nationalist colours freely distributed from the *Comandancia Militar*, and were driven wildly through the thronged streets to the cry of 'Franco! Franco! Franco!'

As if by magic Nationalist colours appeared on all the balconies in the main streets of the town, though in the humbler outlying quarters there was little sign of any change. People who had come down from Madrid after its surrender all agreed that the situation there was less alarming than in Valencia, where far too many youths were doing patrol work either on their own or party initiative, armed with rifles which they all too obviously did not know how to use. And we were told by witnesses of the events of July 1936, when the war broke out, that the present scenes were almost an exact repetition of what had occurred then.

In the midst of the hubbub we managed to get out the National Joint Committee lorry and collect up some remaining members of the International Delegation and a few Spanish friends who were willing to stake a chance on being evacuated at Gandia by British warships lying off that port. By taking to the back streets we steered safely past the patrols and by 5.30 found ourselves outside the town – almost certainly the last lorry to leave Valencia.

Notes

1. The Eckroyds were Quakers living in Spain who supported the Popular Front Government. Russell was British, Maria Spanish.
2. Hugh O'Donnell was administrator with first British medical unit, in charge of SMAC office Barcelona; he subsequently worked with the PSUC.
3. Events preceeding May 1937 fighting in Madrid, between anarchist groups supported by POUM and government forces. Underlying the rivalries between left-wing parties was disagreement as to whether winning the war or the revolution took priority and whether there should be unified control of the army and of war production.
4. Geoffrey Garratt was NJC representative in Spain and author of the Penguin Special *Mussolini's Roman Empire*. Eric Muggeridge was a former Winchester School master, Indian cavalry officer and *Manchester Guardian* correspondent in Abyssinia.
5. Marguerite de Culpeper; later nursed in army base hospitals.
6. Málaga fell to Duke of Seville's regiment, with Italian and Moorish troops on 8 February 1937.
7. After the May conflict in Barcelona Juan Negrín became Prime Minister with a programme of reorganising war industry, and of social reforms aimed at uniting all classes against Franco.
8. Compare this version with Elizabeth Burchill's, pp.194-9.
9. Philip Jordan was *News Chronicle* correspondent; George Steer correspondent of the London *Times*.

10. José Antonio Aguirre; President of Euskadi, the autonomous Basque Republic.
11. Leah's memory was inaccurate. The British government had already agreed that 4,000 children could come in two batches, on 29 April 1937. George VI's coronation was on 12 May. A week later the government agreed that all 4,000 could come together. Leah also recalls Dr Ellis as 'Dr Hill' and the cruise ship *Habaña* which brought the children as a yacht. Nor does she mention that Edith Pye was working jointly with her.
12. Phil Thorne was Secretary of Australian Spanish Relief Committee.
13. Ayuda Infantil de Retaguardia, Spanish Committee for Children in the Rearguard: organised colonies for refugee children.
14. Hotel Colon; headquarters of the PSUC.
15. Alfred Jacob and his wife Norma were in charge of Quaker work in Spain.
16. 28 March 1939; the Military Junta led by Colonel Casado, which had seized control of Madrid in early March, surrendered to Franco.

Part 4

SUPPORTING AND REPORTING

Looking for Evidence

Isabel Brown

Isabel Brown *was from a Tyneside working-class family. A foundation member of the Communist Party of Great Britain, she was twice imprisoned at the time of the General Strike of 1926. In 1933 she helped set up the international Legal Commission of Inquiry into the Reichstag fire, which helped to secure the release of the accused. As Secretary of the Committee for the Relief of the Victims of Fascism she took the initiative in raising medical aid for Spain, and organised the first Labour delegation to go after the start of the war. She worked for the dependents of International Brigaders and was noted for her eloquence in raising money for Spanish Aid.*

The British government took the same attitude as the French government, that it was a civil war that was taking place in Spain, and they would adopt a policy of non-intervention. The Labour Party and the TUC took the same attitude of non-intervention. So we understood there was a political battle to be fought. The suggestion came up that we should get a responsible delegation to go to Spain in August [1936], within weeks of the war starting, to investigate for themselves whether there was any evidence of Hitler or Mussolini intervening with arms in any form. It was my job to get that delegation. So I got Lord Hastings to agree to go, because titled names always count, and two Labour MPs, one was William Dobbie who was MP for York, a railwayman, the other was Seymour Cox, with a Midland constituency. And the fourth was me. And I was very quiet about it. [...]

We finally got to Port Bou, the frontier station, and we had to go through the tunnel, through the Pyrenees. I knew that while there was an independent *Presidencia* in Catalonia, at the frontier post the Anarchists were a very big influence, and a negative influence, in a way ... Well these Anarchists let us through ... And they offered us two cars and armed guards to take us to Barcelona because that was their territory, as it were. So we got finally on the way with armed guards with us [on a] very tragic journey down to Barcelona. We were going through villages and the only protection for the village was a load of hay, a little way across the road and then a gap and another load there, and a boy about fourteen with an old hunting gun guarding the village. That to me was tragic. [...]

Getting to Barcelona this translator said to me, 'They want to take us to their headquarters.' Well, that was just what I was not [having]. So I did something that I never had done before and never have done since. I came over all ladylike and said, 'Oh, that's quite impossible. After this long journey all the way from London we must go to the hotel. We must change our clothes. I won't go to visit anybody's headquarters until I have had a bath and changed my clothes.' And I could see Dobbie looking at me and Jack Hastings looking at me and Seymour Cox saying, 'That's not the Isabel we know.' But it worked. And we got to the hotel. We were all shown rooms. And I got the translator. I said, 'Get on the telephone. Ring up the Presidencia and ask the President,' – he was called Companys.[1] He was subsequently executed by the Francoists at the end of the war. I didn't know anything about him or his politics or anything – but I said, 'Inform him that there is this important delegation from Britain composed of Viscount Hastings, MPs and Mrs Brown.' To my amazement it paid off. We immediately got an appointment to see him towards afternoon, and he would send cars for us. So we escaped out of the hands of the Anarchists. We'd have never fulfilled our job if we hadn't.

We got to the *Presidencia*, were taken into the Orangery. And Isabel does not say one word. She lets Lord Hastings and the two MPs do all the talking, what we were wanting to know. And he said they were being bombed from the Balearic Islands by the Italians already, in Barcelona. But that wasn't true, just him saying it. We had this interview, and then he offered us cars with guards to take us to Madrid the next morning. So we got safely to Madrid where we really could get the information we wanted.

Again I got the translator to ring up the Ministry of Defence. [...] He rang up the Ministry of Defence, told about this delegation, mentioned our two Labour MPs, probably said Mrs Brown. And he came back to me and said, 'Caballero won't receive you.'[2] Now, he had a grievance against the labour movement because of how they'd been treated when they were there as a trade union delegation. So I said, 'Go back again,' I said, 'By the by, there's a Barcelona paper here.' They got hold of the paper, and they'd reported in it that this delegation had been received by the President of Catalonia. They said it was Lord Hastings, William Dobbie, Seymour Cox, MPs, and Lady Brown.

Of course, when they rang up Caballero wasn't wanting to see Lady

Brown or Lord Hastings or Labour people. I said, 'Ring again and say it's Isabel.' He did. We immediately got the appointment and we went to see them. Again I kept quiet except I talked to his secretary, whom I knew very well, privately. But I left the important people to do all the talking. As a result of that we were given two Italian silk parachutes that had been captured. We were given two German incendiary bombs. We were afforded interviews with some Italian prisoners that had already been taken. And we got everything that we wanted about the Italian and German intervention. One of the funny incidents of that was that as we were coming out of the Ministry of Defence Dobbie was carrying the two bombs. They weren't very big, with thermite inside. And he dropped one. Fortunately, nothing happened. When we got back to London Ellen [Wilkinson] and others had organised the press conference for us. Again I didn't speak. The other three of the delegation gave their report. We showed the bombs, the parachutes and so on. Actually, I was ill. I was bitten by some bug in my leg and I was ill for a little while. But the Labour Party Conference was due to meet in Edinburgh shortly after this press conference, which got quite a good coverage, [saying] that there was intervention from the fascist powers. So we had another arm to fight for support for Republican Spain.

All the other people involved had to be at the Labour Party Conference. So we knocked together this report ready to be printed, and they went off to Edinburgh. I stayed behind because it wasn't printed. They promised it for that night. I got a sleeper up to Edinburgh and took this report. [...] Of course, it was a right-wing leadership in the Labour Party then. Bevin was the main speaker in favour of following the non-intervention policy. He said in his speech, 'We have no proof that there has been intervention.' And at once a forest of our pamphlets, which I'd gone without sleep to get there, were waving up in the air. I'll never forget that sight. Now, that had a big influence on the conference.[3]

Dangerous For Us
The Duchess of Atholl

Katharine, Duchess of Atholl was the first Scottish woman MP, Conservative, for Kinross and West Perth. She campaigned in the 1920s against female circumcision in Africa. During the Spanish war she chaired the National Joint Committee for Spanish Relief, the 'umbrella' which united some 850 Spanish aid organisations. In 1937 she led a women's delegation to Republican Spain. In 1938, because of her opposition to Appeasement, she resigned her seat and stood as an Independent Conservative, with popular front support, but lost to the official Conservative. After 1945 she chaired the British League for European Freedom to oppose Soviet policy in Eastern Europe.

In July 1936 the news burst on the world that a Spanish General named Franco had flown from the Canaries to Tetuan and there was assembling an army to fight the Spanish Republican government. I knew nothing about Spain, though friends who had visited the country had told me that the people were extremely poor. A day or two after the news of the rising came, a well-known European Catholic statesman was lunching with us and we asked him what he thought of the rebellion. He replied with great feeling that the Spanish peasants were the poorest in Europe, and that he thought that the Church ought to have done more to help them.

A few days later came a press report that one of several Italian planes on their way to join the General had come down in North Africa. Mussolini was evidently privy to this venture. Again, a few days later, I read in the *Daily Telegraph* that its representative in Gibraltar, Sir Percival Phillips, had just met a man from Seville who had seen German fighters and bombers there. It seemed to me clear that if Hitler as well as Mussolini was helping Franco, his victory would be dangerous for us. [...]

Ellen Wilkinson, who was keenly interested in Spain, asked me if I would consider a short visit there to see what was going on. She was going herself, as were Eleanor Rathbone and Dame Rachel Crowdie,[4] whom I had met on a Red Cross Committee. We went by train to

Toulouse, whence I took my first trip by plane to Barcelona, and in Barcelona we were warmly received at the beautiful old Generalitat by Señor Companys, President of Catalonia.

The seat of the Spanish government had by then been moved and our Minister there, Mr Ogilvie Forbes, was a former officer in the Scottish Horse. We found him both friendly and on good terms with the Spanish authorities, and we were soon presented to the President, Señor Azaña. Azaña was apparently friendly, but rather annoyed at some recent interference by British ships with ships bringing supplies to Spanish ports.

At Valencia the first thing we saw was one of the schools for refugee children, which showed clearly the interest in education taken by the Republican government. Next came a visit to a prison for political prisoners, until lately occupied by the present President and Prime Minister.

The prison consisted of a large well-lit building with a central hall from which radiated staircases to various galleries. Outside these there was a good-sized gravelled recreation ground in which some fifty men were standing about, looking well clothed and fed. We were allowed to call out for men who could speak French or English, and any who could do so were hastily pushed forward. In reply to our questions they said that little was wrong with the food, and that letters and gifts from friends were received regularly. The only complaint made to us was that no visitors had been allowed for a month.

In another prison we visited, two hundred Italian prisoners-of-war, Mussolini's so-called 'volunteers', were confined. We were allowed to talk to them freely and we asked them how they came to be here. Several replied that they had thought they were being taken to one of the Italian colonies. Others had come with their own officers, as a regiment. When we asked them how they were being treated, several ran off to fetch samples of the bread they were getting, which they obviously found satisfactory. They looked well cared for, and happy to be out of the fighting.

The Prime Minister, Señor Caballero, found time to see us, and in reply to a question I put to him, assured me that, in the event of a Republican victory, there would be full religious liberty. But by far the most interesting personality I met was the woman member of the Cortes, Dolores Ibarruri, commonly known as La Pasionaria. I had been reluctant to see her, as her nickname had suggested to me a rather over-emotional young person, but on Ellen Wilkinson's pressure I agreed to meet her.

I have never ceased to be glad that I did so, for the only person with whom I felt La Pasionaria could be compared was the woman I had always regarded as the greatest actress I had seen, Eleonora Duse. She had Duse's wonderful grace and voice, but she was much more beautiful, with rich colouring, large dark eyes, and black wavy hair. She swept into the room like a queen, yet she was a miner's daughter married to a miner – a woman who had had the sorrow of losing six out of eight children. I could understand nothing that she said, and she talked with great rapidity, but to look and to listen was pleasure enough for me.

Naturally our party was pressed to visit Madrid, then under siege by Franco, and we agreed to go there for a night. The country through which we drove seemed barren and poor – almost African – and the occasional houses along it were primitive. The city itself was amazing in its calm courage. It looked almost normal. The shops were open and the streets were full of people. Yet none of it was more than a mile or two from the front line, and the people who were going about their business so casually might at any moment be struck down by a sudden shell-burst.

As it happened, the day we spent in Madrid there was what was described as a heavy bombardment by the insurgents' artillery. A shell hit the official centre just before our party visited it. Another shell exploded at the entrance of the hotel basement where we were lunching, killing three people and wounding five. Three shells fell in the central square; one of them blew a bootblack to pieces, while the client whose shoes he was cleaning escaped unscathed. [...]

In the city, I visited the house of the Duke of Alba, which had been badly damaged, obviously by bombs: I was shown a lovely bathroom with a huge round hole in the ceiling. Yet Franco's supporters were making out that the house had been sacked by the 'Reds'. All of us were received by the government Commander-in-Chief, General Miaja. He spoke to us quite bluntly. The authorities much appreciated our presence in Madrid, he said, but if democracy in Spain were to survive, it needed concrete help rather than sympathy.

I found myself thinking most of the plight of the children. Just outside Madrid, we heard, a community of cave-dwellers were taking children in to protect them from the constant bombardments and were asking, many of them, no money for their pains. In a broadcast I made from Madrid wireless station, I appealed for help for the children of the city.

On my way back from Spain I was the guest in Paris of friends who had entertained me on a previous visit. Another guest was a Frenchman who had just returned home from a visit to Franco's side in Spain. He told us how normal things were in that area: order was perfect, trains were running and children were even going to school. I could not help saying that I had found exactly the same in Republican Spain, and adding that, moreover, new schools were actually being opened. My hosts hardly seemed to believe me, and I almost felt I had made a *faux pas* in mentioning my visit to the Republic.

* * *

The development of primary education has been specially remarkable. Some thousands of new schools were actually organised in 1937, a truly amazing feat for a country in the throes of civil war, and 'flying brigades', consisting of members of juvenile and women's organisations, were called for to endeavour to stamp out illiteracy in the villages, and to give them some rudiments of culture.

But the most interesting features in educational development have been those provided for the army. From the very beginning of the struggle travelling libraries have been sent up to the lines to relieve the tedium of the trenches. There hundred of these were dispatched from Madrid in the first month of the war.

There were many men, however, in the fighting line who could make no use of books, for they could neither read nor write. Classes therefore were gradually organised, either behind the lines or sometimes in the actual trenches, less than one hundred metres from the enemy. [...]

A system of libraries for villages has also been created, and so great is the desire for books that small hamlets without libraries apply direct to the Ministry of Education for literature. The government is devoting millions of pesetas to this work, and its efforts are supplemented by 'Cultura Popular', which is said in recent months to have brought into existence over one thousand of these libraries.

Opportunities for education are also opening for young women who have not hitherto known them. Daughters of working men and peasants are now being admitted to a residential centre of culture for women at Madrid, founded in 1914 for daughters of professional men. The new-comers receive allowances to cover all expenses, and students who come from professional homes are required to give one hour a day to helping them to overcome the handicap of little previous education. Students from peasant homes, on the other hand, give their companions instruction in gardening and the care of animals. It is hoped that residence in this centre will enable the new students to proceed to secondary schools, where they may matriculate or qualify as teachers. [...]

Filming the Internationals

Vera Elkan

Vera Elkan was a South African photographer living in London when, in December 1936, she was asked to take five ambulances to Spain for Medical Aid, and to make a film about the International Brigades.

When the Spanish civil war broke out friends of mine asked if I was willing to take five so-called ambulances for the Spanish Medical Aid down to Spain with their drivers, because I could speak French and understand a little Spanish; and whether I would be willing to make a film of the International Brigade with the equipment that had been used by Ivor Montagu, who had made *The Defence of Madrid* and had just come back with that. I said I would. We were due to leave on the night on which King Edward VIII abdicated.[5] I hadn't met any of the five lorry drivers. I was due to meet them at Newhaven at midnight; and I was staying in a room with breakfast in Robert Adam Street W1. I was all packed up to go when the landlady said would I like to hear his broadcast. I just had time (I think at 9 o'clock) to hear him abdicate down in the landlady's basement, where she sat with a pekinese, a gin bottle and a friend, and tears streaming down her cheeks.

I was also very upset. I got in the train, and I arrived at Newhaven, I had to find my way to some small café by the docks, where I met these five types who hooted with laughter when I said how upset I was by the abdication, because they were very, very left-wing and very anti-royalty. So we started off on that sort of footing. I had my pockets full of letters from Harry Pollitt and other members of the Communist Party, and though I was not a Communist it proved in the end to be my salvation, because showing these letters I got through everywhere. [...]

I got a lift up to Albacete in a small van with a lot of other volunteers sitting in the back, and I was sitting with the driver. We passed

— 254 —

enormous mountains of oranges by the wayside, which nobody had the transport to take away. So we stopped the van and filled it up with oranges for people in Albacete, which was very welcome when we got there. While we were on the road the men in the back were fooling around with their guns and things, and suddenly one of them went off and literally went between me and the driver into the dashboard. I had been near to death.

At Albacete there were a lot of Russians, which surprised me very much, I must say. They really did what you read about in books; questioned poeple in the middle of the night. And they did that to me. But luckily I had met members of the CP. One was Wilfred Macartney and one was Kerrigan.[6] And when they heard my door being opened by these Russians they came to my rescue. I could have been a bit terrorised and got into trouble, but the Russians departed. [...]

I arrived at Madrid in a sort of depôt which was not very nice for sleeping; it must have been a very bad dormitory or something. In the washroom I met J.B.S. Haldane, and we struck up a sort of acquaintanceship. He said, 'Come and live in the Canadian blood transfusion centre, where I am staying,' and I did so. When he left he fortunately left behind his pyjamas and they were the things that kept me warm because I wore them throughout my stay. I wrapped them round me twice.

Then I started filming; and because this was the Canadian blood transfusion outfit – with Bethune who had transport – I used to go along with them when they went to deliver blood to the front. There were also quite a few journalists around like Hugh Slater. I went with him sometimes; sometimes with Claud Cockburn; sometimes with Philip Jordan,[7] whoever was going anywhere interesting which anyone wanted filming, I went along.

I remember I came back one night from the front, and there was a dead child lying on the couch of the room where I wanted to work, and crying relations by its side. It had been shot that day in the street I think. And we were bombed from the air by the Germans, and shelled. But somehow, except one time when I was in Torreledones where Stukas dive-bombed us, I was never frightened. I really wasn't. Once I was in a trench, taking pictures of the other side, and they were shooting straight at me. I couldn't make out why, and then this soldier yelled at me, 'Get down with your camera'. Because the camera of course wasn't black; the telephoto lense was shining. So they shot at it.

I was bitterly cold. It was so cold that when we came in in the evening we had one little round electric heater, and we used to have to warm our hands so that we could pick up a glass. Whisky we had a lot of because the Canadians had that. But we couldn't pick up the glass without warming our hands on this heater. The only food we had was very, very stale bread and lentil soup; and lentil soup I will never eat again. [...]

The way back was quite interesting. I became ill. I didn't realise how ill. When I got to Barcelona they asked me to take five British wounded back to England. I said I would. We were put in a car, and they drove up to cross the Pyrenees. When we got to the top we were horribly storm-tossed. The two frontier sentries came out of their hut and they were literally blown across the road against the barrier. They said, 'You can't go any further, if you do you will be blown off the road.' We had to somehow reverse and get down again. We got down to the bottom, to Port Bou. They said, 'No. No trains. You will have to walk into France.' They gave us each a stick, and we went one in front of the other, the front one with a small torch, and the others had to run the stick along the rails to know where we were. We walked through the tunnel from Port Bou to Cerbère, the frontier town, which took quite a long time and was very tiring. I had to carry all my gear, all the cameras – the lot. [...]

I was beginning to be really ill. And when I got to Paris I phoned London and they said 'take a plane', which I did. I arrived in Croydon, and they held up everything while they went through literally every photograph I brought back – everything. Because Britain at that time was more pro-fascist than pro-the other side. However, they let me take the stuff and my undeveloped film. I was in hospital for about three or four months, and then I went to Switzerland for a holiday. Quite a few months later I came back to England through Folkstone or Dover, I don't remember which, looking quite different and in a mac and in a skirt and not in dirty trousers. I went through passport control, when a man tapped me on the shoulder. 'How do you do, Miss Elkan?' I said 'I'm sorry I haven't met you before.' And he said, 'No, you haven't. I knew you.' And he was an intelligence officer, who said, 'Have you been to Spain again?' And I said, 'No.' I'd been on holiday, and he said, 'Are you quite sure?' I was shaking to the bottom of my shoes that he should recognise me after all that time. But he did.

The POUM Women's Battalion

Mary Low

Mary Low, *an Australian poet, went to Spain from Belgium early in the war, together with the Cuban revolutionary José Breá. In Spain she edited the English edition of the POUM bulletin* The Spanish Revolution, *and joined the women's militia. Low and Breá left Spain in January 1937 after the POUM was expelled from the Catalian government.*

A little later I went to the law-courts with a Spanish friend and the Frenchwoman with whom he had lived for ten years.

'We've decided to get married,' he'd told me. 'It's silly, of course, and unnecessary, and counter-revolutionary, and all that, but I want her to have the nationality. It'll be easier for her here, and she'll be better looked after while I'm at the front.'

Her name was Simone, and her birth certificate and the papers they needed were in Dieppe and could not be got hold of. The men in session at the courts did not seem to mind, and waived it all with charming courtesy and good humour.

'Name? ... Name of mother? ... Name of father ...?'

'I never had a father.'

She said it painfully, and blushed.

They smiled at once, kind and encouraging. They treated it as a fine idea. One of them slapped her new husband on the back.

'Good for you,' they said.

To them it really seemed quite right and sensible.

They asked for the witnesses, and then found that one of them had not brought his identity papers.

'I'll go back and get them. I forgot. I won't be long.'

'It doesn't matter. Don't go, I think I know your father. Didn't he live at 29, Rierez Alta?'

'Yes.'

'Then it's all right. I know who you are and we'll take you on trust.

Come along, sign here. Have a cigarette?'

They shook hands, laughed. It was over and had taken five minutes.

'And the divorce?' I asked.

'That only takes five minutes, too, and it's quite easy.'

'What grounds do you admit?'

'Oh, the wife has all the same permitted reasons for divorcing her husband as he had for divorcing her. Besides that, if two people come to us and want to divorce and seem determined about it, we don't see any reason for muddling their lives for them. We don't prevent them from having a fresh start.'

It seemed to me clean and reasonable.

'Either of the parties can marry again. But they have to wait thirty days to make sure that the woman is not with child so that paternity can be acknowledged by the right father.'

I said: 'I suppose in time they will come to realise that marriage and divorce are equally senseless in the new society, where women don't need men's protection and have their own status and earning powers.'

The Spanish women were anxious to grab their liberty, but they had been closed up and corsetted so long that they didn't know how much of it there was to be had. Often they were content with the little scraps which answered their first call. It seemed so much to them.

The Anarchist trade unions had begun a group, 'Free Women', which issued manifestos and edited a splendid paper.[...]

Gorkin's wife, charming and energetic, decided to build a women's secretariat in the party, and form a women's regiment and women's classes and lectures and centres of education and child welfare. She received more than 500 adherents within the first week (it shows you something of their eagerness), but dozens of full-blown matrons, and young girls confided to me: 'Of course I wasn't able to tell my husband (or my father) that I was coming here, he would have had a fit. I just had to say I was joining a sewing-circle.'

The regiment was composed in large part of these runaways. We used to meet at seven o'clock in front of the local, with the winter morning mist still rolling up the Ramblas and round the trunks of the trees, strapped into our new blue woollen uniforms with divided skirts and stand there blowing on our hands and most of us hoping that our families wouldn't catch us.

I have seldom seen such spirits. They were so glad and gay and seemed like children. While we waited for the members of the Directive Committee to come and lead us to the barracks they skipped on the hard pavement and played little girls' games, singing and holding hands and dancing in their pointed shoes. (It was a long time before we could make them all understand that they must go to drill in flat heels and leave their earrings at home.) In the excitement of being free, they were able to get up carelessly time after time in the rough morning air. They would wait endlessly on the drill-field in the wind. Even the weight of centuries of indolence did not deter them.

We used to go to the barracks, which were a long way out from the centre of the town. On the way, in the tram or the metro, the militia-boys used to chaff us. We sang the 'Internationale' very loudly and tried to convince them that our uniform was as serious as their own. Sometimes they ended by being impressed. They would stand whispering gravely together and looking at us seriously out of their thicklashed eyes.

It was a long road from the tram-stop to the barracks. We swung along it in formation. The men leaned out of passing lorries and grinned at us and raised their fists and yelled: 'Comrades!'

'Comrades!' we yelled back in chorus and raised our fists too.

I remember the first day when we all lined up to file past the guards at the entrance to the barracks. How they stared, and afterwards laughed and cheered us, and all the regiments turned out to see us go by. We felt proud. A French boy ran down into the courtyard from one of the galleries, and demanded crossly:

'Now what do you think you're all doing?' He looked as though he had a grievance. He had come back from the front.

'We're coming to learn to fight,' I said, with some pride. 'We're a battalion.'

'Well, it's no use,' he said, quickly. 'I wouldn't have women at the front at all, if I had the choice. I've been there and I know.'

'Why? Don't you think we're capable? Not brave enough?'

'It's not that,' he said. 'Far from it. There may have been something in that at the first, when crowds of untrained girls went there without knowing what they were going to, and so forth, but that was due to the confusion. Of course, everything had been organised since then. Oh, I haven't a word against the milita-women at the front for their courage, or what they can do, or any of that. Oh, no.'

'Then what are you driving at? Why do you object?'

He gave a little, tired sigh.

'You see,' he said, 'it makes everything altogether too heroic. Especially for the Spaniards. They're conscious of being males every moment of the day and night, you know I mean. They haven't got rid of their old-fashioned sense of chivalry yet, however silly they may think it is. If one of you girls get caught by the enemy, fifteen men immediately risk their lives to avenge her. All that kind of thing. It costs lives and it's too much effort.'

'Then they must get over it,' somebody said.

'And they never will unless we go on as we're doing.'

'In any case,' we explained for his greater comfort and joy, 'you can rest yourself about this battallion. We don't put it up as a principle that women ought to go to the front, we don't think that, we only want to give a hand to all the individual cases who are good at that sort of thing. As for the rest of us here, we all have our own social or political work to attend to.'

'Then why are you drilling?'

'How dense you are,' Louise cried, while the early sun glinted on the polished shoes of the horses which were galloping riderless round and round the yard, 'because human beings should be properly equipped for defence when they are liable to be attacked. Supposing Barcelona was shelled? It would be silly if we couldn't do anything – a bunch of sheep, like in bourgeois countries.'

We went into an underground shooting gallery. It was stone paved, and the echo battered at one's ears, rebounding back endlessly from wall to wall.

The first day we were there the sergeant walked quietly to the back of the gallery while we stood facing the targets and let off a shot behind our backs without warning. Everybody screamed. Louise Gómez came out firmly to the front and said: 'If that ever happens again, that is the end of the Women's Battallion.'

It never did happen again.

We drilled for four hours without stopping, in every weather. The officers took us with full seriousness. They would not let the men come into the field and look on, and walked beside the leaders, patiently stamping the earth flat with their boots while giving us the beat. The drummers walked tirelessly in front of us to mark out the time. It was amazing that nobody ever complained, or fell out, or failed to come again. Some of their bodies were stiff and awkward, out of corsets for the first time. Yet they bore it all, and returned for more.

After the shooting and the drilling we used to have machine-gun practice. 'Just supposing one of these things fell into your hands and you couldn't work it,' as the instructor, with his cap lazily pushed over one eye, used to explain. It was the only thing which was really difficult. We had no mechanical turn, and spent a long time learning to take all the parts of the machine to pieces and put them correctly together again, and besides, the machine was so hard and heavy for us. But we did learn. In the end, I think that we could have assembled the parts of a machine-gun in the dark, without a clank to show the enemy where we were hidden, and fired it off as a surprise.

I remember we were very proud of this, and mentioned it in the next manifesto we issued.

The Women's Secretariat had grown enormous, and every day we requisitioned more rooms to house us all. Hundreds of women came every day to attend classes on socialism, child welfare, French, hygiene, women's rights, the origin of the religious and family sense, and to knit and sew and make flags and discuss, and read books. It was a great success. One had to begin from the first steps, like with young children.

Elopement to a War

Jessica Mitford

Jessica Mitford, daughter of the aristocratic Redesdale family, ran away to Bilbao with Esmond Romily, whom she later married. Romily had fought in the defence of Madrid in late 1936, and went to Bilbao as a correspondent for the London News Chronicle. *As author of* Hons and Rebels *and* The American Way of Death, *Jessica later became a well known writer.*

Our days in Bilbao began to assume a routine. In the mornings we would check at the Press Bureau for news, or interview government officials for background stories. Afternoons would be spent typing the stories for transmission to the *News Chronicle*. There was very little going on in Bilbao at the time. The town seemed to have settled into a state of anxious anticipation. Cafés were crowded with people listening to the news broadcasts, following each of which the crowds would respectfully stand at silent attention for the playing of not one, but four, anthems, symbolizing the United Front – the Basque national anthem, the Spanish anthem, the 'Internationale' and the Anarchist hymn.

I was consumed with curiosity and anxiety about what must by now be happening at home.

One day on returning to the hotel, we were told that the Basque Proconsul of the British Consulate had been round to see us. This was cause for alarm. What could he want? We had carefully avoided all contact with British Consulates in our travels.

The next morning the Proconsul returned. He was a young, good-looking Basque, and spoke English with a strong accent. We learned from him that a 'Proconsul' is a national of the country in which the consulate is located, and that his job is to act as a sort of liaison between the consulate and the local authorities.

'I have received a telegram,' he said, smiling broadly. 'The telegram is in code. It concerns you two, I believe.'

'Could we see it?' asked Esmond.

'Yes, certainly. Here it is, and here is the code book. Let us see if together we can decode it.' We felt that this must be rather an unorthodox procedure, but readily agreed to help with the decoding.

The telegram said: 'Find Jessica Mitford and persuade her to return.' It was signed by Anthony Eden.

'And now I must answer the telegram. What shall I say?' asked the Proconsul. We helped him to draft and code the reply: 'HAVE FOUND JESSICA MITFORD. IMPOSSIBLE TO PERSUADE HER TO RETURN.'

'Normally Mr Stevenson, the British Consul, takes care of all this sort of thing. But unfortunately he is now in Bayonne on Consulate business, and he may not be back for some days.'

We assured the Proconsul that he had handled the affair in the very highest traditions of British diplomacy, that no one could have done better in his place. However, we anticipated the return of Mr Stevenson with great misgivings; somehow, we foresaw that he would prove to be a much tougher nut to crack.

Our meeting with the Proconsul served to focus our attention once more on the urgency of getting married. We made inquiries from the Basque authorities, and were informed to our surprise that even in the middle of a civil war people under the age of twenty-one could not get married without their parents' consent. Some anarchists we met in a café offered the services of a priest they had taken prisoner ('We could find ways of making him do it,' they said), but it would have meant a two-day journey and we weren't sure just how legal such a marriage would prove to be.

A few days later we were summoned to the British Consulate for an audience with Mr Stevenson.

Mr Stevenson, a middle-aged, tweedy man with reddish moustache and balding head, was seated at a large desk in this drab little corner of England on foreign soil. He was surrounded by English neatness and orderliness and exuded English lack of charm, in contrast to the delightful Proconsul. He did not rise to greet us.

'You two have caused a great deal of trouble,' he announced in curt, official tones. 'I have instructions to return you to England immediately, Miss Mitford. When can you be ready to leave?'

'But I'm staying here. I don't intend to leave.'

'Mr Stevenson, I suppose you are aware that you have neither the authority nor the power to make Miss Mitford leave against her will,' Esmond broke in, assuming his out-consulling-of-consuls manner.

He sounded so authoritative and in control of the situation that I almost caught myself feeling a little sorry for Mr Stevenson. How could he hope to win against such an adversary? We argued for half an hour, then we left to return to the hotel. The first round with Mr Stevenson had ended, we felt, in a draw. While he had not succeeded in his objective, our security was badly shattered.

Next day Mr Stevenson came to see us.

'Miss Mitford, I have just received word that your sister and brother-in-law are coming to Bermeo tomorrow on a British destroyer to see you. Now you must realize that you have given your family a very great deal of anxiety by your actions. I think the least you can do is to go and meet your sister. She has come all the way from England with her husband just to see you, and to be assured that you are well and safe.'

'Which sister is it?' I asked

'Mrs Peter Rodd. I am going to Bermeo on business tomorrow, I have to meet the captain of the destroyer. I shall pick you up here at six o'clock in the morning.'

'We'll let you know what we decide,' said Esmond firmly, showing him the door.

We spent long hours discussing whether or not I should go. If I refused, Nancy and Peter would probably come to Bilbao and cause embarrassing scenes. On the other hand, perhaps there was a plan to kidnap me and forcibly take me on board the destroyer.

'Of course, I'm much stronger than Nancy, but Mr Stevenson looks disgustingly fit. He and Peter could probably drag me on to the destroyer.' We finally decided I'd better go; the thought of Nancy and Peter descending on us at the hotel was too awful to contemplate.

The port of Bermeo is only thirty miles from Bilbao, but the drive there took almost two hours of slow progress on the stony mountain roads.

As usual, it was pouring. The Proconsul had told us that the Spanish tend to blame English children for the eternal rain there because of their jingle, 'Rain, rain, go to Spain, and never, never come back again.'

Mr Stevenson led me to a bench on the wharf, and disappeared to do his business.

Hours and hours went by; not a sign of the destroyer. I had nothing to read, no one to talk to, and the wait seemed eternal.

Finally the destroyer appeared and docked, and officers and men came ashore. I was actually very excited at the thought of seeing Nancy and extremely anxious to hear news from home. Had Peter Nevile delivered the letter all right? Did Muv and Farve understand that there was really nothing much to worry about? Had they been unduly worried? Were they frightfully angry, or only fairly cross? I had a thousand questions to ask Nancy.

I searched the group from the destroyer, but there was no sign of Nancy or Peter. The tall, handsome captain of the destroyer came over to me, looking very English and familiar after these weeks spent among a darker race. He might have been one of the Australian sheep from deb-dance days

'Miss Mitford? Look, I'm awfully sorry. Your sister didn't come after all. Bad show. But we do want you to come on board for lunch; you must be starved.' Indeed, I was; I had had nothing to eat all day, as we had left too early for the hotel breakfast of *garbanzo* beans and rice.

'I'd love to, but I can't.'

'Oh, too bad. We'd really love to have you. Roast chicken, bread sauce, peas, mashed potatoes, chocolate cake, all that sort of thing, you know.' He rolled the words slowly, with tantalizing emphasis. 'As a matter of fact, our ship's cook really outdid himself in honour of your visit; we were so sure you'd come.'

I could practically feel my gastric juices working at the thought of the roast chicken and chocolate cake, but I remained firm. I couldn't leave just now. I had come with Mr Stevenson. He might think it rude of me to go off for lunch; but the captain had an answer to demolish each objection.

'Well, I'll tell you the real reason I can't come. I have an awful feeling you'd lock me up as soon as we got aboard, and take me back to England.'

He was outraged. 'What a ghastly idea! What do you take us for, kidnappers? Look here. I give you my word as an Englishman that we'd do no such thing. You would come on board for lunch, then we'd take you right back on shore in plenty of time to go back to Bilbao with Mr Stevenson.'

I looked closely at his boyish, open face. The serious blue eyes gazed back into mine; not a trace of dissemblance there. He certainly did not appear to be a tricky type – he would be incapable of the smallest deceit, I decided quickly, wondering with part of my mind what sort of gravy there'd be with the chicken.

'Well ... let me see if I can reach Esmond by telephone. I promised him I wouldn't go on the ship under any circumstances.'

I reached Esmond at the hotel and told him what the captain had said.

'Don't go,' said Esmond. 'It's obviously a plot. Make them bring the roast chicken on shore – as a matter of fact, you might bring some of it back here for me.'

I told the captain I would have to decline the invitation, and his hurt expression made me so uncomfortable that I couldn't bear to add insult to injury by suggesting that the lunch should be brought on shore.

The long afternoon dragged by. I sat haughtily on the bench until at sundown, stiff with cold and hunger, I joined Mr Stevenson for the return trip to Bilbao. I was inwardly raging at Esmond for being so super-cautious about the lunch. That nice captain certainly would never have double-crossed me, after giving his word of honour.

I got back to find Esmond pacing up and down in a violent temper. He had just received a telegram from Hasties, my father's solicitors. It read: 'MISS JESSICA MITFORD IS A WARD OF COURT STOP IF YOU MARRY HER WITHOUT LEAVE OF JUDGE YOU WIILL BE LIABLE TO IMPRISON-MENT.' I was horrified, and very much disturbed. In all of the many hours I had spent wondering what course of action my parents might take, and what efforts they might make to get me to come home, a threat of prison had certainly never occurred to me. This, then, meant total war. I was beginning to see that Esmond's intransigent attitude to my family, far from being over-dramatized and unnecessarily uncompromising, was far more realistic than my own.

Shortly after this we heard again from Mr Stevenson. This time, he produced an 'ace in the hole' against which there was no possible counter-strategy. He pointed out that the Basque government were counting heavily on British facilities to evacuate women and children, refugees from the anticipated offensive. He threatened to refuse further co-operation in the evacuation programme unless we agreed voluntarily to leave the Basque territory. Since we were staying in Bilbao as guests of the government press bureau and were relying on them for help in getting stories, he would notify the press bureau that unless they severed all relations with us he in turn would withdraw British assistance from the refugees.

This fantastic piece of bargaining brought home to me the strength and ruthlessness of the forces ranged against us. In a final stormy session with Mr Stevenson, we capitulated; but not before Esmond had exacted a bargain that we should return, not to England, but to the South of France. We embarked the next day on a destroyer for Saint Jean de Luz.

Inside Franco's Málaga

Sheila Grant Duff

Sheila Grant Duff became, at the age of twenty-one, the first British woman to work as a foreign correspondent. When Hitler took over the Saar in 1935 she reported for the Observer, *and in 1938 covered the Anschluss when Hitler invaded Austria. From 1936 she was stationed in Prague, and became one of the journalists best informed on Czechoslovakia. Her* Europe and the Czechs, *published as a Penguin Special during the 1938 Munich crisis, had a strong influence on British public opinion. Sheila Grant Duff came from an aristocratic background. She was a friend of Jawahabl Nehru and of Adam von Trott, who was executed after the July plot of 1944 against Hitler's life. In February 1937 Ed Mowrer, foreign correspondent of the* Chicago Daily News, *asked her to undertake a mission to Spain.*

To my generation the Spanish Civil War appeared as one of the great battles of human history and its mythic quality moved us all. It touched, as Arthur Koestler has written, 'the collective archetypes of human memory … and caused the last twitch of Europe's dying conscience'.

In Paris I discovered that my mission was even more directly related to the struggle than a straight newspaper assignment. Málaga had fallen to Franco and no newspaper correspondent had yet been allowed in. Koestler, representing the *News Chronicle*, had been caught there and arrested as a Republican spy. The Spanish government wanted a report on how Republican prisoners were being treated, whether the fascist powers were fortifying Málaga harbour, and information about what had happened to Koestler. Mowrer was prepared to cover this mission with a *Chicago Daily News* press card but he could not send any of their staff correspondents because of the paper's well-known anti-Franco line.

He thought of me, not altogether flatteringly, as someone who might slip in unnoticed. The intermediary with whom all this had been arranged, and whom I met for a short briefing in Mowrer's car as

— 268 —

we drove round Paris, was introduced to me as André Simon. Mowrer had spoken of him highly as 'a Jew with a duelling scar', exactly the combination Mowrer would admire. In fact he was Otto Katz, a Comintern agent later executed after the Stalinist trials in Prague in the 1950s. It was he too, I learnt later, who had been responsible for sending Koestler into the Civil War.

I protested my total ignorance of both Spain and its language and made the point that I had never flown in an aeroplane or been outside Europe. I was told that I had to take a circuitous route through North Africa and approach Málaga from the south. Tickets would be provided for me as far as Tangier but then I was on my own; all I had to do was to get to Málaga. 'How?' I asked. 'Oh, stand by the side of the road with a bunch of flowers in your hand and an Italian officer will give you a lift,' said Mowrer sarcastically, and more reassuringly, 'Once you're there all you have to do is to contact the American consul. He is a stout supporter of the Spanish government and will tell you everything we need to know.'

I reached Málaga, unaided I am glad to say, in a bus from Algeciras. To find the consul was more difficult, since there were no taxis, the streets were deserted after nightfall and when I reached his house, it was protected by a huge garden wall which I had to climb. The maid who came to the door would not let me in till the consul himself appeared. He invited me in to dinner, but my fellow guests were Nationalist staff officers and it was clear, from the few moments that I was alone with him, that this was the side that had his sympathies. Conversation at dinner was exclusively about the horrors of Red rule, and when my fellow guests conducted me back to my hotel, which turned out to be Franco's staff headquarters, they insisted on producing photographs of the horrors they had been describing. One of them became angry when I showed unwillingness to look at these pictures, but the other two were bright and friendly. On their part it was more a flirtation than a political encounter. Suddenly one of them looked at his watch. 'Good heavens!' he said. 'Twenty minutes to midnight! Do you want to come to the execution with us?'

Silence fell and all three looked at me. I felt confronted, as I had never been confronted before, with a stark choice the consequences of which would stay with me for ever. For a young journalist it would be a sensational coup; for a spy it was precisely one of the things I had been sent to find out; for a human being, it would be to stand and watch people whom I regarded as friends and allies being put to death in cold blood. I knew I would never be able to live with this. I did not go.

I awoke to spring sunshine and went down to the terrace. Little orange trees in tubs had been rolled into the garden and the fruit was warming in the sun. There were swallows flying low over the water and the sky and the sea were shades of the same deep azure blue. The young men were having their breakfast. Still in military uniform, they now had revolvers at their belts. I thought of Prague with its leaden skies, the snow piled in sodden heaps in the gutters, the ill-clad Czechs shuffling along with their shoulders hunched against the cold. I turned to one of the officers and said: 'How can you have a civil war when you have a country like this where the skies are blue and the sun is warm in February and the swallows are here already?' 'You are talking like a Red,' said the angry one of the previous night. 'May I see your passport?'

Mowrer had made me ask the British Consulate in Paris for a new passport because my old one had a Soviet visa in it. The effect of this three-day-old passport was dramatic, and immediately raised the questions of who I was and what I was doing so near the front when no journalist had yet been given permission to come there. Luckily they were due at the front themselves, but the angry one said he would be back that evening and would have me sent to Seville for a full investigation.

I had no intention of going to Seville or being investigated, so I had only this one day to find out what Mowrer wanted. I bluffed my way through the juvenile guards on the harbour gate and ascertained that no fortifications were being built. I attended a summary court trying Republican prisoners and learnt how the sentences carried out at midnight were reached. The British consul told me that Koestler was probably in Seville, awaiting investigation.

That evening I went early to bed and next morning I caught the first bus to La Linea. I strolled past the long line of cars held up at the frontier and walked, trembling but safe, into Gibraltar.

Guernica

Elizabeth Wilkinson

Elizabeth Wilkinson *was a member of the British Women's Committee Against War and Fascism. She was Secretary of the Spanish Women's Commitee for Help to Spain, a grouping of women's organisations. In the spring of 1937 Elizabeth went to the Basque country as* Daily Worker *correspondent. Later she and her husband ran a progressive school.*

Bilbao 27 April 1937

Yesterday at about 1.30 pm[8] I arrived in Guernica, the ancient capital of the Basque country. It was a peaceful town, with no factories, no munition works and no troops stationed there. Peasant women and children were going quietly about the streets.

Then at four o'clock the rebels began a brutal bombardment which continued without stopping until seven in the evening.

More than fifty German planes rained bombs on the town and machine-gunned the streets incessantly. The surrounding villages were similarly bombarded. The rebel planes even machine-gunned the flocks in the fields.

At eleven o'clock at night the whole town was in flames, not a single house standing. The streets and the square were crammed with goods and chattels snatched from the inferno. The people are still searching for missing relatives, for wives, daughters, husbands, sweethearts and children.

During the first few minutes of the bombardment the Catholic priest blessed the people, Socialists and Communists included.

The roads out of Guernica are now thronged with refugees, driving their sheep and cattle and carrying their rescued goods with them. Eleven thousand more people are coming to Bilbao. Eleven thousand more to be fed.

Bilbao 29 April 1937

There were no air-raids on Bilbao yesterday, owing to bad weather, but at the village of Amorebieta near the front, a Red Cross hospital was bombed and machine gunned. [...]

Peasants are bringing their cattle into the capital. There is a constant stream of oxen. Calves with broken legs are carried in carts, while their peasant owners walk beside them. [...]

Bilbao 9 May 1937

Heavy bombing still continues, including bombs having set the pine woods at Solluse alight.

The militia, however, are still holding the crest, and the last line of fortifications outside Bilbao has been constructed.

Only two days before an appeal was made in the press for the work to be done, and 500 people volunteered immediately.

Particularly fine has been the response of the women, married women whose husbands are at the front, mothers whose children have been taken away to safety, refugees from San Sebastián.

Bilbao lies in a deep hollow, and the fortifications have been built on the edge of the hills dominating the roads.

Work went on from seven in the morning until seven at night. A young girl said to me, 'It is better up here than down below. Although there is so much bombing, we get down into the trenches. They waste their ammunition.'

On the way back I had twice to take refuge. I counted six bombers with eight chasers. They dropped many bombs.

The big asylum at Zamudio was ablaze. Women and children were hastening from the farms nearby. Aeroplanes came suddenly and caught numbers of them.

Bilbao 12 May 1937

Hitler is celebrating Coronation Day with the biggest air-raid and bombardment on this city since the offensive began.

As I write this, at mid-day, in the centre of Bilbao, I can see a tremendous pall of black smoke darkening the bright sky.

There at La Campsa in the outskirts of Bilbao, a huge petrol dump is in flames. When I was out in this area I could feel the intense heat from the tremendous conflagration on the other side of the river, where the roads and the embankment were pock-marked by machine-gun bullets. And the dump is still flaming.

A little later a house in front of where I was standing was completely destroyed. The people who had lived there talked to me just a little, and one of the things they said was: 'I should like to put the London Non-Intervention Committee right in the middle of all this.'

I counted nine bombers and seven chasers come over. They bomb and machine-gun everything the pilots can set eyes on. They have even bombed a herd of cattle coming along one of the roads into Bilbao.

The people streaming in along those roads say they are strewn with dead and dying cows.

Already the Nazi pilots have dropped thirty big explosive bombs and hundreds of incendiary bombs on the city. They dropped them when you in England were laughing and shouting.

As I write the sirens, signalling a raid, are sounding again. I cannot tell what will happen.

An Anarchist Call

Ethel MacDonald

***Ethel MacDonald** was Secretary of the Anti-Parliamentary Communist Movement in Glasgow. At the end of 1936 she went to Spain to work as a radio announcer at the headquarters of the Anarchist trade unions (CNT). Ethel suffered from a nervous breakdown, and on her return from hospital played a part in the Anarchist and POUM revolt of May 1937. She was imprisoned but released after representations from the British and American Consuls. She returned to Glasgow saying, 'I went to Spain full of hopes and dreams. It promised to be Utopia realised. I return full of sadness, dulled by the tragedy I have seen'. Afterwards she printed the Anarchist paper the* Word, *and stood firm against trade union denial of the right of women to set type.*

Comrades, Workers, I ask you to consider the great battle of the Spanish people. Parliamentarianism placed the military fascists in military power, hesitated to give effect to constitutional reformist demands. The common people of Spain armed, sometimes battled with only their bare fists, and walked heroically to their deaths to vanquish fascism. The ill-equipped and betrayed people were winning. So fascist Portugal, fascist Italy, fascist Germany stepped in. [...] They warred secretly whilst France and Britain, especially Britain, played at democracy, spoke non-intervention, and behind non-intervention assisted fascism and Franco. [...] Despite the governments of the world, despite the apathy of British Labour, the workers of Spain won. They checked fascism. [...] Franco marched his Moors on Madrid, his Christian Mahommaden Moors, with their Sacred Hearts, and still the workers won! [...]

You recall the occupation of Germany. You recall the Black troops imposed on Germany.[9] You recall the protests of Germany, and of all that was best in Britain, in France, in America. If it was wrong to impose black troops on Germany, is it not wrong to use black troops in Spain. Why not organise, demonstrate, strike against your government standing by and passively, if not actively, aiding Franco and his black troops. Without your apathy the Moorish troops could never have entered Spain. [...] English-speaking workers, why are you sleeping while your Spanish brothers and sisters and comrades are being murdered? Where are your traditions? Speak! Act! – and overthrow fascism. Emancipate Europe, the world. End class society now!

If you are men and women, if you sense the class struggle you will permit no ban on volunteers. Spain does not want British volunteers. Spain wants action. Spain demands the historic loyalty to their own class interests of the British proletariat. Workers act!

There is no doubt that the magnificent struggle of the Spanish workers challenges the entire theory and historical interpretation of parliamentary socialism. The civil war is a living proof of the futility and worthlessness of parliamentary democracy as a medium of social change. It clearly demonstrates that there is but one way, the way of direct action. And that but one class can make the change – the working class. Social democracy has lived too long. It is said Spain has killed it. And now it is merely necessary that the corrupted body be burned.

The struggle in Spain is maintained by the Anarchists and without the Anarchists the war would have been lost for the workers before this. And it is because of this fact that the Socialists, and those who call themselves Socialists, refuse to have anything to do with the Spanish Revolution. It is true that those persons organise collections for the poor children of Madrid who have lost their parents as the result of barbarous bombardments, and it is true that those persons are collecting clothes and food and dispatching them to Madrid. But that is all. The Spanish conflict is regarded as a case for charity, something on the same footing as the poor of the Salvation Army. This is typical of the social democrats. It exposes them clearly as petty bourgeoisie with hearts that beat warmly for the poor starving children of Madrid. But speak to them about the revolution and they gooseflesh all over. To them revolution is illegal and unlawful, and as good law abiding citizens and subjects, they refuse to have any association with it. That is the treachery that is perpetrated on the working-class by those individuals and parties. They claim to be socialists and with that label attached to them they seduce the working-class.

And so they are willing to give their petty assistance to the victims of the Spanish war because they feel that by doing so they will not lose anything, will not suffer any inconvenience or hardship. But at the first breath of suspicion that the help were for the Anarchists their assistance would be brought to an end. They are capitalists in excelsis.

The Revolution is Slipping

Jane Patrick

Jane Patrick *broadcast for the Anarchist political organisation (FAI) and trade unions (CNT) in Madrid and Barcelona.*

The workers of Spain are giving of their very best because they have something to fight for. They know that the workers are already in possession and will hold fast to what they have won and fight unceasingly for what they must still wrest from their enemies. And they know that when the war is over they will own every foot of the country. And they will build newer and finer buildings in the place of those that have been destroyed, useful buildings that they can use and enjoy. They will carry on industry under the control of the syndicates they have already established. Everyone will be well-housed and well-fed and they shall be neither privileged nor oppressed. All shall be equal and have equal opportunity to (be) useful and happy, understanding and managing their own affairs without owners and without masters, working under the best possible conditions for the good of all, and free to develop their own personalities and idiosyncrasies at the same time. And that ideal sustains the workers of Madrid and the whole of Spain. The ideal gives them something to fight for and an incentive no capitalist army can have.

Barcelona March 29th '37.

What do you think of the situation in Spain now? Do you think that the revolution is progressing? For my part I see it slipping, slipping, and that has been the position for some time. However, perhaps it will be possible for it to be saved. Let us hope so, but it seems to me that reaction is gaining a stronger hold each day. [...] What do you expect Britain and France to do about Italy, now that she has so openly declared her intentions? Do you think they will rush an armistice or will they just let things slide? In my opinion they cannot afford to let things slide as there is no limit to what the Duce will do, and I don't think they will be prepared to declare war, so the only alternative, so far as I can see, is an armistice. I think an armistice would be a disgraceful thing, and the Anarchists of Spain would not stand for it. But I am afraid the government cannot be trusted. The government and its Communist Party allies are capable of anything. What will follow? Of course, I do not know what will take place. It is all speculation on my part but things seem to me to be in a very bad way.

Tension in Barcelona, May 1936

Mary Lowson

Mary Lowson *was an orphan, born in Hobart, Tasmania, and brought up by distant relatives. After teaching in a primary school she trained as a nurse. At the Lidcombe State Hospital in Sydney she was so shocked by conditions that she joined the Communist Party. She was 41 when the Spanish War started and went as leader of the Australian group. Much of her work in Spain was as an administrator and in politics. In Australia she returned to civil nursing.*

Well after midnight the train reached Barcelona. The last tram had gone. I tried to secure a taxi. Some men on a loaded horse taxi heard my voice. They called out derisively, 'English', and went off shouting. People were singing noisily. The whole atmosphere had changed from when I had left for Madrid. There was no taxi available. I did not wish to remain in this atmosphere until morning. From a telephone bureau on the station I rang the International Flat and told them to expect me within an hour.[10] I hoped I would find my way in the moonlight.

Away from the station everything was quieter. Groups of men and women were on the Ramblas but there was no unusual behaviour. I walked on in the bright moonlight, up the Ramblas, across Plaza Catalunya, into Paseo de Gracia. I was tired and sat for a while on a stone seat almost opposite Casa Carlos Marx. [...] I continued my walk, over Piy Margall, passed the statue of Liberty, and reached Calle Muntaner. It was just daylight and there I saw again something which made me know something was wrong. Groups of guards were assembled around small fires which had been lit at the sides of the street. They merely glanced at me as I went by. Finally I reached the building where the International Flat was. I was too tired to make any enquiries, went to bed as soon as possible and tried to get some sleep. [...] As I lay in bed a violent fit of trembling seized me, after a while the trembling ceased and I slept for some hours.

When I got up Hugh O'Donnell told me that things were serious in Barcelona, perhaps through the whole of Republican Spain. However for the present we were to carry on as usual. I went on to the small balcony outside my room. There was a stillness over everything, a stillness which makes an explosion more startling when it occurs. We went down to the office. A large mail had arrived. Amongst it were some notices that there were some parcels at the railway station. One of them was for Aileen Palmer. She was with the British Medical Unit somewhere on the Madrid Front so I decided to collect it and send it to her. A young English girl who had spent most of her life in Barcelona called at the office. She said she would return at two o'clock and help me to collect the parcels. [...]

I went out to lunch. I was returning along a side street near the Telephone Exchange when a guard ordered me to go back.[11] I stepped back and waited. Nothing happened. There were no bombers, no rifle fire, only the curious atmospheric tension. I started to go on again. The guard became agitated and said there was danger. I was mystified. I went back along the street, took another turning and came out on the Ramblas. When I came to the Telephone Exchange again it was being silently watched by a group of people. I stood and watched too, a young Frenchman from the Foreigners' Office came and stood near me. I asked him what was wrong. 'Some trouble in the Telephone Exchange,' he told me. We remained silently watching the building. No one entered or came out. A policeman asked us to go away. The crowd dispersed and we returned to the office.

G. called as she had promised and we went by bus to the railway station to collect the parcels. On the way we passed the Telephone Exchange. Groups standing near the building were becoming larger and more excited. Some of the passengers on our bus nearly fell off as we were passing trying to see what was happening. At the railway station everything was paralysed. In the whole place there were two groups, three men in each. They were evidently discussing something of serious importance. Five men went off to act as special police leaving one man in charge of the station.

There were four of us there. G., a Spanish woman and myself and the railway worker. The Spanish woman had come to see if she could trace her fourteen-year-old son who was supposed to arrive by train from Madrid that morning. It was of course impossible to collect the parcels. All the departments were closed. The tension increased minute by minute. We left the almost deserted railway station. No taxis or buses were available so we were forced to walk. When we reached the street where the office was groups of people were standing in the doorways looking anxiously first one way then another. We had received orders to return home until the position was calmer. [...] All kinds of wild rumours were spreading. Some were started by fifth columnists, others by the uncertainty of the situation. We tried to get some supplies on the way home but very little could be procured. None of us knew where the fighting would break out or where the traitorous elements had hidden themselves. Everything remained quiet.

We had a meal and then went on to the balcony to watch the scene in the street. Workers from the office were now staying in the flat. Many more police and militiamen could be seen. Shutters were being closed on most buildings. There were hardly any pedestrians on the street.

All cars were being stopped and their occupants being asked to produce papers. An anarchist leader had been assassinated.

Apart from these happenings a heavy silence had fallen over Barcelona. [...]

Before we went to bed we had another look at the city from our vantage place. Men were now beginning to build barricades. I had often read of these things and had seen the barricades in Madrid. Now I was seeing them prepared for action. They were neither as high or as solid as the ones in Madrid. The large stone blocks in the pavements were prised loose and formed into barricades about three feet high. Everything was done with calmness. There was no excitement, no hysteria. Just the attitude that this, too, would be overcome.

The Point of Truth

Ellen Wilkinson

Ellen Wilkinson *was Labour MP for Middlesbrough East from 1924 to 1931 and for Jarrow from 1935 to 1947. She took part in the Jarrow March of 1937, drawing attention to the town's plight. In 1934 she visited northern Spain to investigate Franco's suppression of the Asturian miners, for which she was censured by the Labour Party. She campaigned for Republican Spain and was one of the women's delegation led by the Duchess of Atholl. She opposed Labour Party support of 'Non-Intervention' in Spain and supported 'People's Front' politics in Britain. She was Minister of Education in the post-war Labour government.*

There is one remark of the hon. Member with which I agree.[12] He said that this is not only a fascist and Communist fight in Spain, but that we have to remember the condition of the people of Spain for the last 100 years. That is true, and it is also tremendously true, as he said, that in Spain the point of death is the point of truth. To tens of thousands of oppressed workers and peasants in Spain this civil war is just that. It is the point of truth. The grandees and the big landlords of Spain have been known for long as being the rottenest set of landlords there are in Europe. They are absentee landlords, men who have wasted their substance in the bars and casinos of Biarritz and Monte Carlo. They leave their land to be farmed out by *caciques* [local bosses], and we know what that means. If ever there was a day of reckoning at the point of death it is the reckoning that the grandees of Spain have deserved, and it is happening now. General Franco knows that, and he knows that though he holds those districts of Spain that are in his hands today he cannot keep them unless he shoots practically every able-bodied man behind the lines, except those who are willing to join his army.

Mr Donner: Does the hon. Member suggest that the human failings of individual persons justify murder?

Miss Wilkinson: I am not talking of individual failings. I am talking of the deliberate military policy of General Franco. I can refer the hon. Member not to something that the *Daily Worker* says, but to an article written by a Conservative, which appeared in a rather pro-fascist journal, the *Evening Standard*, in which he pointed out that:

> It was a mistake to say that 15,000 working men had been shot at Corunna; General Franco had admitted that only 10,000 workmen had been shot there.

That has been the deliberate military policy, and it is today the deliberate military policy of Franco, because he knows that he is really fighting the people of Spain. The question about the priests and so on falls into insignificance compared with such a slaughter as that. The Spanish people are really at the point of truth, and they are determined to sweep away the results of centuries after centuries of tyranny.

It was an awful humiliation for the deputation that went to Spain to have to realise the changed attitude in Spain to this country. Britain had been looked upon as the leader, almost the prototype, of democracy. The Spanish people realised that when we had sent volunteers to Spain we had sent them on the side of the people almost exactly 100 years ago. What they could not understand was not the idea of non-intervention, but that non-intervention should be used by this country in such a way as to form the most effective weapon that General Franco had. [HON. MEMBERS: 'General Franco has also objected!'] I have not noticed that General Franco has asked for anything except more of the kind of thing that he is getting. The letter that has been read from the Marquis del Moral shows that he had applied for more neutrality on the same lines. This non-intervention has given aid to General Franco. If non-intervention were worked as non-intervention we would not object to it, but the Foreign Secretary knows perfectly well that this non-intervention has worked on the side of General Franco.

The Secretary of State for Foreign Affairs (Mr Eden) *indicated dissent.*

Miss Wilkinson: Let me put a few points to the right hon. Gentleman. Franco got the army, or most of it, but one advantage which the Spanish government had, although it was bereft of the means of obtaining order, was that as the legal government of Spain it had control of the finances of the country. It was expected that Franco was going to get control of Spain in 48 hours. In that he failed. Then Germany and Italy promised to supply him with everything he wanted until December. Almost the next day France and Britain came forward with the declaration of non-intervention. By that declaration they cut through and made nugatory the one advantage that the government of Spain possessed, namely, that they had control of the national finances, and therefore had the power and in international law the right to buy arms. The Non-Intervention Committee neutralised that one advantage. That is why I say that this country came to the aid of General Franco. I have been among the soldiers and the young officers. [*Interruption.*] Really, the sense of humour in this House becomes almost indecent. It is offensive.

Mr Denville: No offence is meant on this side of the House.

Mr Gallacher: Their humour is as smutty as their politics.

Miss Wilkinson: These people whom you call murderers had built up their army from among the workers. Then came the Russian tanks and the Russian aeroplanes. That was making all the difference to them. It means such a lot when you can see aeroplanes on your own side, when you are being bombed from the other side. Therefore, they were very grateful to the Russians. They had built up their army almost from the ground, and one big advantage was the Russian aeroplane. It gave them the one way of protecting their women and children from the awful air raids that had been taking place before the Russian aeroplanes came. Almost immediately came the second act of the Non-Intervention Committee, when again the Non-Intervention Committee came to the aid of Franco. The Foreign Secretary knows that I am not accusing him in any personal sense. What I am trying to put is how it seems to the men who are doing the fighting. The Germans and the Italians are within a night's flight of Spain. Thirty-six Junker aeroplanes arrived three days before our deputation got there, and they went to the north. The Russian aeroplanes have to come in by sea. Let us be perfectly frank about it. It is ridiculous to deny facts. The Russian aeroplanes had previously been able to use Czechoslovakia as a half way house. That is not possible now for the Russian aeroplanes. Whereas the aeroplanes from Italy and Germany can fly into Spain, the aeroplanes from other countries have to go by sea, and they have to pass through the German and Italian ships that are there in the name of the control scheme.

By what logic we can justify putting German and Italian ships, which have overwhelmingly intervened on the side of Franco throughout, in control of the government coast of Spain I have never been able to understand. The case as has been put to us on behalf of the Non-Intervention Committee is that they have no power to stop ships but only power to observe. But all the English ships have been withdrawn from the Spanish East coast. German and Italian warships on which there is no observer can bring in what they like and are also in a position, if they observe any neutral ship, to signal to the rebel fleet and thus put an absolute blockade on the government coast. [...]

The facts are there, and the world knows them; and to do General Franco justice, he does not seem to take great pains to hide the facts. Are we going to say to the Spanish government: 'No intervention; you shall not have the right to buy arms to defend yourselves'; and then to have our leading newspapers sneering at them because they have not enough planes to defend their people. That is not a very pleasant thing for the people of this country, which is supposed to be a democratic country, to know; and there is only one consolation: it is that when we have done mean things such as that, they will come back on us, and the British people will pay, and pay heavily, for what their government have done to poor little Spain.

University City

Frida Stewart

Frida Stewart *from Cambridge worked as an organiser for the
National Joint Committee for Spanish Aid. In the spring of 1937
she and a young Irish woman, Kathleen McCoggan, took an
ambulance, donated by Scottish miners, to Murcia. She worked
there with Francesca Wilson, and broadcast from Madrid Radio.
Back home she took concert parties of Basque children round
Britain and the Continent. After Franco's victory she worked with
Spanish refugees in France. Frida was interned by the Germans
but escaped with the help of Spanish prisoners. She brought
messages from the French Resistance to General de Gaulle, and
worked with the Free French Forces.*

Against the blue distance the buildings of the Ciudad Universitaria
stood up, looking, with their square dignified forms and yellow
and russet tone, like the Greek temples at Paestum or Girgenti.[13]

They are indeed temples, temples of learning and culture, and like
Girgenti ruined now, but still beautiful.

The university city was planned five or six years ago by several
Spanish architects as a group of buildings, each distinct, but
harmonious as a whole. There was to be one for each faculty, with a
specially large and fine one for medicine, and one great hospital for
treatment and practice. These buildings were to be constructed
during the years 1932 to 1940, when the whole university would be
complete, a small city of culture and science, unique in the world. [...]

We go downstairs and out into the sun-baked street, and turn right,
in the direction of the University city. It is ten minutes' walk to the
trenches. We go with one of the young officers from the house, a
trench specialist, who had originally studied medicine in the very
building where he now commands a section. 'I studied here for two
years,' he said as we walk towards the *Casa de Medicina* and it almost
hurts to go back to it. 'We were so proud of the building and the rooms
were so beautiful, and now ...'

We pass through a sort of courtyard, an open space with a fountain
where soldiers are splashing and lying about sunbathing in groups.

We go into the building by a side door; there is the beautiful entrance-hall, large, simple and airy, with a stone staircase with tall pillars leading up to the first floor.

There are heaps of rubble lying round and in one corner of the ceiling of the hall is a gaping hole, where a shell hit the building, knocking down plaster and bricks everywhere.

We go upstairs and look at the classrooms and lecture hall.

This is one of the most tragic sights I have seen in Spain, this huge amphitheatre with its broken blackboards, and the benches that should be filled with eager students, turned upside down, battered, smashed and scattered, lying in heaps, torn out of their positions by shells that have fallen through the roof or shaken the buildings with their explosions. [...]

We plunge into a trench which leads down into the bowels of the earth and for a bit we totter forward, feeling our way along the walls in pitch darkness. At last a glimmer of light, and we come out into the front line of trenches proper. It is difficult to believe that these really are the '*primeras lineas*'. We have heard so much about the trenches in other wars, in the Great War ... about the horrors of mud, of wet, of cold; or of dust and dryness, and burning heat, with lice and rats and conditions of indescribable misery. Here our ideas are completely changed. These trenches are the little alleys of a miniature city, a trench-city, of which the dugouts are the houses, miniature palaces cared for by their inmates with a pride that is touching when one thinks of the impermanent character of the buildings. [...]

Some have planted flowers outside their door, which cheers the whole trench as well. Inside they have panelled them with oak panels carried down from the *Casa de Medicina*. They have brought other equipment from there as well ... chairs, desks, benches, washing apparatus and so on, and have invented ingenious devices for fixing up clothes rails, making folding tables and adaptable furniture.

Outside the doors the names of the palaces vaunt their pride. 'Casa Florida', 'Hotel Victoria', 'Hotel Rusia', 'Villa Pasionaria', and many others.

We go on along the trench. Strains of music can be heard. Guitars are brought into the trenches and nearly every one can sing and absolutely everyone can enjoy the flamenco music. 'Casa Miaja' even has a gramaphone. The Miajans invite us to sit down and hear a record, which we do. It is a *fandanguilla*, a very cheerful tune, but alas! almost inaudible, so husky and well-worn it is from much playing and trench wear and tear. It happens to be the only record they possess, which explains its condition!

In the next 'palace' a soldier is sitting bent over a piece of wood which he is carving into a beautiful foliage pattern. It is to be the door of the dug-out. The boy comes from Córdoba and he was learning his profession when the war broke out.

Next door to this is the company '*Oficina*' which is full of people working and reading by electric light (which is fixed up everywhere in these trenches). We are invited to look at the library ... all sorts of books are there, ranging from arithmetic textbooks to economics, from thrillers of the peculiarly lurid Spanish variety, to serious novels and plays. Over the door some one has stuck a picture of Goethe.

We feel more and more that this is really a university city after all, a trench university. They say that they have classes every day for the illiterate soldiers, and more advanced ones for anyone who cares to join. Here at least war has been a breeding ground for culture and education.

Soldiers and Sickles

Sylvia Townsend Warner

Sylvia Townsend Warner *the English writer, campaigned for support and aid for the Spanish Republic, and wrote numerous articles, poems and reviews with the conflict as their focus. She visited Spain, together with Valentine Ackland, on two occasions during the war. In late 1936 they went to Barcelona and worked at the base of the British medical unit, reporting to the SMAC and the Communist Party in London. In July 1937 Sylvia and Valentine went to Madrid and Valencia as part of the British delegation to the Second Congress of the International Association of Writers for the Defence of Culture.*

It is unusual for writers to hear such words as 'Here come the Intellectuals' spoken by working-class people and common soldiers in tones of kindliness and enthusiasm. And it was a new experience to see a harvest being reaped with sickles, and trodden out upon threshing-floors.

This harvest on the long plain east of Madrid is significant in many ways. While the strange workings of Non-Intervention impede even foodstuffs from reaching that part of Spain which is loyal to the government, every ear of corn is important. I was told a story about this, while we sat quenching our midday thirst in the inn of Utiel, sitting in a large, bare, half-darkened room, while, silhouetted against the blazing light of the open doorway, the children of the town came in, at first shyly, then confidently, to walk exploringly around us, murmuring to each other those words we had already learned not to flinch at, 'These are the Intellectuals.' It was a writer who told me the story, Jef Last. But he spoke as a soldier, for he has been fighting since the outbreak of the Franco revolt. This year, he said, the corn had ripened early. His regiment was holding a section of the line which runs through cornfields. The men, very many of them peasants, watched the corn with interest; presently, with passionate concern. For it was ready to reap, and in these acres dominated by war there was no one to reap it. They watched the corn as patriots, too, knowing the important of the harvest. They held a meeting, and decided that they themselves would reap it. Sickles were got and the corn behind the lines was reaped and stooked. But there was corn in front as well, in no man's land. Crawling out on their bellies, under threat of fire always and often under fire, working in the time allotted to them for rest, they reaped the no man's land corn also. Between them and the enemy was an array of neat stooks. But who was to carry it? Each soldier is equipped with a blanket, and they carried the corn in their blankets, carrying the treasure back behind the lines to where common life began again, to where the mules trudged on the threshing-floor and the barns could store the harvest.

That story was in my mind as we drove all day across the melancholy plain, with its few huddled villages. Scattered groups, elderly men and women mostly, stooped over the corn, repeating that movement that looks so harmonious, that in reality entails such ruthless fatigue. So they reaped when the corn was carried to the windmills of La Mancha against which Don Quixote aimed his spear.

But this year's harvest was different. It is the first of a new lineage of harvests, the first these peasants have reaped for themselves. But it is also the last, if things go as they should, of the old lineage of harvests. Those leagues of corn-land, immemorially fertile, vast rolling stretches of shallow tilth, demand a stronger technique of agriculture. It would be a perfect country for tractors. When the Spanish government can beat its swords into plough-shares there will be deep-ploughing here, the internal combustion engine will take the place of the mule and the donkey, science will reinforce the patient traditional skill of the *campesino* [peasant]. When those days come, I thought, these lands will show a harvest worthy of those who will reap it. And afterwards, as though it were a promise of what should be, I saw, stepping down a hillside in the early golden dusk, a rank of pylons, ghostly silver, their delicate geometrical beauty most perfectly assorted to the austere landscape of Castille.

How would they seem to Don Quixote, these strange apparitions? They might pull him out of his romances by what they could promise, a stranger news in this countryside than any romance, speaking of power and light coming to the darkened and the exploited, of education in the stead of ignorance, of houses for hovels, of the lives of free men for the lives of anxious bondage. But it is the children of Sancho Panza and Maria Gutierrez his wife who will best understand these promises.

Two Poems

Sylvia Townsend Warner

Port Bou

Through these ruined walls
the unflawed sea.
And to the smell of sunned
earth and of salt
sea is added a third
smell that cries: Halt!
I am what will be

familiar to you
by this journey's end.
I am, stale, the smell
of the fire that quenched
the fire on this heath, that brought
down these walls, that wrenched
this wound in the ground.

I am the smell
on all the winds of Spain.
I am the stink in the nostrils
of the men of Spain.
I have taken the place
of the incense at the burial,
I have usurped the breath
of the rose plucked from the bridal,
I am the odour of the wreath
that is held out for heroes
to behold and breathe,
I cordial the heart,
I refresh the brain,
I strengthen the resolved fury
of those who fight for Spain.

Journey to Barcelona

In that country pallor was from the ground,
darkness from the sky,
As the train took us by
we debated if it were mountain we saw or cloud.

The bleached fields are pallid as truth might be.
Men move on them like clouds.
Dwellings like hempen shrouds
wrap up squalor with a grave dignity.

Pale is that country like a country of bone.
Dry is the river-bed.
Darkness is overhead,
threatening with the fruitfulness implicit in storm.

The willows blanch, and catch their breath ...
It rains in the hills!
The parched river-bed fills,
the sky thunders down fruitfulness.

Faithful to that earth the clouds have gathered again.
If the people unknown
were cloud, it will be stone
before long. Rain from the red cloud, come to Spain!

Writers in Madrid

Valentine Ackland

Valentine Ackland *the English writer, visited Spain in late 1936 and again in July 1937, the second time to attend the Second Congress of the International Association of Writers for the Defence of Culture.*

There has never been a Congress like this before. More than sixty delegates from all countries met together in the front line held by the fighters for freedom and intellectual liberty – Madrid. Gathered there as honoured guests of the Republican government of Spain, we discussed the present phase of the World War from our various national points of view and, as always, from the unanimously agreed decision to combat fascism as Intellectual Enemy No.1.

Among hundreds of happenings, here are two ...

Going by car from Valencia to Madrid we stopped for lunch at a small village. During the fine meal spread for us we heard a crowd of children gathered outside the hall. They started to sing and sang us the war songs of Spain, 'Riego's Hymn' and the 'International'.

After exchanging shouted greetings with them, when we came to embark again for the journey, we found their mothers waiting to greet us with handshakes, embraces, tears. These women told us that they were refugees from Badajoz and Madrid, sacked villages and towns.[14] ('My husband was shot in the massacre at Badajoz ... I am alone here, I and my child, we have no one left ...') They thanked us with tears for coming to Spain, telling what we must write when we returned – what we must say – and always ending up with, '*Viva La Republica!*', '*Viva los Intelectuales!*'

Casals, who conducted a concert in our honour at Barcelona, asked the leader of our delegation whether we could not now return to England satisfied that Republican Spain was *not* a country of barbarians? It was a serious question, but if it had been a jibe it would have been amply justified.

Badajoz to Dorset, August 1936

Valentine Ackland

Telephone wires cry in the wind
& make song there. I stand in the misty night
& listen. Hear voices from a far distance
hear sounds from further, outside the wires,
than ever inside. Hear sounds from Spain.
The mist muffles all but these; blankets perhaps the reply –
But the wind plays the wires still, & the wires cry.

Things That Have Never Been Funny

Dorothy Parker

Dorothy Parker, *poet, writer and celebrated wit of the New York literary scene in the 1920s and 1930s, was also one of the founders of the Anti-Nazi League in Hollywood. She visited Spain in October 1937 and made a broadcast from Madrid Radio (below). As chair of the Women's Committee of the American Committee to Aid Spanish Democracy she helped to raise $1.5 million ($50-60 million in present value) for Republican refugees. During the 'time of the toad', as she called the McCarthy era, she was blacklisted and her career was blighted on account of these activities.*

I came to Spain without my axe to grind. I didn't bring messages from anybody, nor greetings to anybody. I am not a member of any political party. The only group I have ever been affiliated with is that not especially brave little band that hid its nakedness of heart and mind under the out of date garment of a sense of humour. I heard someone say, and so I said it too, that ridicule is the most effective weapon. I don't suppose I ever really believed it, but it was easy and comforting, and so I said it. Well, now I know that there are things that have never really been funny, and never will be. And I know that ridicule may be a shield, but it is not a weapon. [...]

In spite of all the evacuation, there are still nearly a million people here (in Madrid). Some of them – you may be like that yourself – won't leave their homes and their possessions, all the things they have gathered together through the years. They are not at all dramatic about it. It is simply that anything else than the life they have made for themselves is inconceivable to them. Yesterday I saw a woman who lives in the poorest quarter of Madrid. It has been bombarded twice by the fascists; her house is one of the few left standing. She has seven children. It has been suggested to her that she and the children leave Madrid for a safer place. She dismisses such ideas easily and firmly.

Every six weeks, she says, her husband has 48 hours leave from the front. Naturally he wants to come home to see her and the children. She, and each one of the seven, are calm and strong and smiling. It is a typical Madrid family. [...]

Six years ago, when the Royal romp, Alfonso, left his racing cars and his racing stables and also left, by popular request, his country, there remained 28 million people. Of them, 12 million were completely illiterate. It is said that Alfonso himself had been taught to read and write, but he had not bothered to bend the accomplishments to the reading of statistics nor the signing of appropriations for schools.

Six years ago, almost half the population of this country was illiterate. The first thing that the Republican government did was to recognise this hunger, the starvation of the people for education. Now there are schools even in the tiniest, poorest, villages; more schols in a year than ever were in all the years of the reigning kings. And still more are established every day. I have seen a city bombed by night, and the next morning the people rose and went on with the completion of their schools. Here in Madrid, as well as in Valencia, a workers' institute is open. It is a college, but not a college where rich young men go to make friends with other rich young men who may be valuable to them in business with them later. It is a college where workers, forced to start as children in fields and factories, may study to be teachers or doctors or lawyers or scientists, according to their gifts. Their intensive university course takes two years. And while they are studying, the government pays their families the money they would have been earning.

In the schools for young children, there is none of the dread thing you have heard so much about – depersonalisation. Each child has, at the government's expense, an education as modern and personal as a privileged American school child has at an accredited progressive school. What the Spanish government has done for education would be a magnificent achievement, even in days of peace, when money is easy and supplies are endless. But these people are doing it under fire. [...]

Their fight is the biggest thing, certainly, that we shall see in our time, but it is not a good show. This is no gay and handsome war, with brass bands and streaming banners. These men do not need such assurances. They are not mad glamorous adventurers, they are not reckless young people, plunged into chaos. I don't think there will be any lost generation after this war.

But I, as an onlooker, am bewildered. While I was in Valencia the fascists raided it four times. If you are going to be in an air raid at all, it is better for you if it happens at night. Then it is unreal, it is almost beautiful, it is like a ballet with the scurrying figures and the great white lights of the searchlights. But when the raid comes in the daytime, then you see the faces of the people, and it isn't unreal any longer. You see the terrible resignation on the faces of old women, and you see little children wild with terror.

In Valencia, last Sunday morning, a pretty, bright Sunday morning, five German bombers came over and bombed the quarter down by the port. It is a poor quarter, the place where the men who work on the docks live, and it is, like all poor quarters, congested. After the planes had dropped their bombs, there wasn't much left of the places where so many families had been living. There was an old, old, man who went up to everyone he saw and asked, please had they seen his wife, please would they tell him where his wife was. There were two little girls who saw their father killed in front of them, and were trying to get past the guards, back to the still crumbling, crashing houses to find their mother. There was a great pile of rubble, and on the top of it a broken doll and a dead kitten. It was a good job to get those. They were ruthless enemies to fascism. [...]

It makes you sick to think of it. That these people who pulled themselves up from centuries of oppression and explotation cannot go on to a decent living, to peace and progress and civilisation, without the murder of their children and the blocking of their way because two men – two men – want more power. It is incredible, it is fantastic, it is absolutely beyond all belief ... except that it is true.

Hunger is Awful

Lillian Hellman

Lillian Hellman *is best known for her plays* The Little Foxes *and* Watch on the Rhine *which were made into popular films, and for her memoirs,* An Unfinished Woman, Pentimento *(on which the film* Julia *was based) and* Scoundrel Time. *In the first of these she records her visit to Republican Spain in November 1937.*

Tonight I took the peaches, two cans of anchovies, a box of crackers to the dinner table. I asked the hand-shaking German to open them, but he put his hands in his lap and smiled. I passed them to the young man from the press office, but he shook his head. I was puzzled and thought I had offended all of them until the English doctor wrote something in his address book and passed it to me. 'They are shy about taking other people's food. Open the cans yourself and pass them around.' I started to open the anchovies, but the key got stuck. The doctor opened the cans, and gave them back to me. Nobody would have an anchovy, but each passed the can to the next person with great politeness. When the can came back to the Englishman, he kicked me under the table and said, 'You are leaving tomorrow. You have brought these down to have a kind of party. You will be unhappy if we don't share your party, yes?'

I liked him very much as he rose and served each person one anchovy and a cracker. Everybody ate very slowly, and there was no talk. I served the peaches and they stared at their plates, almost as if they were frightened to eat. There were still a few anchovies and so I gave one to the German lady, one to her husband, one to the press attaché. There wasn't any for the doctor or for me. The German immediately put his anchovy on my plate and the German lady leaned over to give hers to the doctor.

The doctor said, 'No, thank you. In England we eat them as a savoury and I don't like them. Miss Hellman told me that she doesn't like them either.'

I said that was true, I was sick of anchovies, and suddenly both the doctor and I were talking at once. It was a long time before they finished their anchovies, and when the oil of the can was passed around, I heard the German lady make a sound of pleasure. I didn't want a peach, but there was such disbelief when I said so that I ate part of one. This small party had taken an hour and had acted on my table companions as if they had drunk a case of champagne. For the first time in the weeks I had known them they chatted and laughed, and the German told an elaborate joke that everybody pretended to understand. As we left the table, we all shook hands. At the door, I turned to speak to somebody and saw that the German lady was wrapping my half peach in a piece of paper. She handed it to her husband. He shook his head and gave it back and she gave it back to him and this time he took it and kissed the hand that gave it to him. The doctor had waited at the door for me and had seen what I had seen.

In the hall he said, 'My God. Hunger is awful.'

Ideals and Realities

Emma Goldman

Emma Goldman, *anarchist and feminist, was 67 when she visited Spain at the invitation of the Comité Anarcho-Syndicaliste in September 1936. After meeting the anarchist militia on the Aragon front she opened a propaganda office for the FAI-CNT in London, where she edited the English-language edition of their bulletin. She formed a Committee to Aid Homeless Spanish Women and Children, with the support of the actress Sybil Thorndyke, and an International Anti-Fascist Solidarity body with Rebecca West, Fenner Brockway and the philosopher C.E.M. Joad among its patrons. But she lamented the lack of support in Britain for the anarchist cause. Emma returned to Spain in September-October 1937 and again in the autumn of 1938. After her second visit she defended the policies of the FAI-CNT at the Congress of the ('Black' or Anarchist) International Working Men's Association in Paris.*

I have seen from the moment of my first arrival in Spain in September 1936 that our comrades in Spain are plunging head foremost into the abyss of compromise that will lead them far away from their revolutionary aim. Subsequent events have proved that those of us who saw the danger ahead were right. The participation of the CNT-FAI in the government, and concessions to the insatiable monster in Moscow, have certainly *not* benefited the Spanish revolution, or even the anti-fascist struggle. Yet closer contact with reality in Spain, with the almost insurmountable odds against the aspirations of the CNT-FAI, made me understand their tactics better, and helped me to guard against any dogmatic judgment of our comrades. [...]

I returned to Spain with apprehension because of all the rumours that had reached me after the May events of the destruction of the collectives. It is true that the [Communist-led] Lister and Karl Marx Brigades went through Aragon and places in Catalonia like a cyclone, devastating everything in their way; but it is nevertheless the fact that most of the collectives were keeping up as if no harm had come to them. In fact I found the collectives in September and October 1937 in better-organised condition and in better working order – and that, after all, is the most important achievement that must be kept in mind in any appraisal of the mistakes made by our comrades in Spain. Unfortunately, our critical comrades do not seem to see this all-important side of the CNT-FAI. [...]

The revolution in Spain was the result of a military and fascist conspiracy. The first imperative need that presented itself to the CNT-FAI was to drive out the conspiratorial gang. The fascist danger had to be met with almost bare hands. In this process the Spanish workers and peasants soon came to see that their enemies were not only Franco and his Moorish hordes. They soon found themselves beseiged by formidable armies and an array of modern arms furnished to Franco by Hitler and Mussolini, with all the imperialist pack playing their sinister under-handed game. In other words, while the Russian Revolution and the civil war were being fought out on Russian soil and by Russians, the Spanish revolution and anti-fascist war involves all the powers of Europe. It is no exaggeration to say that the Spanish Civil War has spread out far beyond its own confines.

As if that were not enough to force the CNT-FAI to hold themselves up by *any* means, rather than to see the revolution and the masses drowned in the bloodbath prepared for them by Franco and his allies – our comrades had also to contend with the inertia of the international proletariat. [...]

With the most fervent desire to aid the revolution in Spain, our comrades outside of it were neither numerically nor materially strong enough to turn the tide. Thus finding themselves up against a stone wall, the CNT-FAI was forced to descend from its lofty traditional heights to compromise right and left: participation in the government, all sorts of humiliating overtures to Stalin, superhuman tolerance for his henchmen who were openly plotting and conniving against the Spanish revolution.

Of all the unfortunate concessions our people have made, their entry into ministries seemed to me the least offensive. No, I have not changed my attitude toward government as an evil. As all through my life, I still hold that the State is a cold monster, and that it devours everyone within its reach. Did I not know that the Spanish people see in government a mere makeshift, to be kicked overboard at will, that they had never been deluded and corrupted by the parliamentary myth, I should perhaps be more alarmed for the future of the CNT-FAI. But with Franco at the gate of Madrid, I could hardly blame the CNT-FAI for choosing a lesser evil – participation in the government rather than dictatorship, the most deadly evil.

Russia has more than proven the nature of this beast. After twenty years it still thrives on the blood of its makers. Nor is its crushing weight felt in Russia alone. Since Stalin began his invasion of Spain, the march of his henchmen has been leaving death and ruin behind them. Destruction of numerous collectives, the introduction of the Tcheka with its 'gentle' methods of treating political opponents, the arrest of thousands of revolutionaries, and the murder in broad daylight of others. All this and more, has Stalin's dictatorship given Spain, when he sold arms to the Spanish people in return for good gold. Innocent of the jesuitical trick of 'our beloved comrade' Stalin, the CNT-FAI could not imagine in their wildest dreams the unscrupulous designs hidden behind the seeming solidarity in the offer of arms from Russia.

Their need to meet Franco's military equipment was a matter of life and death. The Spanish people had not a moment to lose if they were not to be crushed. What wonder if they saw in Stalin the saviour of the anti-fascist war? They have since learned that Stalin helped to make Spain safe against the fascists so as to make it safer for his own ends.

The critical comrades are not at all wrong when they say that it does not seem worthwhile to sacrifice one ideal in the struggle against fascism, if it only means to make room for Soviet Communism. I am entirely of their view – that there is no difference between them. My own consolation is that with all their concentrated criminal efforts, Soviet Communism has not taken root in Spain. I know whereof I speak. On my recent visit to Spain I had ample opportunity to convince myself that the Communists have failed utterly to win the sympathies of the masses; quite the contrary. They have never been so hated by the workers and peasants as now. [...]

If our comrades have erred in permitting the Communist invasion it was only because the CNT-FAI are the implacable enemies of fascism. They were the first, not only in Spain but in the whole world, to repulse fascism, and they are determined to remain the last on the battlefield, until the beast is slain. This supreme determination sets the CNT-FAI apart in the history of indomitable champions and fighters for freedom the world has ever known. Compared with this, their compromises appear in a less glaring light.,

True, the tacit consent to militarisation on the part of our Spanish comrades was a violent break with their Anarchist past. But grave as this was, it must also be considered in the light of their utter military inexperience. Not only theirs but ours as well. All of us have talked rather glibly about antimilitarism. In our zeal and loathing of war we have lost sight of modern warfare, of the utter helplessness of untrained and unequipped men face to face with mechanised armies, and armed to their teeth for the battle on land, sea, and air. I still feel the same abhorrence of militarism, its dehumanisation, its brutality and its power to turn men into automatons. But my contact with our comrades at the various fronts during my first visit in 1936 convinced me that some training was certainly needed if our militias were not to be sacrificed like new- born children on the altar of war.

While it is true that after 19 July tens of thousands of old and young men volunteered to go to the front – they went with flying colours and the determination to conquer Franco in a short time – they had no previous military training or experience. I saw a great many of the militia when I visited the Durruti and Huesca fronts. They were all inspired by their ideal – by the hatred of fascism and passionate love of freedom. No doubt that would have carried them a long way if they had had only the Spanish fascists to face; but when Germany and Italy began pouring in hundreds of thousands of men and masses of war material, our militias proved very inadequate indeed. If it was inconsistent on the part of the CNT-FAI to consent to militarisation, it was also inconsistent for us to change our attitude toward war, which some of us had held all our lives. We had always condemned war as serving capitalism and no other purpose; but when we realised that our heroic comrades in Barcelona had to continue the anti-fascist struggle, we immediately rallied to their support, which was undoubtedly a departure from our previous stand on war. Once we realised that it would be impossible to meet hordes of fascists armed to the very teeth, we could not escape the next step, which was militarisation. Like so many actions of the CNT-FAI undoubtedly contrary to our philosophy, they were not of their making or choosing. They were imposed upon them by the development of the struggle, which if not brought to a successful end, would exterminate the CNT-FAI, destroy their constructive achievements, and set back Anarchist thought and ideas not only in Spain but in the rest of the world. [...]

Our comrades have a sublime ideal to inspire them; they have great courage and the iron will to conquer fascism. All that goes a long way to hold up their morale. Airplanes bombarding towns and villages and all the other monster mechanisms cannot be stopped by spiritual values. The greater the pity that our side was not prepared, nor had the physical means to match the inexhaustible supplies streaming into Franco's side.

It is a miracle of miracles that our people are still on deck, more than ever determined to win. I cannot but think that the training our comrades are getting in the military schools will make them fitter to strike, and with greater force. I have been strengthened in this belief by my talks with young comrades in the military schools – with some of them at the Madrid front and with CNT-FAI members occupying high military positions. They all assured me that they had gained much through the military training, and that they feel more competent and surer of themselves to meet the enemy forces. [...]

Since I have been privileged to be in Spain twice – near the comrades, near their splendid constructive labour – since I was able to see their selflessness and determination to build a new life on their soil, my faith in our comrades has deepened into a firm conviction that, whatever their inconsistencies, they will return to first principles. Tested by the fires of the anti-fascist war and the revolution, the CNT-FAI will emerge unscathed. Therefore I am with them, regardless of everything.

Black Fighters
Eslanda Goode Robeson

Eslanda Robeson, a prominent campaigner for black rights in the USA, accompanied her husband Paul when he visited Spain in 1938 and sang to International Brigade audiences.

Wednesday 26 January: Back at Albacete ... in our so-called Grand Hotel. Off to Tarazona, the training camp for the International Brigade. Arrived about twelve, had a good lunch with the men.

Saw lots of Negro comrades, Andrew Mitchell of Oklahoma, Oliver Ross of Baltimore, Frank Warfield of St Louis. All were thrilled to see us and talked at length with Paul. All the white Americans, Canadians and English troops were also thrilled to see Paul.

A Major Johnson – a West Pointer – had charge of training.

The officers arranged a meeting in the church and all the Brigade gathered there at 2:30 sharp, simply packing the church. But before they filed in, they passed in review in the square for us, saluting us with *Salud!* as they passed.

Major Johnson told the men that they are to go up to the front line tomorrow. The men applauded uproariously at that news ...

Then Paul sang, the men shouting for the songs they wanted: 'Water Boy', 'Old Man River', 'Lonesome Road', 'Fatherland'. They stomped and applauded each song and continued to shout requests. It was altogether a huge success. Paul loved doing it. Afterwards we had twenty minutes with the men and took messages for their families.

Monday 31 January: [...] We had a good talk over lunch and afterwards over coffee in the lounge, and then we went off to the border. Fernando, in civilian dress, accompanied us, and Lt. K., armed in full uniform, was our official escort. [...]

As we drove along, K. got talking and told us the story of Oliver Law. It seems he was a Negro – about 33 – who was a former army man from Chicago. He had risen to be a corporal in the US Army. Quiet, dark brown, dignified, strongly built. All the men liked him. He began here as a corporal, soon rose to sergeant, lieutenant, captain and finally was commander of the Battalion – the Lincoln-Washington Battalion. K. said warmly that many officers and men here in Spain considered him the best battalion commander in Spain. The men all liked him, trusted him, respected him and served him with confidence and willingly.

K. tells of an incident when the battalion was visited by an old Colonel, Southern, of the US Army. He said to Law – 'Er, I see you are in a Captain's uniform?' Law replied with dignity, 'Yes, I am, because I *am* a Captain. In America, in *your* army, I could only rise as high as corporal, but here people feel differently about race and I can rise according to my worth, not according to my color!' Whereupon the Colonel hemmed and hawed and finally came out with: 'I'm sure your people must be proud of you, my boy.' 'Yes,' said Law. 'I'm sure they are!'

K. says that Law rose from rank to rank on sheer merit. He kept up the morale of his men. He always had a big smile when they won their objectives and an encouraging smile when they lost. He never said very much.

Law led his men in charge after charge at Brunete, and was finally wounded seriously by a sniper. K. brought him in from the field and loaded him onto a stretcher when he found how seriously wounded he was. K. and another soldier were carrying him up the hill to the first aid camp.

On the way up the hill another sniper shot Law, on the stretcher; the sniper's bullet landed in his groin and he began to lose blood rapidly. They did what they could to stop the blood, hurriedly putting down the stretcher. But in a few minutes the loss of blood was so great that Law died.

A Visit to the British Battalion

Charlotte Haldane

Charlotte Haldane, the writer and traveller, was Secretary of the Dependents Aid Committee, which raised money for the families of International Brigaders. In 1937 she worked in Paris transmitting volunteers through to the Brigades. In 1938 she accompanied Paul and Eslanda Robeson to Spain, where she visited the British Brigaders. On her return she went to China for the Communist International. During the Second World War she was a correspondent in Russia. On her return she broke with the Communist Party.

The machine-gun battery had been installed on a cliff overlooking a valley, two hundred feet below, where the infantry were holding the most advanced part of the line. A fascist counter-attack was expected, but this did not take place until some weeks later, when Franco's forces recaptured Teruel. On this night all was quiet. The boys presented me with a souvenir, an empty cartridge case, in which was inserted a tiny scroll of paper on which they had written in indelible ink: 'We, the machine-gun Co. of the British Battalion, warmly greet our comrade, Charlotte Haldane, and desire to express our deep appreciation of her work at home in England.' It was signed by 32 of them, and on behalf of eight others, who were sick or wounded. I felt deeply honoured to receive this precious testimonial, and have it still. [...]

When it became sufficiently dark, Rust, Tapsell,[14] myself and the boys carrying the food supplies from the cookhouse to the men in the advanced lines, set out to climb down the two hundred feet of cliff into the valley below. I am one of those people who are terrified of heights, and have frequently become almost paralysed by fright when I have had to descend more than twenty feet or so. On this night, however, I found my qualms vanish as soon as we started. Tappy supported me over the roughest parts of the ground. Whether it was the strength that came to me from the loving comradeship of the Brigaders, or whether it was due to the darkness, and the fact that I could not look down and see the drop below us, I do not know, but I negotiated the cliff quite easily, with no dizziness nor nausea.

It was nearly five o'clock in the morning when we returned to Teruel. Later that day we set out on the backward journey to Barcelona. There was a wonderful deep, new, spring mattress on the floor of the van, extracted no doubt from the marital bed of one of the abandoned houses. As we drove off, Bill Rust drew out a souvenir he had acquired for me – a rather worn and shabby dark red Spanish silk shawl.

Back in Barcelona, I was particularly anxious to meet La Pasionaria, the famous Spanish woman Communist leader. After I had been kept waiting for some days, an appointment was made for me through the British political commissar. I bought a huge bunch of scarlet gladioli – there was no food in the shops, but there were plenty of flowers – and presented myself at the headquarters of the Spanish Communist Party, a large building, as closely fortified and guarded as a fortress. There were armed men everywhere. In due course I was ushered into an important and well-furnished office. Dolores Ibarruri rose from her seat behind a big mahogany desk, and came forward to greet me. She had a matronly but magnificent figure, and bore herself with that unselfconscious nobility and dignity that is so characteristic of certain Spaniards, irrespective of birth or class. Her features were regular, aquiline; her eyes dark and flashing. She had splendid teeth, and her smile was young and feminine. The voice that in public meetings could enthral thousands was, in private conversation, low and melodious, though still decisive. She told me with gleeful amusement stories of the terrible tales that had been spread about her by her political enemies. To the fascists she was a dread, Medusa-like legend. In fact, she was the daughter of an Asturian miner, and from childhood had been used to abject poverty and violent political strikes and battles to gain even the slightest amelioration of the living and working conditions of her people. She had been illiterate until her 'teens. Against tremendous odds, however, she had educated herself whilst earning her living. Her devotion to the Spanish working class was absolute and completely sincere. She became one of the greatest orators her country has produced, on a par with such oratorical stars as Jaurès and Cachin in France. Her nickname was due to the fact that the passion which filled her whole personality and her voice when she defended her people or attacked their enemies was a mystical one, and the *pasión* with which she preached her cause was akin to religious fervour. The hatred which she was certainly capable of feeling as well as inspiring was due to an unusual sensibility, an outraged compassion for her fellow men and women, the inversion of the immense love and loyalty by which she was equally inspired.

Notes

1. Luis Companys was President of Catalonia during the war.
2. Largo Caballero was Socialist Prime Minister and War Minister from 4 September 1936 to 17 May 1937.
3. The Labour Party Conference in October 1936 voted to support the non-intervention policy.
4. Eleanor Rathbone was Independent MP for Combined English Universities 1929-45, a leading campaigner for women's rights and the originator of the plan for family allowances. Dame Rachel Eleanor Crowdy (not Crowdie), trained as nurse, commanded VADs (voluntary nurses) in France and Belgium in the First World War and was Head of Social Question Section League of Nations.
5. Edward abdicated on 10 December 1936; the broadcast was made the following day.
6. Wilfred Macartney was Commander of No. 1 Company of British Battalion at the time; Peter Kerrigan, a leading CP member, was British Political Commissar at Albacete at the time.
7. Claud Cockburn was the *Daily Worker*'s correspondent in Spain; Philip Jordan was a *News Chronicle* correspondent.
8. She probably wrote 11.30, as she told the editor (J.F.) that she went to Guernica with George Steer (see Leah Manning's contribution, pp.222-4), immediately after the bombing.
9. MacDonald is referring to the colonial troops which were part of the French force which occupied the Ruhr in 1923, when Germany defaulted on the war reparations imposed by the Versailles Treaty. Protests against the French occupation included protests against the use of black troops, an indication of racist attitudes among left-wing and other progressive people at the time.
10. In Calle Muntaner, for SMAC personnel while in Barcelona.
11. Tension in Barcelona reached a peak on 2 May 1937 when government forces tried to take over the telephone exchange from the FAI. Heavy street fighting began two days later. Mary speaks of the rebels as 'fascists', echoing the CP line of the time that the POUM were consciously Franco agents.
12. Ellen is speaking in the House of Commons on 6 July 1938. Mr Donner and Mr Denville were Conservatives, Mr Gallacher was a Communist.
13. The University City, Madrid, was the scene of heavy fighting in November-December 1936 when Franco's troops failed to enter the city.
14. Rebel forces took Badajoz in Estremadura on 14 August 1936 and massacred thousands of local Republicans in the bull ring.
15. Bill Rust was a *Daily Worker* correspondent in Spain. Walter Tapsell, previously the circulation manager of the *Daily Worker*, Political Commissar of the British Battalion at Teruel, was killed during fascist break-through in Aragon in April 1938.

Part 5

THE OTHER SIDE
OF THE LINES

The Men are Working Better

Eleanora Tennant

Eleanora Tennant *was of Italian origin, from Australia. By marriage she was related to the aristocratic Glenconner family. Always interested in politics, she visited Franco Spain, via Portugal, early in the Civil War, publishing her observations under the title of* Spanish Journey.

We passed through mile upon mile of pine forests, olive groves and orchards of fig trees. There were no barricades across the roads, and we were only once held up to show our passes. Motor-cars were gaily beflagged, and all, even lorries, bore a distinguished mark. This was either the old yellow and red flag of Spain, now re-adopted by the Nationalists, or a white flag bearing wording such as 'Long Live the Army', or 'Long Live the Glorious Cadets of Toledo'.[1] Once, when our own flag blew away, my chauffeur got extremely worried as he thought we might appear to be unpatriotic.

After passing for three hours through undulating country rising at last into foothills, we arrived at Tharsis, where I called on the mine manager. It was interesting to hear this intelligent Scotsman tell of what had occurred in Tharsis on the outbreak of the rebellion. These ancient mines, now under British management, have been worked at different periods since the days of the Phoenicians. They employ thousands of men. The moment it became known that General Franco had rebelled, the men downed tools and did not return to work for a fortnight, although they carried on the essential services. The province of Huelva boasted a Red Governor, therefore no one knew what was going to happen. The British women and children living at the mines were evacuated to a British destroyer lying in Huelva harbour. At 3 a.m. one morning the manager was awakened by violent knocking. On opening the door he was greeted by a party of Communists, all armed – an unpleasant situation to face in pyjamas. They ordered him to hand over all the dynamite on the company's premises. This he refused to do without an order from the Governor. The following day the men returned with the order duly signed by the Governor of Huelva and they took away a considerable quantity of dynamite.

Tharsis was one of the first places to be captured by the Nationalists, and fortunately the time factor spared this little bit of Spain from any major tragedies, although a certain amount of shooting was necessary before the Reds were dislodged. The Red leaders bolted into the hills as soon as they realised that the Nationalists were approaching.

As conditions were so peaceful at Tharsis (the men are working better than they have done for years), I moved on to Huelva. Huelva, unlike what I saw later on, was again a surprise, and showed no signs of serious damage, except for the Church of Asunción, which was in ruins. The streets were crowded with people shopping and talking in groups. There was complete law and order. Shops were full of food and merchandise. The only sign of military activity was the fact that almost every man wore a uniform of some sort.

From Huelva I motored to Seville. [...] Seville was teeming with people; trams were running as usual, taxis were good and numerous, and there were many horse-drawn cabs. Perfect order was to be seen everywhere, and I was surprised to find Seville so full of life and bustle and the municipal services so efficient. 'Business as usual' was the order of the day, except, I gather, that there was far more business than at any time since the fall of the monarchy in 1931. [...]

The service at the Hotel Madrid, where I stayed, was comparable to that in a first-class London hotel, but less expensive. The food was plentiful and good. I received telephone calls in my bedroom from as far away as Salamanca. [...]

A hairdresser I visited in Seville told me of the improved conditions under the Nationalists. He was a German who had lived in Spain for many years. Before the rebellion he had been on the point of cutting his losses and returning to Germany. He said that his custom had almost vanished because no ladies ventured out of their houses for fear of being shot or worse. Now his trade was returning, as the ladies were having their hair attended to again and everyone could now venture out with complete safety. [...]

Having secured a military pass to enter the war zone, I decided to proceed to Toledo *via* Merida and Talavera de la Reina, a distance from Seville of 500 kilometres over two ranges of mountains. The manager of the Hotel Madrid helped me to hire a car and a chauffeur. I was somewhat disturbed to find, after we had started, and were well out of Seville, that José, the chauffeur, had never been to Toledo before, as I had been warned that if we made any mistake in the roads we might easily find ourselves in Red territory. Fortunately, José proved a treasure and thanks to my precious map we kept to the right road. [...]

In a small village beyond the town of Merida, José halted the car so that I might examine a wall surrounding the village cemetery which had been used by Red firing-squads as a place of execution. This wall was about 7 feet high, and part of the wall, about 12 feet in length, was pitted with hundreds of bullet-holes. Only a space about a foot in width at the top and a foot wide at the bottom was free of bullet-marks. [...]

Talavera had suffered the usual Red atrocities before the Nationalists arrived. More than 100 of the inhabitants were shot, including a number of priests and nuns. Many of these suffered appalling tortures. The prison conditions as recounted by a refined English woman (married to a Spaniard), who had been in Talavera under the Reds, are too horrible to record in detail. Suffice to say that over 50 men and women were imprisoned for many weeks in one small room and never allowed to leave it under any pretext. Hardly any furniture and no conveniences of any kind were supplied. The centre of the room had to be used as a public latrine. The atmosphere became so unbearable that some died and others continually lost consciousness. No one had any opportunity of changing clothing of any kind. [...]

A Shining Light

Florence Farmborough

Florence Farmborough *left Russia during the revolution, and from 1926 to 1936 lived in Valencia. After the military revolt she made her way to Salamanca, in Nationalist territory, where she broadcast to English-speaking countries each Sunday evening. Her account of her experiences was dedicated 'with pride and humility to Generalissimo Franco'.*

Now I should like to say something about the conditions prevailing in National Spain. Strange as it may seem, life in liberated Spain is almost normal.

And this atmosphere prevails even in the villages and towns separated from the front line by a distance of only two or three miles. Market-days come and go with clockwork regularity; fiestas are never forgotten and are celebrated with enthusiasm and sincerity, especially those connected with the church: bullfights, and other forms of popular amusements, are not wanting. The booming of guns and the bombardment of enemy 'planes, make but a slight diversion from the daily routine of the people; they are noises, so usual, so familiar, that the average person pays little heed to them!

Food-stuffs abound and prices are very little higher than they were prior to the 18th of July, 1936. [...]

And the youth of Spain turn towards their Leader, Generalissimo Franco, as towards a shining light; he is the beacon that guides them to their highest goal. In all people this great faith in the Caudillo is to be found; in the highest and lowest, in the richest and poorest, in the oldest and youngest, for even the very small children are taught to play their role of loyal subject to National Spain. And that reminds me of an incident which I witnessed the other day, an incident which amused me and yet seemed to touch a deeper chord. I was walking through the Arcade of the Plaza Mayor in this city of Salamanca (one of the most beautiful old squares in Europe, surrounded by a columned promenade, lined on one side by shops), when I saw in front of me a woman of humble station in life, holding a small boy of some three years by the hand. Suddenly the child stopped, turned towards a shop-window and, relinquishing his mother's hand, drew himself up to his full height (about ¾ yd.!), clicked his tiny heels together and, standing to attention, was about to raise his arm in the Phalangist salute[2]. His mother, unconscious of his action, grasped his hand and dragged him along with her – none too gently! The wee boy's face was a study in expressions of anger and disappointment. But, with sudden determination, he turned, manfully resisting his mother's display of force, and, nearly toppling over himself in his anxiety that his heels should touch each other, he stiffened his small round body and saluted, solemnly and ceremoniously, in Phalangist manner! His unheeding mother, sensing rebellion, seized him so vigorously that the child stumbled and nearly fell – but he was docile now, he had done his duty. He had saluted a large portrait of Generalissimo Franco in the shop-window! [...]

And what of the woman's role in the great Movement of Liberation in National Spain? The answer comes readily: the woman of Spain is not found wanting. Her place is in her home, miles away, perhaps, from the front line, but her heart is in the trenches. How could it be otherwise? Is not every soldier a mother's son? And has not every soldier a mother, sister, or sweetheart, who are daily, hourly, experiencing anxious thought for his welfare? 'Men must work and women must weep.' And though it may be true that the women of Spain, by reason of the greatness of their heart's pain, have, and still do, shed tears for their absent ones, it is also true that this pain is mitigated by pride, a pride born of self-sacrifice and patriotic abnegation in the heart of every woman who gives her best-beloved to her country that he may defend it in its evil hour.

Spain is awakening to a new era. '*Autres temps, autres moeurs!*' And this new era may perhaps be most vividly illustrated by the sudden 'leap' into public activity of the women of Spain. Before the National Movement there were, it is true, many feminine institutions, chiefly connected with the Church; certain sports also, especially tennis and riding, were bringing the girls to the fore, but the old Spanish custom of chaperone (*carabina*, as they called her) of the girl youth of Spain was still in vogue, and many a girl was unable to go out shopping or even for a walk, because her chaperone was not available at the desired hour!

Now it is different, everything is different. A young girl has duties to perform, public duties, outside her home; she goes here, there, everywhere, occupied with this or that organisation; all disinterested action; she is conscious only that her efforts, co-operating with those of her girl friends, are of enormous importance to her country. She, too, places herself in the category of combatant in the service of the Mother-Country and of the State. She is not forced to give her time, there is no law to oblige her to do so; it is the call of her native-land that she hears, the sacred duty of patriotism that she fulfils, an intimate impulse of her heart, of her national feeling, that she obeys ...

There are so many ways and means by which the Spanish woman shows her patriotism, so many organisations for women of merit and utility, that it is impossible to enumerate them all today. The Red Cross has no lack of helpers, and countless deeds of heroism could be narrated of those great-hearted women who, braving danger and death, devote their days and nights to the nursing of the wounded and sick. Every province contributes its quota of philanthropic service to the Cause, and with thoughts ever engrossed the Spanish woman goes about her daily task. In her spare time she is not idle, her hands are light and her fingers dexterous. She sews, by hand and by machine; she knits; she crochets; all with will, with solicitude, knowing that there is someone in the trenches whose life will be made a little more comfortable by this – the tangible result of her labours.

I remember my first impression on seeing a group of these workers. It was in Seville. I had entered the office of the *Falange Española Tradicionalista* (Spanish Traditionalist Phalanx), in the *Sección Feminina Valenciana* (Women's Section), and I saw some twenty to thirty young women seated in a large circle, all knitting steadily; to me, a non-knitter (I confess it with shame!), it seemed almost fiercely, so energetically did the long needles dart in and out of the soft woollen threads. On the ground at their sides were baskets containing balls of wool in all shades of grey, brown and dark blue, which were rapidly being converted into the useful garments, lying in various stages of progress on their laps, for the 'boys at the front'. Their faces were serious, their eyes absorbed. Then I became aware that they were reciting something; I listened more attentively: it was the Rosary. One of their number was reciting the prayers to the chorus of responses. It was my first meeting with the 'Women Workers of the Rear', and I must admit that it made a great impression on me. The note it struck seemed a very healthy one: this assembly of young girls, playing their part resolutely, hopefully, their fingers swiftly working, their minds intent on the prayer to the Virgin Mary. Surely here was the true woman's spirit, and surely that softly uttered prayer would call down a divine blessing on the work of the women of New Spain.

The Woman's Section of the Spanish Traditionalist Phalanx, with Pilar Primo de Rivera at its head, is undoubtedly the leader of the organisations for women in National Spain. Its branch institution, the Sisterhood of City and Country (Hermandad de la Ciudad y del Campo) does a splendid work; the young girls place themselves at the service of those families, either in city or in country, who are in need of extra assistance, owing to the fact that the men whose hands had previously performed the tasks are now occupied fighting in the National trenches. Much good and important work has been accomplished during the past year; at the reaping of the large crops of grain in Castille, at the vintage of the grape and at the harvesting of the olive in the southern provinces, these 'sisters' are ever to be seen, full of life and enthusiasm, carrying out their duties to the letter and glad of the opportunity of lending a helping hand to their country.

And the Social Aid or Welfare Institution (Auxilio Social)! I should like to have several hours at my disposal to describe all its endless activities. It had its birth in Valladolid, under the direction of Mercedes Sanz Bachiller, and began by opening one dining-room in the city and ten in the villages of the province; now there are hundreds distributed throughout National Spain. [...]

I should like to give you a quick sketch of what takes place within these dining-rooms. At noon the rush hour begins. The young girls, all enthusiastic volunteers, all staunch followers of the Phalanx, are standing about in groups; white aprons over their dark dresses, their badge of red yoke and arrows showing up plainly against the navy-blue of their blouses; they are ready to begin their work of serving. The doors are opened and men and women enter. In their hands are pots and large muglike receptacles. Food is given to all in abundance; no documents are required, no personal questions are asked. What does it matter if they are White or Red! What *does* matter is that they are hungering – that is sufficient for the Phalangists. And, if they are Reds, all the better! Let them learn the great lesson that although they clench their fist in hatred – to take by force, the Phalanx opens its hand to give – with love ...

The old people have special dining-rooms arranged for them, from which a portrait of the Leader, Generalissimo Franco, and the flags of Spain and of the Phalanx are never absent. Girls and women are working in them from morning to night, some of them so assiduously, as scarcely ever to see the light of the sun! One senses the atmosphere of sacrifice which pervades these busy centres; the work goes forward with a will; the girls give to it all their time and thoughts. And the care and service are duly appreciated by the old people. After a meal their time-worn faces are a study in happy expressions; satisfied and grateful they sit there, nodding their heads and smiling, their old wrinkled hands folded on their knees. Sometimes they sing a patriotic song in honour of Spain; for, strange to say, in their old age they are beginning to learn and understand exactly what the Mother-Country *stands for* and *is*; they are being taught by those who wear white aprons and the badge of red arrows yoked in union, that the Mother-Country is not merely an empty name, but a living breathing existence, whose first and last thought will ever be for the well-being of her children. The old people, replete and content, file out; the tables are cleared, clean crockery is placed on them, for another hungry batch is about to enter. In a few minutes, the girls are again moving swiftly in all directions, serving ... chatting ... smiling ... Again the hard faces relax into softer expressions; again the quavering old voices are lifted in hymns of praise ...

The Bishop's Equipo

Gabriel Herbert

Gabriel Herbert was the only English-speaking woman with Franco's medical services. The Bishop's Fund for Relief of Spanish Distress sent a hospital unit, and Gabriel Herbert, whose uncle, Lord Howard of Penrith, was chairman of the fund, went as enlacé, *or 'middle-man' as she described it, with the unit.*

The *Equipo Anglo-Español* came into being through the generosity and help of the Bishop's Committee; it consisted of a group, who all had ties with Spain, and were anxious to help the Spanish Nationalists; the members were all Catholic, I think; the 'Bishop' was the Cardinal of Westminster, Cardinal Hinsley. Without being an official member, he gave the Committee much help and encouragement with their project.

The Committee decided that the first priority should be medical supplies and assistance; they would collect money for this through appeals in the press, meetings, lectures, etc. This scheme was accepted by the British Foreign Office, with the proviso that all goods for Spain should be bought outside that country. The best help appeared to be concentration on supplying hospital needs. In the event we ended by supplying our *own* hospital. [...]

The Spanish were obviously pleased at the suggestion and made one condition; that all the hospital staff should be Spanish; the reason was, of course, the language barrier; which, in a hospital, would make havoc.

I was excluded from this veto; became a sort of *enlacé*, or middle-man; who could travel more freely than the Spanish could, between frontiers, report to the Committee, and act as their representative; as my Spanish improved, I could translate the orders for urgent needs for the doctors, and, when convenient, go to London to check the orders, and convoy them back to Spain. There were one or two embarrassing moments for me; a confusion between the meaning of words: *agujas*, meaning needles; *angulas*, meaning baby eels. It was pointed out, very kindly to me, that what I was asking the bewildered Committee to send us, urgently, was 10,000 baby eels of different sizes!

Improbable as it sounds, I was also in charge of stores; keeping tally of them; later, when we had our own transport, travelling with the material when possible; was responsible to see that we had sufficient, *and that it was where it was where it was needed.* During the latter part of the war, in order to secure its safety, we rented a barn, near Zaragoza, and fetched the material as required. One of the nightmares was the possibility of success in an attack by Red forces, and loss of all the Committee's hard work and valuable drugs.

I went out to Biarritz in early September [1936] to await the arrival of a promised permit for Spain. The Duke of Lécera, at about the end of the month, drove me into Spain. It was the day of the taking of Irún, which was burning, or smouldering rather, in a wet, raw mist, and the bridge closed. [...]

I was less than hopeful the next morning when we set out for Burgos to see what view the government took of the suggestion of the doctors [for the organisation of the *Equipo*, J.F.]. I saw General Mola, at the time Chief of Staff, later killed in an airplane crash (certainly the most impressive of the Generals) and his Aide General Cabellas.

On my return to London, the doctors had already made out their first list of requests, and I took it with me. This was really the end of the first stage. The Committee was delighted with the list. Cash had been flowing in and with actual things to be bought the flow doubled.

I saw the list agreed; the two ambulances full. Then they were blessed by the Cardinal, ready to go. I left myself to await their arrival at the frontier.

And wait indeed was what I did; so did we all. There were quite important losses before the things got to the frontier. One of the ambulances got through customs, the other was held up by a curious rule that cotton wool was material of war. (The French customs were undisguisedly hostile.) The second ambulance, carrying one ton, had to be re-dispatched by sea to Lisbon. [...]

Finding a suitable chief doctor was not difficult, owing to the contact between Committee members and their Spanish friends. An excellent surgeon-physician, Don Ignacio Urbina, volunteered for the *Equipo*, and agreed to act as chief.

It was Don Ignacio who selected the doctors and nurses to work with him. Both doctors and nurses came as volunteers, as he had done. As soon as a doctor had joined the *Equipo* he was given a military rank and paid by the army. Neither by *Sanidad* [medical authorities] nor any other body were any of our staff transferred to strange hospitals during the war. This was an enormous help to the solidarity of the group. We worked together, played together, laughed together and became friends. *Sanidad* had designated us as an *Equipo Móvil de Servicio al Frente*. We were to be a unit and a self-sufficient one.

Equipo Móvil is a sort of mobile first aid post; we followed the armies, and, when necessary sent forward parties of three to suitable villages: a surgeon, a nurse and an *ayudante* (surgeon's assistant in operations, who also supervised dressings). These small posts were very useful indeed, especially in winter, especially on the Northern Front. This front stretched back from the coast towards, and into, the Picos de Europa. There were no roads there, for the region was mountainous, and getting the wounded back to hospital a most difficult task. One of the nastiest things in that region was the prevalence of minerals, and also and particularly gangrene in the soil. The posts, dotted about in small villages, were invaluable, for they could treat the wounded earlier, and therefore with greater chance of success. Penicillin was, in 1936, unknown, at any rate in Spain and the only hope of saving the men infected, was gangrene serum, at the earliest possible moment.[3]

Samaniego was the first post we were sent to, on this coast, in (I think) November 1936. It made a splendid hospital, adjacent to Vittoria, with three stories, in which we and two other *Equipos* worked independently; the main part of our job was to nurse the wounded from the Northern Front, which the *Requetés* (the Royalist army) were struggling to clear.[4] They were charming men, immensely brave, and devoted to their cause; at one moment we had, side by side, in the hospital, three generals; grandfather, son and grandson. The grandfather had presented himself to take the place of the other two when they were wounded, as a matter of course. [...]

We left Samaniego in October '37 (I think) for Huesca, a small city, north-east of Zaragoza. When we arrived, it was very empty; there were, I believe, only 2,000 inhabitants left, for the city was under siege, and supplies very short. To the east and west arcs, the heavy guns of the Red forces had the range of Huesca; the south their light infantry with machine-guns dominated the Zaragoza road. It could only be travelled in the half-light, early morning or dusk, and we could only use side lights. The town council of Huesca had the duty of supplying its people with necessities; drinking water, food, oil and petrol, which were all in short supply; this they decided to do by donkey train. It was the most extraordinary sight. The first four to six kilometres of the Zaragoza road were sunk below the verges on either side; a heavy mist covered the road, and the donkey's legs hidden in it; only their bodies visible, bobbing along, or floating, like little boats, drifting.

We were given a really rather nice house as hospital; fairly capacious, and with glass in many of the windows. When the cold became excessive we brought in large buckets, filled with alchohol, which were lighted with a match and burned out. It was surprising what a difference this made, and how long the effect lasted. We also had sufficient fires and stoves to heat water for the patients. Some of the patients (civilian) in the town hospital were moved into ours on our arrival, where they had more comfort, and we were able to help their town hospital when we replenished our supplies from the Zaragoza barn, where the bulk of our material was stored.

Huesca was relieved in April '38 by the [Foreign] Legion, who arrived overnight, and the Reds were gone before I woke up next morning. Before we left Huesca the Council, in the name of the people, made the gift, to every man or woman who had been in the *Equipo*, of the '*Medalla de Huesca*' which I expect they embroidered themselves, for there was no one to do it for them, 'For our friends, who came to help when we were beseiged'. They were such a friendly and welcoming people. I passed through there once again, carrying material for the *Equipo*, in a new post: the number of people that came up, when they saw the lorry, whose faces I knew, but not their names, to ask news of the *Equipo*, and send them messages and good wishes, was extraordinary. They were the friendliest place we were ever in. [...]

All of our equipment proved to be of immense use. During the spring and summer of '38, when we were following the armies across Aragon and Catalonia, in the campaign to open the way to Barcelona, I doubt if we could have found any village with enough beds to supply a field hospital. When we came to Barcelona and to Madrid, the *Equipo* was more than pleased to find enough mattresses to unroll on the floor of the Ritz and sleep on.

Assisting the Task of Appeasement

Lady Chamberlain

Lady Chamberlain *chaired the Relief Fund for Depressed Women and Children of Spain. Her former husband, Sir Austen Chamberlain MP was British Foreign Secretary from 1924-29, and her brother-in-law, Neville Chamberlain MP, was Prime Minister from 1937 to 1940. In September 1938 Lady Chamberlain visited Franco Spain, and stayed with Doña Carmen Franco, the general's wife, at her country home near La Coruña. At Burgos she met Franco and said she was 'most favourably impressed with living conditions' in insurgent territory. On leaving Spain she said that her journey 'had no political significance'. Asked if she intended visiting Republican territory, she replied that there was no reason why she should. On 12 November she appealed in the* Times *for her fund.*

Two and a half years of bitter fighting on fronts that have changed with the fluctuating fortunes of war have resulted in the devastation of scores of towns and villages. The inhabitants, homeless and destitute, have sought refuge in the hills or in overcrowded cities behind the lines, where hunger, disease and the constant fear of air-raids have added to their misery.

It is these refugees, and particularly the children, we have tried to help. We have sent out food, clothing, blankets and medicines. We have opened milk canteens at which over 6,000 children and nearly 2,000 mothers, aged people and invalids draw their modest daily supplies. We have helped to maintain the British hospital at Barcelona, a peacetime institution which provides a temporary home for crippled children, and endeavours to carry on its work among the remaining British residents. More than one British sailor on patrol duty with the Fleet in the Mediterranean owes his life to the hospital's doctors and nurses. We have also been able in a few instances to deliver supplies to men and women in prison.

All this work has been of a non-political and impartial character. Supplies have been sent to both sides in equal proportion. Their distribution has been controlled by our own representatives, on the Nationalist side by a committee with which HRH the Infanta Beatrix is associated, on the government side by the British hospital.[5] Care has been taken to avoid any step that might be considered as intervention, and our committee is in no way responsible for the separation of children from their parents or their removal from Spanish soil.

Unfortunately we are now faced with the prospect of having to suspend our work owing to lack of funds. Of the £13,000 raised so far less than 6 per cent has been required for expenses, and of the rest very little remains. We are urgently in need of a further £3,000 to tide over the next few months.

Winter is approaching and distress is increasing, and again it will be without Christmas cheer. Must those to whom our help has meant so much look to us in vain for further help?

I appeal to all those who have the suffering of humanity at heart, and particularly to those who care for children, to contribute as generously as they can. Everything which tends to keep burning among the Spanish people the flickering flame of sympathy and kindness is a contribution towards their ultimate reconciliation. Perhaps, in the case of Spain, it is also the best way of assisting the task of general appeasement.

Notes

1. The Alcazar Fortress in Toledo was besieged by Republican militia in August and September 1936 until relieved when Francoist troops captured Toledo on 27 September.
2. Falange Español, a fascist party formed soon after the Republic was established in 1931, by José Antonio Primo de Rivera, son of the former dictator.
3. Gas gangrene was virtually eliminated in the Republican army by good surgery in front-line hospitals. Gabriel describes hopsital organisation similar to that in the First World War.
4. *Requetés* were Navarrese forces of the extreme right-wing royalist and clerical Carlist party, supporting the rival Bourbon line to that of Alfonso XIII.
5. Cousin of Alfonso XIII, she attended the first meeting of the NJC in London, but withdrew. On the fall of Barcelona she arrived at the Quaker centre to take over relief work.

Part 6

A PEOPLE IN
RETREAT

A Tragedy So Immense
Edith Pye

Edith Pye, *the veteran Quaker relief worker, has been made a* Chevalier *of the Legion of Honour for her work in France with refugees during and after the 1914-18 war. She was a member of the Friends Service Council Spain Committee and visited Barcelona in December 1936 to supervise the establishment of canteens for refugees. She worked with Spanish refugees in France, and after Franco's victory visited Spain from where she reported that food sent to relieve distress was being seized by the military, and that all the Quaker canteens had been closed and the food sold.*

Perpignan
29 January 1939

Dear Hilda,
It is a really terrible tragedy here – up till today the pass leading to Spain has been one solid block of refugees, of all ages, wounded soldiers, etc., and I understand they spent the nights standing, as one stands in the tube in rush-hours. They were prevented from coming into France by Senegalese soldiers. (They said 'Moors behind us and now Moors in front!' and the crowd simply got wedged tighter and tighter.) Some of our people set up a canteen on the French side giving a piece of bread and a drink of hot milk to all the women and children and old people. Miss Vulliamy with National Joint Committee money set up another for wounded and worn-out men, but up till now there has been *no chance* of getting to the Spanish side of the frontier.[1] Even del Vayo had to give it up.[2] The only way to get there would be by walking on their heads and shoulders.

Today things are a little better. They are letting a few thousand through and they have at last begun to issue rations. The French intend to feed 150,000 on Spanish soil but there is no sign and no possibility of their beginning this at present. These poor people have absolutely no shelter – it poured in buckets all last night and thou can imagine what it was like. Today we met the Gerona lot of workers at the frontier and have brought them back. They were bombed out of Gerona and out of Figueras, had been three days on the way and slept two nights in the lorry. Poor Cuthbert Wigham is very spry but he looks as if he had been through something. Dr Audrey [Russell] Ellis had an awful time in a car on the road full of refugees that they were bombing and machine-gunning. She was alone and said the road was full of bodies of refugees.

I spent the morning at Le Perthus watching the crowd – in the middle of it a poor woman went suddenly mad, stripped off every stitch of clothes and ran down the middle of the road screaming. She was very fat and pink, and it made the most awful contrast. The gendarmes were very nice about it, *very* decent; I offered to help and said I was *infirmière* [a nurse] but they said they did not need help – the poor thing was out of her mind. I saw her after in an ambulance.

We shall see tonight what more can be done – nothing in Spain itself I fear, except on the border.

29 January 1939

No time to write – a tragedy so immense that one hardly sees how to tackle it. Margarita has a canteen for milk and bread at the frontier, but the French are only beginning today. Refugees have had five nights in the open – and last night pouring wet. All our workers out safe. Shall not be here long.

A Whole Landscape Moving

Nancy Cunard

Nancy Cunard, *the writer and campaigner for black rights, was one of the first British observers to go to Spain after the army revolt. She attended the International Writer's Congress in Madrid in 1937. She wrote many poems and articles on Spain, and in 1937 circulated British writers to ask them which side they supported. One hundred replied supporting the Republic, five supporting Franco and sixteen said they were neutral. In February 1939 she reported to the* Manchester Guardian *on the plight of Spanish refugees at the French border.*

8 February 1939

Vans, trucks, lorries, and buses continue to bring refugee women and children across the frontier at Le Perthus. The road is much better organised, and half of it is now free for cars to pass in and out of Spain. Pitiful little groups of refugees are still camping out, washing their clothes in the streams. At night there are small camp-fires all along the mountain. There are many babies in arms and infants at the breast. […]

When I was sitting on a bench in Perpignan today an old peasant woman came up to ask me for a little money. These were her words: 'I left Gerona with my husband the night before last. Eight 'planes followed us out of the town to the last bridge, machine-gunning us. We got to Figueras. If only you could see it – nothing but ruins, smashed to pieces. I made my husband get into a lorry there; he is ill, so I walked to La Junquera. We had 11,000 pesetas we had saved; we have worked all our lives. They gave us 28 francs for this at the frontier, and the bus from Le Boulou to Perpignan cost us 16.'

This disastrous situation of the exchange is beyond words. Nearly all Spaniards arrive with various sums of money, but cannot, or can hardly, pay for a hotel room or a meal.

It is fit to pay tribute to the leaders of a nation in its present agony who care in the way they do for the cultural heritage of their people. Perhaps one of the last official documents to bear the signature of Señor del Vayo in the old Castle of Figueras was that accepting that the Spanish paintings and works of art be taken to Geneva for safe keeping by the League of Nations. [...]

The report that some of the lorries transporting Spanish works of art were attacked by 'planes is confirmed in the local press here today. It adds that José-Maria Sert (famous Spanish painter whom I have known personally and whose work decorated the chapel of the Duke of Alba's palace of Liria, in Madrid) sent a telegram to the Duke of Alba in London asking that there should be no bombardments during the transport of the pictures and art treasurers. These contain 400 or more paintings by Velásquez, El Greco, and Goya.

Yesterday, on Spanish territory between Le Perthus and La Junquera, I passed ten huge vans carrying these treasures; immense, solidly packed trailers attached to special motors and driven by French chauffeurs. The one I talked with was indignant over the conditions in which this work has to be carried out. 'They attack even the works of art of a country,' he said. 'Can you imagine what it has been like getting away from Figueras during these air raids?'

9 February 1939

At Le Perthus, from nine o'clock this morning until 4.30, I have been watching soldiers pass between the two stone posts that are actually the frontier-line. They have come by in thousands and thousands, in groups, singly, and in numberless lorries. At the posts stand the French soldiers, who immediately search them for arms. The Spanish soldiers give up their arms in an orderly fashion. The pile of rifles, revolvers, cartridge belts, dirks, and even a knife or two grow throughout the day. Two machine-guns have been brought in; farther up, an armoured car.

But all this is only the beginning; we are told: 'Tomorrow the rearguard of the army, and afterwards – the army that has fought.' On the mountains each side they come, so that the whole landscape seems to be moving. Soldiers on horseback, wounded men, women, children, a whole population, and cars and ambulances. Many of the ambulances are British and of the 'Centrale Internationale Sanitaire', one of whose doctors tells me of the appalling lack of supplies, of staff, and of help.

In fact, there is enough of nothing save the now excellently distributed food rations which are made by France. There was a good supply of food at La Junquera, as the food parcels that had been intended for parts of Catalonia now taken by the enemy were being used there. All medical centres and staffs are over-powered, however; at Cerbère, for instance, a doctor told me, are 1,500 wounded soldiers with hardly any sanitary necessities at all. Lack of sufficient transport for them is another difficulty. Dr Audrey Russell, who is well known for her fine work in Spain for many months, said that she had just been able to get her last canteen into French territory.

General Molesworth was another English worker at Le Perthus, where he was indefatigably trying to get the internationals together. 'Only a handful have come through so far,' the General told me.

10 February 1939

Some of the camps to which the Spanish refugees are going are not fit to receive human beings. The problem has been too vast to be dealt with as yet.

At the great central camp at Le Boulou are thousands of men, women, and children. On one side of the road is an enclosure with wire fencing. On the other the refugees who walked down from Le Perthus yesterday are lying, sitting, standing, doing nothing this cold end of a February afternoon. It is a horrible sight, and all of them, men, women and children, are in the utmost depression. This 'camp' is a large, flat, bare area, the grass trodden down into a sort of grey compost. They sleep here, in the open. A few have rigged up some vague kind of shelter.

As for medical aid – just one case I saw will show the state of things. A woman lamented that she could do nothing for her child. She took off the little girl's bonnet and said: 'These dreadful sores are the result of typhus.' They come and stand around you and talk; they argue among themselves in front of you: 'Are we worse off here today than we might be in Spain?' Then a woman cries out, 'I shall never get into a train without knowing where it is going, for I have heard that they want to send us back to Franco.' Other voices broke out: 'Ninety-five per cent of us want to go to Mexico – anything rather than return to Spain as it will be under the fascists.' At the village town hall a girl I knew in Spain says she thinks the women she is one of in a long queue may get a permit to go to Perpignan some time soon. All the men, says a French guard, are going to Argelès; when? No one knows. In all of this families get separated; the men are taken from their families in some cases. Every phrase ends in 'I don't know.' As for the wounded – they are lying in the ditch among their crutches; a man limps by in obvious agony.

Somehow one becomes accustomed to such sights after ten days. But they become more real again when I try to set down just a fraction here and compare this mass-wretchedness with the 'business-eye' of some Marseilles white-slave traffickers who have made their appearance. There are many pretty girls in the Spanish migration.

Concentration Camp

Lillian Urmston

The things seen during the last days of our retreat from Spain, and the experiences undergone in the concentration camp of St Cyprian, near Perpignan, I shall never forget ... The last few days spent in Spain, working close to the front, yet within sight of the Pyrenees, were utterly ghastly. Operating work was done, *and efficiently*, just inside houses by the roadside. In innumerable instances, we came upon families of refugees wounded whilst fleeing to safety. We cared for them and kept them with us if they were seriously wounded ...

On the late evening of the 8th we received orders to go into France. Although sad at leaving our Spain, we all realised that this had to be and looked forward to a rapid reorganisation in France which would result in our going back to another sector of Spain to carry on the struggle against Fascist aggression.

But we were soon disillusioned ... We were led to believe that France had opened her frontiers to receive our soldier refugees and wounded, thus preventing a complete massacre. We expected sympathy and humane treatment. We had neither.

The vigilance of hundreds of armed guards made sure that all people entering France entered the concentration camp. Ours was a stretch of sandy desert land, surrounded by the usual formidable barbed wire. Wounded men were even without treatment for about six days. We were *not* allowed to tend our sick comrades. One small spring supplied water for about 15,000 to 20,000 people. Food was not supplied until the fifth day ... Men attempting to dodge out to buy bread and send letters were treated brutally by the guards. Our comrades received bayonet wounds at the hands of these soldiers of the French army. My Spanish friends turned to me and said: 'Would we be treated like this in England?' And I wonder, would they?

Spahi soldiers told our men to return to Franco Spain and then they would get away from all this.[3] Our soldiers felt deeply about this, and called out to those men who were collected to be sent to Barcelona, deploring their conduct. Then the camp resounded with '*Viva la Republica! Viva nuestra Independencia!*'

A Ship for Mexico

Nan Green

The National Joint Committee quickly set to work to send relief, and in particular to collect the money for the chartering of an entire ship to send refugees to Mexico, whose government had generously offered asylum. A French vessel was chartered, the SS *Sinaia*, whose usual run was to take pilgrims to Mecca. It could hold about 2,000 passengers. [...]

Now a relatively small problem came up. The ship held only a limited number of people. Observers must go with it, but every observer would occupy a place which might have been used by yet another refugee. Sir Richard Rees and William Brebner, a Quaker, were to go from the National Joint Committe but if anyone else went it ought to be someone who could be useful on board and who could come back and campaign for more money, for yet another ship was the intention. I could speak Spanish; I could be useful on board, and could return with first hand information to tour the country appealing for more funds. Leah Manning, bless her, suggested me, and the Committee agreed. Hastily borrowing a number of white coats, to make me look a bit professional on board ship, I packed up and set off for southern France where the ship lay ready. [...]

The voyage took twenty-three days. My job, I discovered, was to see to the feeding of the very young children for whom no arrangement existed in the ship's facilities. On the first day, a group of (refugee) doctors interviewed all the infants and children under two years of age and allocated them to one of five or six diets. Supplies of various kinds of infant food had been brought on board. I co-ordinated the diets into quantities, and every three hours descended to the galley where I stirred, with the aid of two hard-working Spanish girls, great saucepans full of milk and different paps, distributing them in a made-over barber saloon to the mothers, either in bowls or in feeding bottles which had to be sterilised between feeds. I hardly ever got up on deck.

There were two interesting breaks in the voyage. The first was at Madeira, where the ship stopped to take on water, and the Captain asked some of us who possessed passports to go ashore and buy him some wine. Sir Richard, William Brebner and I, together with

Georges Soria, a French journalist, who was to write up the voyage for the French press, went off into the hills to some cellars, furnished with tables, and chairs made from barrels and 'tested' glass after tiny glass of Madeira. Having made our purchases (I have absolutely no 'palate' and could not tell one from another, but someone must have been proficient) we returned a bit tipsily through Funchal, where we were held up by a procession of Fascist Youth, armed in black shirts and jackboots. Soria, with whom I had up to the point spoken only in French, suddenly leaned over my shoulder and said, in excellent English: 'Fuck them all!' to my great delight.

Our second stop was Puerto Rico. Here, the island's supporters of Republican Spain had arranged an absolutely magnificent reception and treat for the refugees, with a huge banquet and a fleet of charabancs in which they proposed to take everyone for a tour of the island.

Alas, the American authorities refused permission for them to land. There was a lot of altercation, in which the Mexican Ambassador took part, but to no avail. Only those four of the passengers who had gone ashore at Madeira were permitted, and even then the Yanks tried to stop me on the grounds that they had not got a *woman* officer to search me; I stepped defiantly before the Marine officer and *dared* him to go ahead. Shamefacedly and grumpily he let me pass. We talked with the 'Spanish Aid Committee' which had organised the reception. They took us to see the scene of the banquet which had been prepared, and for a brief run by car to show the beauties of the countryside. Meanwhile, a portable platform had been brought to the quayside, where local worthies made speeches of solidarity and affection. When we got back to the ship, we were stunned to see that the mountain had come to Mahomed!

The whole side of the ship was festooned with ropes and lengths of string, to which a crowd of Puerto Ricans were fastening sausages, roast chickens, joints of meat, loaves of bread, baskets of fruit, cakes and biscuits, every imaginable kind of food which was being hauled aboard by their Spanish friends lining the rail above, while speaker after speaker on a platform below addressed them through a megaphone. It was a scene of sheer love, and difficult to describe whether those on the ship or those on the shore were more moved. I caught sight of a very small ragged boy, probably a bootblack, tying a sandwich – probably his lunch – on to a string and smiling angelically to see it hauled above. The scene continued all day and the crowd stayed until we sailed in the evening. [...]

Shipboard is one of the classical sites for *rumours*. As we neared

Veracruz and people began to express their uncertainty as to what would happen when we reached shore, the strong rumour went round that all the women were to be put in convents and all the men in barracks. The Mexican Ambassador and his wife, who were not themselves sure of exactly what was planned, went round with reassuring words which did something to allay the mischief.

What happened when we finally docked I did not see, as I was below in the galley preparing the last baby-foods so that the children should leave the ship with contented tummies. But I found when it was all over that after a number of Mexican government figures – and Dr Negrin[4] who had come to welcome his fellow-countrymen – had made brief speeches, the refugees simply walked ashore, being handed as they reached the bottom of the gangway a printed, addressed card saying 'This is where you will eat. This is where you will sleep.' They could then step into freedom! Two luxury liners which were lying in Veracruz Harbour had been made ready for children, a big warehouse had been cleared and fitted up with beds and showers, linen etc. for men. Someone handed me a note from Dr Negrín saying he couldn't stay to see me but thanked me for my help. I went ashore and wherever I walked, fellow-passengers rushed to embrace me exclaiming: 'Look! We are free!'

Notes

1. Chloe Vulliamy worked for the NJC during Spanish war with Basque children and other refugees. In 1963 she was arrested in Spain while taking money to the families of political prisoners, and was very badly treated.
2. Julio Alvarez del Vayo was Socialist Foreign Minister of the Republic in 1936-37 and 1938, and Spanish representative at League of Nations from 1937 to 1939.
3. Spahis were Algerian cavalrymen in the French army.
4. Dr Juan Negrín, Socialist Prime Minister of Spanish Republic from 17 May 1937 until fall of the Republic in March 1939.

Part 7

AFTERWORDS

The Undefeated

Martha Gellhorn

Martha Gellhorn *the American writer, began her career as a war correspondent in Spain in 1937. There she met Ernest Hemingway, whom she married. She later reported from Czechoslovakia after the Munich agreement, from the Second World War, the Korean war and the Vietnamese war, as well as from other areas of trouble and conflict.*

At the end of the gray unheated ward, a little boy was talking to a man. The boy sat at the foot of an iron cot and from this distance you could see that they were talking seriously and amiably as befits old friends.

They had known each other for almost six years and had been in five different concentration camps in France. The little boy had come with his entire family in the great exodus from Spain at the end of the civil war in 1939, but the man was alone. He had been wounded at the end of the war and for six years he had been unable to walk, with a wound in his leg that was never treated and had never healed. He had a white, suffering face and cheeks that looked as if the skin had been roughly stitched together in deep hunger seams and he had gentle eyes and a gentle voice.

The little boy was fifteen years old, though his body was that of a child of ten. Between his eyes, there were four lines, the marks of such misery as children should never feel. He spoke with that wonderful whisky voice that so many Spanish children have, and he was a tough and entire little boy. His conversation was without drama or self-pity. It appeared that the last concentration camp was almost the worst; he had been separated from his mother and father. Also the hunger was greater, although the hunger had always been there, and one did not think about it any longer.

In the last camp they all ate grass, until the authorities forbade them to pull it up. They were accustomed to having the fruits of their little communal gardens stolen by the guards, after they had done all the work; but at the last camp everything was stolen. And there were more punishments for the children: more days without food, more hours of standing in the sun; more beatings.

'The man who guarded us in our barracks was shot by the Maquis, when they came to free us,' the boy said. 'The Maquis shot him for being bad to children.'

His mother was here with him, and three sisters, too. An older brother was somewhere fighting with the French Maquis.

'And your father?' I asked.

There was a pause and then he said, in a flat quiet voice, 'Deported by the Germans.' Then all the toughness went, and he was a child who had suffered too much. He put his hands in front of his face, and bowed his head and wept for his father.

There were other men in the ward, waiting for this day to pass, as six years of days had somehow passed before. They were all veterans of the Spanish Republican army who had either been wounded in the war or destroyed by the ill usage of the concentration camps. There were the faces of tuberculars among them, and men without arms, and one-legged men, and all of them were ravaged by the long hunger and the long imprisonment. They came around the bed now to comfort the boy.

'Come, man,' one of them said, 'courage! Thou must not despair. Here is this *señora* who knows more than we know, and she will tell you, the Americans will free your father in Germany. He will come back. The war is almost over, man, you will see your father.' We all told the child consoling lies, speaking earnestly and with great conviction, and we all wished to believe what we said.

The child did not believe us, but he put his grief away where he kept it always, behind the anguished eyes and the lined forehead. His name is Fulgencio López and there are thousands like him; and no country, no government, no charity takes care of him. It is hard to know whether it is worse to be Fulgencio López or to be his mother, who had to watch those lines forming in his forehead and the pain growing in his eyes, and has been helpless and is still helpless.

Fulgencio wished to introduce me to his comrades in another ward. Having been removed from their last concentration camp a few weeks ago (because even though France was freed, there was no place to free the Spaniards in), they were now given temporary shelter in a Red Cross hostel in Toulouse. They could be considered lucky because there were cots and the building was not as cold as it might have been and there was food and no one would be cruel to them.

Other Spaniards were not nearly so fortunate; they slept on straw in cement huts that had no heating and no windowpanes; they lay wounded in hospitals that are tragic in their poverty; they lived in various cold empty schools, factories, barracks, surrounded by wastes of mud, and waited while tuberculosis gnawed the sick and threatened the sound.

By contrast, the gray wards of the hostel were a palace. So Fulgencio introduced me to his friends, about twenty of them. The youngest was six and the oldest was sixteen and they were all smaller than they should have been, but they were all wondrously alive and funny, and beautiful to look at, for the Spanish make lovely children. And also they make brave children, for if you are a Spanish Republican you have to be brave or die.

The children rocked with laughter as they told about climbing illegally into their barracks to get drinking water; the authorities locked the barracks all day long and the children were simply to suffer thirst between meals. The littlest ones wriggled in the windows and handed out water a cupful at a time. This was a huge joke apparently. Also they sang in the dark in their lonely barracks, separated from their parents, and when the guard came in to stop them and to punish the guilty ones, they acted as if they had been asleep all the time. (And how do you like that picture: the child voices inside the prison, singing defiantly in the night?)

There were two little blond characters of six, a girl and a boy. The little boy had a pair of cheap goggles on his head (he planned to be an aviator one day), which was the only toy or semi-toy in the place. These two were called the fiancés! They had refused to be separated since they had been able to walk, and they knew nothing of life except jail.

The little boy's father had been killed in the war in Spain; the little girl's father had been deported in a German labor battalion. It must have seemed to them that only children could stay together in an unsafe world. When they went down the hall they held hands as if they were crossing a dangerous stretch of country, where enemies might fall on them and tear them apart.

The children wanted a bicycle: one bicycle for all of them. He who rides a bicycle is free and going somewhere. They said it must be a woman's bicycle so that even the smallest could ride it. If a bicycle was too much to ask they would like one Meccano set and one doll: these too would be shared amongst them all. They had never had any toys but they were full of hope, because some of them had ridden on the streetcar in Toulouse and for the first time had seen toys in shop windows. So, since these things existed, one day they might exist for them.

There are many Spaniards in Toulouse, and all up and down the

Pyrenees frontier, and generally scattered in the villages and towns of France. You can go to a half-burned-out former French fascist youth camp and see there the men who fought for their faith and their country, and in so doing became what is called *grands mutilés* – the armless, the legless, the blind. They lie on straw on cement floors, in cement buildings that are without heat or window-panes, and in one building half the men – twenty-four out of forty-six – have tuberculosis.

But there are no vital statistics for the Spaniards in France for no one was concerned with their living or dying.

All we do know is that there were ten concentration camps in France from 1939 on. It is alleged that half a million Spanish men, women and children fled to France after the Franco victory. Thousand got away to other countries; thousands returned to Spain tempted by false promises of kindness. By the tens of thousands, these Spaniards died of neglect in the concentration camps. And the German *Todt* organizations took over seven thousand able-bodied Spaniards to work as slaves. The remainder – no one knows certainly how many – exist here in France. The French cannot be blamed for their present suffering since the French cannot yet provide adequately for themselves.

The Third French Republic was less barbarous to the Spaniards than was the Pétain government, evidently, but it would seem that all people who run concentration camps necessarily become brutal monsters. And though various organizations in America and England collected money and sent food parcels to these refugees, nothing was ever received by the Spanish. Furthermore, they were constantly informed by all the camp authorities that they had been abandoned by the world: they were beggars and lucky to receive the daily soup of starvation.

The only way to get out of these French concentration camps was to sign a labor contract: any farmer or employer could ask for two or ten or twenty Spaniards, who were then bound over to him and would have to work for whatever wages he chose to pay under whatever living conditions he saw fit to provide. If a Spaniard rebelled, he could return to the concentration camp. A well-known Barcelona surgeon worked as a wood-cutter for four years at twelve cents a day. He is sixty-two and there is nothing unusual about his case.

Behind the Spanish refugees were two years of a fierce and heartbreaking war, and most of them left their families locked inside their own country. They have of course not seen any of them for six years at least, and mostly they are without news. All they know is that there are a half million Republicans in prison in Spain and another million working at forced labor, and that the executions in the Spanish prisons have never stopped.

The generally accepted figure is 300,000 executions in the six years since Franco won power. The total present American casualties, killed and wounded in all theaters of war, are about 475,000. It is obvious that the only way to defeat these people is to shoot them. As early as 1941, Spanish Republicans were running away from their French employers and disappearing into the Maquis. From 1943 onward, there was the closest liaison between the French Maquis and the Spanish bands throughout France.

That the work of the Spanish Maquis was valuable can be seen from some briefly noted figures. During the German occupation of France, the Spanish Maquis engineered more than four hundred railway sabotages, destroyed fifty-eight locomotives, dynamited thirty-five railway bridges, cut one hundred and fifty telephone lines, attacked twenty factories, destroying some factories totally, and sabotaged fifteen coal mines. They took several thousand German prisoners and – most miraculous considering their arms – they captured three tanks.

In the south-west part of France where no Allied armies have ever fought, they liberated more than seventeen towns. The French Forces of the Interior, who have scarcely enough to help themselves, try to help their wounded Spanish comrades in arms. But now that the guerrilla fighting is over, the Spaniards are again men without a country or families or homes or work, though everyone appreciates very much what they did.

After the liberation of France, the Spanish Maquis in the southwest made the now famous forced entry into Spain, in the Val Daran section of the Pyrenees. This attack has been wildly reported and wildly misunderstood. It was a commando raid, purely and simply, and was never intended as anything more. The Spanish Republican soldiers involved were too few in number and too lightly armed to expect to overthrow Franco. But it was a gesture that worked.

It drove news into a country where there is no news, for inside those closed frontiers only word of mouth can travel. It was a call from the outside world where dictatorships were being destroyed and it was a call of hope to people who have lived in fear and misery for a long time. And though many of the Spanish Republican soldiers were killed, and though most of them withdrew into France as scheduled, many got through, and they have work to do inside their country. Because of that armed entry, the world was forced to remember the men who had started fighting Fascism in 1936. It is interesting to note that two thousand people suspected of Republican sympathies were arrested in Barcelona alone after the frontier attack. [...]

After the desperate years of their own war, after six years of repression inside Spain and six years of horror in exile, these people remain intact in spirit. They are armed with a transcendent faith; they have never won, and yet they have never accepted defeat. Theirs is the great faith that makes miracles and changes history. You can sit in a basement restaurant in Toulouse and listen to men who have uncomplainingly lost every safety and comfort in life, talking of their republic; and you can believe quite simply that, since they are what they are, there will be a republic across the mountains and that they will live to return to it.

I Shall See Their Like Again

Dorothy Parker

I was in Paris in 1937, a year when 'Not Valid For Travel in Spain' was stamped across American passports. So I went to our embassy to see what I might do to have my passport so altered that I might visit Spain.

The American embassy in Paris was – and, surely, still is – a lovely place, calm and spacious and dignified, and as you came through its massive portal, you had the feeling that all was to be done for you, that you would be served with courtesy, with understanding, almost with compassion.

Deep inside the building, one of the most courteous young men in the world listened to me. He wore admirable clothes, not new – oh, God, not new! – and the freshness of the handkerchief four-pointed in his jacket pocket was less like snow than like snow-drops. He was called – this I gathered from other young men who kept running in and out of the stately room – Pinky. But maybe my memory is wrong there. He may have been Binkie. He had the tidy face that you see atop the fine, hard, sedulously tended bodies of the young men like him, with whom he went to prep school and to college; young men who are always young men and, no matter where you see them, in whatever calm and spacious places their careers lie, are always at prep school and at college; the tidy face that you cannot for the life of you remember ten minutes after seeing it.

The young man with the tidy face and the admirable clothes was gentle and soft and patient with me; and patience, with its implication of time, was no easy matter for him. For those were tough days in the American embassy in Paris in the summer of 1937. There was tension in the air; there was strain and uncertainty and anxiety. The golf team of the embassy was about to set forth for Brussels, to play the team of our embassy to Belgium. My young man, high man of his team, had yet to do his packing; hell brewed. You know what he was laboring under, and so his courtesy was doubly to be commended.

Fortunately, the matter of the passport was simple. It was just the business of taking a look at it, and then telling me where to go to have it approved for Spain. The young man looked at it, wrote something on something, and then said to me, 'Oh, by the way' – for such young men keep conversation going by such phrases as 'by the way' – 'which side of this Spanish fuss do you want to go in on?' He said it with a little laugh, as who should imply, 'These formalities – but after all, tradition –'

I said the Loyalist side; and I am not at all sure that I did not add, for such young men reduce me, and you, too, to the texture of a milk pudding, 'if you don't mind, please.'

He looked up then. 'Really?' he said. 'Well. Well, if that's what you think you want. But of course, you'd have much more fun on the Franco side.'

I have not followed farther the track of the young man of the embassy. I cannot tell you, heaven help me, if his team won its match. I cannot tell you what ever happened to him. My guess would be: nothing. But I can tell you what happened to me. I went to Spain, on that side of the fuss where there was less fun, and I became a member of the human race.

I stayed in Valencia and in Madrid, places I had not been since that fool of a king lounged on the throne, and in those two cities and in the country around and between them, I met the best people anyone ever knew. I had never seen such people before. But I shall see their like again. And so shall all of us. If I did not believe that, I think I should stand up in front of my mirror and take a long, deep, swinging slash at my throat.

For what they stood for, what they have given others to take and hold and carry along – that does not vanish from the earth. This is not a matter of wishing or feeling; it is knowing. It is knowing that nothing devised by fat, rich, frightened men can ever stamp out truth and courage, and determination for a decent life.

It is impossible not to feel sad for what happened to the Loyalists in Spain; heaven grant we will never not be sad at stupidity and greed. To be sorry for those people – no. It is a shameful, strutting impudence to be sorry for the noble. But there is no shame to honorable anger, the anger that comes and stays against those who saw and would not aid, those who looked and shrugged and turned away.

Letter from the Underworld: For the English

'Caliban' (Aileen Palmer)

Me lords and ladies, you'll forget,
no doubt, that we have ever met,

Or may think, with a spasm of pain,
'One of the crowd I knew in Spain ...'

Our underworld is different now:
folk live in affluence, and how!

Old boys get knighthoods, and get Thistles:
with aristocracy it bristles,

But, lords and ladies, don't forget
somewhere on Freedom Road we met ...

Acknowledgements

We are grateful to the following for permission to use extracts from the sources given:

Patience Edney, Anne Knight, Vera Morley, the late Joan Gilchrist and the late Portia Holman: taped interviews, transcripts lodged in the International Brigade Archive (IBA), Marx Memorial Library, London.

Thora Craig: taped interview and family letters (IBA).

May Pennifather and Amirah Inglis: taped interview (IBA).

Isobel McGuire and New Zealand Radio: taped interview (IBA).

International Brigade Archive and Marx Memorial Library: Winifred Bates, *A Woman's Work in Wartime*, unpublished memoir; Leah Manning, report to SMAC from Catalonia, September 1938; Louise Jones, letter to SMAC, 1937.

IBA/Marx Memorial Library and the Hoover Institution, Stanford, California: extracts from SMAC bulletins (Anne Murray and Lilian Kenton, February 1938, Rosaleen Smythe, May 1938, Phyllis Hibbert, June 1938, Lillian Urmston, October 1938 and March 1939).

Veterans of the Abraham Lincoln Brigade: Muriel Rukeyser, 'Mediterranean' from *The Heart of Spain* (ed. A. Bessie), New York 1952; Rose Freed and Fredericka Martin, letters from *From the Spanish Trenches*, New York and London, 1937; Celia Seborer, letters from *The Volunteer*, Vol. VII, Nos 2 and 3, 1935; Dorothy Parker, *No Axe to Grind*, from *Volunteer for Freedom*, 15 November 1937, and Introduction to *The Heart of Spain*.

Editor of *The Friend*: Francesca Wilson, *The Friend*, 2 September 1938 and 25 November 1938; Bronwen Lloyd Williams and Lydia Gee, *The Friend*, 23 April 1937; Barbara Wood, *The Friend*, 21 April 1939.

The American Friends' Service Committee: letters of Lydia Elliott Morris, Esther Farquhar, Florence Conard, Emily Parker, Judith Cope and Martha Rupel.

The National Library of Australia, Manuscript Collection: Aileen Palmer, *Pilgrim's Way* (unpublished manuscript), family letters and 'From the Underground'.

Australian National University, Archives of Business and Labour, Phil Thorne Collection jointly with Phil Thorne: May MacFarlane, letter to mother, 27 December 1937; Una Wilson to Phil Thorne, 18 March 1938.

The same jointly with Ralph Tonkin and the late Agnes Tonkin: Agnes Hodgson, letters to Phil Thorne, 30 December 1936, 15 April 1937 and 23 October 1937, and diary extracts.

Phil Thorne, Laurie Aarons and Red Pen Publications: letters to Thorne from Una Wilson, Agnes Hodgson and Esme Odgers, in *From the Battlefields of Spain*, Red Pen Publications, 10 Smith St., Collingwood 3006, Melbourne, 1986.

Acknowledgements

The State Library of Western Australia: Mary Lowson, *Love Thy Neighbour* (unpublished manuscript).

George Jackson and Yvonne Shadbolt: letters of Rene Shadbolt.

Lawrence and Wishart: *Felicia Browne, Drawings*, Lawrence and Wishart, London, n.d.

Aurora Edenhoffer, Irene Spiegel and Esther Blanc: unpublished memoirs (IBA).

Tanya Ossack: letters from Madge Addy to Dr N. Mallimson (IBA).

Martin Green: Nan Green, *A Chronicle of Small Beer* (unpublished manuscript).

Mildred Rackley Simon and Brandeis University, Special Collections: Mildred Rackley, *It Isn't Romantic, But ...* (unpublished manuscript 1938?).

Ray Marantz: letters to J. Fyrth, 1987-88 (IBA).

Mary Lee Thompson: *Up From the Cellar*, Lini de Vries © Vanilla Press, Minneapolis, 1979.

Dr Walter Lear and *Health and Medicine*: *While Passing Through*, Salaria Kea O'Reilly, *Health and Medicine*, Chicago, Spring 1987, and unpublished extracts.

Ruth Waller: Madrid Radio broadcast, 10 January 1938 (IBA).

Sam Sills and ALB Film Project: Evelyn Hutchins, extract from script of ALB film, *The Good Fight*.

Marrion Merriman Wachtel and Warren Lerude: *American Commander in Spain:* Marrion Merriman and Warren Lerude © University of Nevada Press, Reno, 1986.

Helen Grant: Spanish Diary, March-April 1937 (unpublished manuscript, Cambridge University Library).

John Murray (Publishers) Ltd: *In the Margins of Chaos*, Francesca Wilson © John Murray, London, 1944.

Sister Elizabeth Burchill: *The Paths I've Trod*, Elizabeth Burchill © Spectrum, Melbourne, 1981.

Hugh R. Loader: *Six Months in Spain*, Dorothy Davies (unpublished manuscript, 1939) Society of Friends Library, London.

Victor Gollancz Ltd: *A Life for Education*, Leah Manning © Gollancz, London, 1970.

Norma Jacob and *Quaker Monthly*: *Spain's Agony*, from *The Wayfarer*, April 1938.

Kanty Cooper and Elaine Greene Literary Agency: *The Uprooted*, Kanty Cooper © Quartet Books, London, 1979.

Muriel Nicholas: *The Fall of Barcelona*, unpublished diary, 1939 (IBA).

The Imperial War Museum, London, Sound Records Dept.: Isabel Brown, recorded interview, 000844/08.

Grizel Warner: *Working Partnership*, Duchess of Atholl © Arthur Barker Ltd, London 1958, and *Searchlight on Spain*, Duchess of Atholl © Penguin Books, Harmondsworth, 1938.

Acknowledgements

Sheila Sokolov Grant: *The Parting of Ways*, Sheila Grant Duff © Peter Owen, London, 1982.

The Mitchell Library, Glasgow: Ethel MacDonald and Jane Patrick, *News from Spain*, Guy Aldred, Glasgow, 1 May 1937.

City Lights Books: *Red Spanish Notebook*, Mary Low and José Breá, copyright © 1979 by City Lights Books, San Francisco.

Susanna Pinney and William Maxwell: Sylvia Townsend Warner, two poems from *Collected Poems*, and 'Soldiers and Sickels', from *The Countryman* (to which also acknowledgement), October 1937; and Valentine Ackland, 'Badajoz to Dorset', from *Life and Letters Today*, Spring 1937, and 'Writers in Madrid', from *Daily Worker*, 21 July 1937.

Jessica Mitford, *Hons and Rebels*, Jessica Mitford © Gollancz, London, 1960.

Macmillan and Co and Little Brown and Co: *An Unfinished Woman*, copyright © 1969, by Lillian Hellman.

Frida Knight: 'University City', Radio Madrid broadcast, 1937 (IBA).

Paul Robeson Jnr: Eslanda Goode Robeson, diary extract, from *The Heart of Spain* (ed. A. Bessie), New York, 1952.

Herbert Dru and Michael Alpert: Gabriel Dru, letter and manuscript memoir to Michael Alpert.

Sheed and Ward Ltd: *Life and People of Spain*, Florence Farmborough, Sheed and Ward, London, 1938.

Martha Gellhorn: 'The Undefeated', from *The Heart of Spain* (ed. A. Bessie), New York 1952.

Drusilla Pye and David Pye: Edith Pye letter to Hilda Clark, from *War and Its Aftermath, Letters from Hilda Clark*, Edith Pye (ed.), Clare Son and Co, London, n.d.

Eyre and Spottiswode: Eleanora Tennant, *Spanish Journey*, London 1936.

Morning Star: Elizabeth Wilkinson, *Daily Worker* reports, 28 April 1937, 29 April 1937, 10 May 1937; Valentine Ackland, 'Writers in Madrid', *Daily Worker*, 21 July 1937.

Penelope Feiwel: Penelope Phelps, 'English Penny', Speech for Spanish Medical Aid, 1937 unpublished memoir, IBA.

Alix Kates Schulman: Emma Goldman, Address to the International Working Men's Association, from *Red Emma Speaks: Selected Writings and Speeches of Emma Goldman*, Alix Kates Schulman (ed.), © Wildwood House, London, 1972.

Every effort has been made to trace authors and holders of copyright. The editors and publishers apologise for the few cases where these efforts have failed, or if in any cases the rights have been incorrectly ascribed.

Name and Place Index

Bold type indicates a person's contribution to this collection.

Subject Index

Note: Military engagements are in the Name and Place Index

(SMAC): British, 24, 25, 27, 29n, 63, 68, 78, 81, 90, 99, 104, 125, 172n, 242, 288; North Manchester, 75-8, 172n; New Zealand, 26, 173n
Spanish Women's Committee for Aid to Spain, 271

Times, 242n, 323
Trades Union Congress, 23, 49

Unión General de Trabajadores (UGT), 117, 180
University City Madrid, 285-7, 308n

Women in British Aid Spain Movement, 23
Women in medical and relief services

in Spain (numbers of), 29n
Women in Nationalist Spain, 315-7
Women in Republican militia, 19, 24, 49-50, 186, 257-61
Women in Spanish society, 20, 185, 186, 257-8, 315
Women's Committee Against War and Fascism, 15, 271
Women's Committee, New Zealand, 126
Women's support for fascism, 22n, 257-8
Workshops for refugees, 190-1, 193
World War, First, 13, 188, 327; Second, 13-14, 16, 61, 73, 78, 101, 116, 125, 136, 146, 172n, 173n, 188, 194, 200, 235, 285, 306, 339-44 *passim*